LIGHTNING
STRIKES TWICE

—————————— Second Edition ——————————

Discover the Private Face of Public Universities

LIGHTNING
STRIKES TWICE

—————— Second Edition ——————

MAC O'SHEA

YorkshirePublishing
www.yorkshirepublishing.com
Write Now.

ISBN: 978-1-947491-63-2
Lightning Strikes Twice
Copyright © 2015 by Mac O'Shea

Acknowledgements: the author gratefully acknowledges and thanks the open access
provided by several websites as facts, dates and quotations were researched and
interspersed throughout this story. Also, grateful acknowledgment is extended to the
Yorkshire Publishing Team for their support and assistance as this manuscript was
carefully transformed into a book.

This novel is a work of fiction. Names, descriptions, entities, and incidents included
within this story are products of the author's imagination. Any resemblance to actual
persons, events, locations and entities is entirely coincidental.

You may contact the author at macoshea14@gmail.com or visit the macoshea.com
website for more information about other books and future events.

For permission requests, write to the publisher at the address below.

Yorkshire Publishing
3207 South Norwood Avenue
Tulsa, Oklahoma 74135
www.YorkshirePublishing.com
918.394.2665

Second Edition

It has been two years since the first edition of this book was released. Now, after more than twenty bookstore events and multiple book festivals, I am pleased and grateful that Yorkshire Publishing has agreed to release this Second Edition.

This book has taken me on an unexpected journey into the complex world of publishing and book marketing. It has been a rewarding challenge to encounter the nuances, and protocols while conquering a significant learning curve. After talking with hundreds of readers and completing several interviews and group presentations, I have discovered most adult fiction readers prefer stories with conflicts that are resolved by happy endings.

Lightning Strikes Twice introduces a cast of fictional characters who interact within the social and political context of a fictitious university. I originally anticipated this book's primary reading audience would be folks who either have direct contact, affiliation or casual interest in public universities. I have been pleased, however, to discover during my book event travels a much broader reading audience. Moreover, several months ago, I was delighted that *Amazon*. UK started selling this book in England. It seems that many of the same people who enjoy *Law and Order or Bluebloods* on television appear to also enjoy this story.

We expect, or perhaps, accept ongoing struggles of good-vs-evil and truth-vs-untruth to permeate the streets of London or New York City. However, few readers anticipate such mean-spirited behavior within the hallowed halls of a campus. Generally, a university's Camelot-like mystique hides the fog and friction caused by intense human dynamics. This story lifts the serene veil. The reader is introduced to the private face of an organization where the undercurrents of power politics and the foibles of human nature thrive while brutal maneuvers are negotiated within a culture dominated by compelling silence. The reader is invited to encounter timeless human struggles as well as intense human drama, intrigue and leadership challenges that unfold within one of society's most complex institutions.

This Second Edition has provided me with the opportunity to correct a few grammatical errors and improve the timeline that anchors the sequence of events and character development within this story. I hope you enjoy this revised edition.

Best wishes for much success and happiness, Mac O'Shea.

Blessed are those who hunger and thirst for righteousness,
for they will be satisfied.
Matthew 5:6

Contents

PART I

A Ship in the Harbor Is Safe

A ship in the harbor is safe, but that is
not what ships are built for.

—William G.T. Shedd, 1820–1894

1

Why the Winds Die

Pilgrim, how you journey

On the road you chose
To find out why the winds die
And where the stories go.
All days come from one day
That much you must know,
You cannot change what's over
But only where you go.
One way leads to diamonds,
One way leads to gold,
Another leads you only
To everything you're told.
In your heart you wonder
Which of these is true;
The road that leads to nowhere,
The road that leads to you.

Pilgrim it's a long way, to find out who you are…

—Enya, "Pilgrim," 2000

June 21, 1971
Road Town Tortola, British Virgin Islands

As I walked across the stage of life, the curtain was closing on the first act, but I did not realize it. With the advantage of hindsight, I now understand it was the beginning of the end of my wide-eyed innocence. My childhood was never the same after that incredible day. I was so immersed within the fun of the party, I missed all the signals. I remember the excitement of my thirteenth birthday like it was yesterday. I had arrived! Finally, I could brag to my family and friends that I was a teenager.

As I crossed this significant milestone in the aging process, I was in transition between the toys of a boy and the tools of a man. Standing exactly six feet tall and weighing 120 pounds, I was lanky and ready to secure a more mature profile in the adult world. On that date, I started counting the number of days until I could get my driver's license. With an enthusiastic attitude, I pursued the good things young teenagers dream about. Oblivious to the shifting sands in my life, I stood on the launchpad like a homeless, confused pilgrim completely unprepared to start anew.

In my young mind, those endless days of June existed for a single purpose. Every morning, I got out of bed and dedicated the routines in my life to the pursuit of happiness. I foolishly assumed that everyone lived with this same lighthearted attitude. As I completed my daily chores and played with my friends, it seemed like God had arranged the summer sun to linger in the sky so we would have extra hours of light each evening to hunt clams and play soccer on the beach.

Sometimes in the summer, when the sky was aglow with a phenomenal sunset, my mom would sit next to me on the old Fort Burt pier. We would dangle our feet in the water and savor the cool evening breeze that hit us in the face. Occasionally, I tried to skip stones if the water's surface was calm. Mom always took the time to tell me magnificent island tales. These age-old stories recounted the brave deeds and incredible hardships suffered by the men and women who settled our native homeland. Each folktale offered a piece of uplifting advice regarding courage, perseverance, and trying to do the right thing. At the time, I thought she was attempting to entertain me. But now I realize she was trying to develop my moral compass.

I was born during the summer solstice. My mother always told me that God made my birthday a special occasion because on this day, he gave everyone the longest possible extension of daylight. These abundant hours of sunshine were a gift that only happened once each year when the good earth positioned itself so we could have extra light to enjoy the best things in life.

In 1958, when I was three months old, I was baptized Samuel Brendan Boswell. My first name was given to me by my father. Everyone called me Sammy Junior. My mother wanted St. Brendan to be my patron saint because he is an ancient Irish sailor known as the protector of those who make difficult journeys beyond the familiar and into the unknown.

As a young boy, I was shy, carefree, and innocently believed everything I was told. I learned to live by the golden rule. My dad taught me to always tell the truth, and my mom insisted that I go through each day without causing harm to others. On the beach, I chased seagulls across the wet sand as the Caribbean sun glistened against my sun-bleached hair. My all-time favorite song was written by Mother Nature and sung by the waves as they crashed against the shoreline. I was certain all good things were possible. My dreams and hopes knew no bounds.

When I was in primary school, my favorite subject was recess! I remember the lighthearted fun of skipping across the playground and many sunlit days meandering on the water's edge, gathering beautiful seashells and shiny stones. I collected these priceless treasures in large glass jars that previously preserved my grandfather's famous moon-glow rum. This homemade elixir was legendary! The secret ingredients within this cure-all brew had to boil in the light of a full moon before it was worthy to be consumed.

As the old jars filled with my collectables, my mom humored this childish hobby of mine and cheerfully labeled each container Summer-in-a-Jar, with the appropriate year carefully written across the old metal lid. How I savored my time on the beach! For me, it was the only occasion in my life when I felt like I was touching infinity. On the beach, the sun slowly warms the fine white sand. The wind moans as it skips across the endless horizon. The birds sing and soar through the blue sky while the rhythm of the waves smash upon the coastline like a man buried alive and relentlessly pounding on the coffin's lid. Overhead, I was certain that God's angels happily danced on top of silver clouds that casually floated past me like huge soft marshmallows.

I also remember riding my new red Schwinn AeroStar bike on warm sunny days as I proudly delivered the San Juan daily newspaper to thirty-seven customers. Each afternoon, I waited at the ferry terminal for the diesel boat from Puerto Rico to arrive. Once I had my paper bundle, I raced from house to house, trying to set a new speed record for completing my paper route. As I madly peddled my bike up and down our hilly cobblestone streets, I periodically shouted words of encouragement to my golden cocker spaniel, Tuffy, as he followed me around town like a dedicated friend and faithful guardian.

That turbulent summer, when I turned thirteen, remains a special memory for me because it was the last summer I walked the beach holding my mother's hand. I had just graduated from eighth grade at the Isabella Morris Primary School. This school, coincidentally, is named in honor of my mother's grandmother, who worked there for forty years before she retired. As I confidently looked forward to beginning my freshman year at St. Andrew's Catholic High School, I never dreamed my mom was dying with liver cancer while we laughed, talked, and made delightful footprints together in the powdery white sand near the Old Tobacco Wharf.

At this early stage of my life, I had not encountered the face of death, nor did I recognize the evil that lurks inside some people. I assumed their pleasant smiles and cheerful voices were an accurate reflection of their kind souls. And I am sure I could not spell the word *slander*, and if I did, it would have been a lucky guess. I had no idea we needed a noun in our language to describe the actions of some people who actually enjoy telling mean lies to discredit their friends and harm their neighbors.

Six months after my mother died, the extreme sadness and grief caused my father, Samuel, to have a fatal heart attack. At that time, he was a forty-six-year-old professor at the H. Lavity Stoutt Community College, where he taught English composition. Some of his friends said he simply died from a broken heart. I remember the deep sadness and overpowering sense of loss that I felt as I stood next to his casket during the funeral. It seemed to me that death always comes out of season. After leaving the cemetery, everyone gathered solemnly in our backyard to eat sandwiches and drink ice tea. While mingling in the crowd, I accidentally overheard my aunt Isabella talking about the need to send me back to Missouri so I could be raised by my grandparents on my father's side of our family.

Less than two weeks after my dad's funeral, my youthful island pilgrimage came to an abrupt end, and the winds of change launched me on a new journey into the unknown. I said good-bye to the sea turtles at Smuggler's Cove and made my farewell visit to Elizabeth Beach near Lambert Bay. During the last night in my private bedroom, I kept the window open and tried to memorize the sound and rhythm of my favorite song: the roaring echo of the waves as they hit the beach near our family home.

The next morning, my aunt and uncle drove me to the ferry dock. My good-byes were rushed and impeded by the turmoil of my feelings. I tried to hide the tears in my eyes. I could not talk because of a lump in my throat about the size of a grapefruit. I boarded the diesel boat with a one-way ticket to San Juan.

Emotionally overcome, I only thought about the end of my childhood lifestyle and the fear of starting a journey into an unfamiliar world. I was too immature to realize that Father Time carries a double-edged sword. One side cuts the time remaining before the end of something. The other side, however, clears the way to start a new beginning.

With a sad heart and a sharp wind in my face, I stood on the boat's rear deck and stared at my island home until it was lost behind the rolling waves that swept across a horizon that looked like an infinite sea of deep blue. That day, I reluctantly accepted my fate and moved two thousand miles north across the Caribbean Sea to live in a small rural town with my grandparents in Kennett, Missouri. In less than thirty hours, this journey thrust me from the tropical sandy beaches of Sugarcane Country to the sandy loam fields in the Bootheel of Missouri.

I woke up the next morning, and everything was different. The Bootheel is a unique section of Missouri where the cotton plant is king and the cotton gin stands as a queen for every community's economy. With an expanse of 1.2 million acres of land that becomes flat as a pancake south of Crowley's ridge, this six-county region contains some of the most fertile soil in the world.

The western edge is defined by the southern flow of the Saint Francis River. About seventy-five miles east, the mighty Mississippi River rambles south and traces the boundary between Missouri and Kentucky. Further downstream, the river's relentless current bends southwest as it arcs around Reelfoot Lake and begins to carve the state line between Missouri and Tennessee. This land, once an uninhabitable swamp within the Mississippi floodplain, is only 230 feet above sea level. The ancient rich soil and abundant virgin cypress tree lumber was reclaimed by the

Little River Drainage project between 1914 and 1928. At the time, it was the world's largest drainage project ever completed. This effort required more earth to be moved in southeast Missouri than moved by the construction of the Panama Canal. A massive network, with more than 950 miles of ditches and 300 miles of levees, forms one of the largest drainage systems in the modern world and sustains a rural economy that is primarily agricultural.

For the first time, I experienced culture shock! The familiar foundations in my life had been shattered. I felt like an unwelcome stranger who had just entered a large room where everyone stops talking and stares. I had to learn the harsh traditions of an economy driven by the cotton market and fueled with secretly stolen labor from poor tenant farmers who owed their soul to the landlord's gin.

In the hallways of the old high school building, I developed a crush on my first girlfriend—a beautiful young Hispanic teenager named Patricia. She had a contagious smile and raven-black hair that always glistened in the sun. We all called her Patty. My friends and I mourned the day she moved with her parents to Cape Girardeau.

My fondness for books compelled me to become a daily visitor at the Kennett City Library. There, I fell in love with Jack London's great adventure books about the Klondike Gold Rush and his picturesque tales about the exhilarating life of the South Pacific. It was London's ability to vividly describe the changing moods of Mother Nature that motivated me to start a daily diary. I wanted to learn how to write like Jack London. Instinctively, I knew it would take a lot of practice.

After thoughtful retrospect, it seems like my high school years were uneventful, and they passed rather quickly. I never really felt like I belonged in Kennett. My comfort zone had been uprooted when I lost sight of the weather-beaten ferry dock. During those formative high school years, my diary was filled with countless memories of my favorite routines at Tortola.

The sand in the hourglass never stands still. I ultimately turned eighteen and graduated as the high school valedictorian. My grandparents organized a big family celebration after I received a certified letter that announced a full-ride academic scholarship in the honors program at Southern Illinois University-Carbondale.

But I must slow down in order to accurately explain where my story goes. I want you to meet the people who shaped my career and forged my character. For years as a young man, I hopelessly chased after gold and diamonds. At one point when I turned thirty-seven, I felt lost, out-of-place—like I was on the road to nowhere. I worried because I was a long way from the house that built me. But eventually, I found the path that revealed why the winds die.

Today I have found peace of mind. I still miss the elegant simplicity and eighteenth-century rhythm of Caribbean life. But I clearly understand how Father Time turned the wheel of fortune and gave me my destiny. Most of my adult life has been a great struggle. Using the criteria of that 1930s parlor game, I lived like the proverbial fox rather than a hedgehog. I studied many things and enjoyed entertaining a variety of concepts postulated by some of the world's greatest thinkers and writers. I chased illusions and tried to fit these scattered ideas into a clear picture. Just when the meaning of my life started to come into focus, the lines rapidly blurred in the midst of turbulence, and I felt compelled to renew my quest for understanding.

But now I have found the courage and serenity to accept my purpose in life. Using a telescope rather than a microscope, I perceive a universal texture within human life. The fragment of time that defines our life belongs to a divine plan and becomes meaningful only when viewed in the perspective of centuries. While individual actions uniquely manifest themselves within a specific social context, the malicious aspects of human nature seem to be constant. Father Time simply reshuffles the deck and deals each of us a new hand using the same tattered, tarnished cards held by our ancestors.

We are born as woeful prisoners within a sinful environment just as Chaucer's mighty Palamon was perpetually condemned to the castle's dungeon. I accept the toil and heartache in this corrupt world with a sense of tolerance. Like the legendary hedgehog who knows one big thing, I have discovered the insight that guides my journey through stormy waters.

Life calls us into many battles between good and evil. Each day, I strive to touch at least one heart with kindness. With a sense of discretion, I try to change the things I can with the hope that my actions, in some small way, make this world a better place. It is my goal to inspire and encourage good people to live by the golden rule. I deliberately look for that fulcrum in time—the precious moment of decision. Those fleeting seconds of opportunity that always wedge between what is and what could be. And so, I want to share this story. I am convinced there are no coincidences in life. We live in the constant sight of a Divine Judge who sees every step we take and every move we make. As our experiences accumulate layer by layer, we slowly discover who we are.

2

Red Dragon Lady

Legends and myths about dragons can be traced back to approximately 4000 BC. There are Legendary beasts in the folklore of many cultures; Dragons are traditionally portrayed as ferocious beasts that represent the evils fought by human beings. There are many important differences between Eastern and Western Dragons. The Eastern cultures value dragons for their magic, charm, beauty, power and good luck. In the West, dragons are viewed as fierce monsters with cruel, mean-spirited personalities. They kill people by breathing out fire. They also are known for their great wings, sharp claws, deadly poison, and five-toed feet. In the great classic, *Beowulf,* the fire-breathing dragon is killed by the King, but the mortal wounds inflicted by the dragon eventually cause Beowulf's death. Legendary tales suggest both Apollo and Saint George fought and killed powerful Dragons. In the Bible, Dragons are mentioned many times where they symbolize the Devil or his evil deeds.

—The World Book Encyclopedia & Internet Research

November 25, 1971
Kearney, Nebraska

In the silence of his living room, Gaylon prays like a man begging to save his soul! Tonight he is alone in the darkness. Racked with spiritual anxiety, he is nervous and overcome with fear. A chill of terror runs down his spine. Desperate, Gaylon leaves the comfort of his La-Z-Boy recliner feeling compelled to fall on his knees. With unprecedented intensity, he prays like he has never prayed before.

~~~

Across town, in a luxurious two-bedroom apartment, a young blonde is finishing a brief entry within her private journal. The closing sentence reads, "Our campus is a special place with dedicated faculty who always go the extra mile to help their students have great sex!"

Diana smiles. She finds private humor and a bit of irony within tonight's journal entry. After a wild afternoon of illicit sex, she has creatively modified the college's original marketing slogan by attaching three extra words to the end of a phase her mom has repeated countless times during their heated arguments.

The hour is late, and she is tired. Reaching across the bed, she places her pen and black leather journal inside the nightstand drawer. Sitting upright, Diana drapes her robe across the back of a nearby chair, turns off the lamp, and climbs under the covers. Her naked body presses against smooth silk sheets and her thoughts drift back to an extraordinary afternoon in a sleazy motel room.

In many ways, she relishes today's sexual conquest like a deer hunter admiring the mounted head of his recently killed twelve-point buck. The sensual memories of her two climaxes are fresh, and she can smell a faint hint of her professor's British Sterling cologne as she squirms against the silk surrounding her body.

As she closes her eyes, the images from this eventful day race through her mind.

—⁕—

A single beam of afternoon sunlight stretches across the badly worn blue shag carpet. The drapes facing the motel parking lot window are not completely closed because the rod is bent after years of use and abuse. When the radio is off, the drone of eighteen-wheelers can be easily heard as they cruise down Interstate 80. Thirty years ago, this room represented the best quality Super 8 could offer to its customers. But on this November afternoon, a young man rents the dingy room and pays $29.95 cash.

It is almost 4:00 p.m. The bed squeaks under the pressure of passionate lovemaking. The moans and groans of pleasure are briefly overcome as the radio announcer screams, "Holy man, woman, and child! Ladies and gentlemen, I have never seen such an exciting punt return. This is one of those runs destined to become a legend. Amazing! Johnny Rodgers, the Jet, just set a new Big 8 Conference punt return record with this incredible ninety-eight-yard touchdown sprint that now gives Nebraska the lead. And, with just two minutes remaining in the fourth quarter, Nebraska leads 34 to Oklahoma's 31. Hold onto your hat, folks, as we wait for the extra point attempt! I believe this incredible run will convince many that Johnny the Jet truly deserves this year's Heisman Trophy. And here we are! The Nebraska Cornhuskers, undefeated this year and the defending national champion from last year, are leading the number two team in the nation, the undefeated Oklahoma Sooners. Wow, this has to be the game of the century! If the Huskers win today, it looks like they are on their way to the Orange Bowl! Let's take a break for a thirty-second commercial. You are listening to KFAB, Omaha, Nebraska. We are the official voice of Husker football."

On the old, double-sized bed, two sweaty, naked bodies reposition in unison. Like skilled Olympic wrestlers locked together, the two roll, and a young Diana Everett emerges on top of her lover. She leans forward with her arms braced against the bed's headboard. Like an orchestrated dance, the two lovers thrust with a single rhythm. Lost in the bliss of an incredible organism, Diana stares at the drab white ceiling with glazed eyes as she transforms a deep groan of pleasure into guttural words, "Ohhhhh myyy gggggod!"

She is nineteen, a freshman at Kearney State College, and her one-track mind is addicted to the excitement of sex. As she glances across the modest motel room, she smiles in triumph, having just seduced her nineteenth man. In the afterglow of this sexual intercourse, Diana feels a deep sense of accomplishment. A major goal has been achieved. Just think—she has slept with as many men as she has celebrated years of age.

And what a man—this number 19! He is a twenty-eight-year-old hunk-of-a-guy. Married, he teaches freshmen algebra at the college. This morning, he fakes being sick with the flu and convinces his wife that he needs to stay home in bed. But, with carefully selected words, he insists that she go ahead and travel with her parents to Lincoln for the great annual football shootout between Nebraska and the Oklahoma Sooners.

Diana stares at her perfectly proportioned algebra professor. With blonde hair and a chiseled body that reflects his athletic prowess as a collegiate swimmer and diver, he looks like an ancient Greek Adonis. It has taken about three weeks of flirting before Diana realizes that his morals are not ruled by the cognitive power of his mind. After this initial discovery, she uses every opportunity after class to tempt his magnificent penis. She is convinced his primary brain hangs below his beltline. Two months later, after consistent effort, her plan is working.

Relishing her success as she stacks two old tattered pillows on the bed, she turns to her lover.

"Honey, that was really great! You are such a stud, and I am so glad I have you as my algebra teacher! I know I am young and kind of inexperienced, but you just gave me the best sex I have ever had!"

She is lying. Diana says that to all the men she takes to bed. She learned quickly at the age of fourteen that every man wants to hear that he is the best in bed.

The young professor smiles contentedly as he opens the cooler and grabs a cold can of Budweiser. Sarcastically, he says, "You know, Diana, our college marketing slogan says we must go the extra mile to help our students! Never let it be said that I shirked my teaching duties!"

They both laugh.

Diana climbs seductively out of bed. Walking around naked in front of the professor, she steps over the scattered pile of blankets. She confidently showcases her vibrant body as she teases him with her moves. Placing both hands under her breasts, she pushes them forward toward her newest conquest and casually smiles. While his eyes are fixed upon her light brown nipples, Diana says, "Did I ever tell you that I really wanted to attend the University in Lincoln, but my mom would not let me go to a big campus? She was convinced I would be just a number there, lost among several thousand other freshmen. So, she insisted that I must go here because that dumb college slogan promised I would receive personalized attention with my classes."

"Well, your mom was right! Don't you agree that I just gave you special, personalized attention?"

Gaylon tries to be casual and funny, but he is dressing quickly. In the afterglow of this forbidden sex, part of him wants to linger and flirt while drinking beer. But another part of him feels uneasy. Perhaps it is just intuition, but he is overcome with bone-deep fear. Torn between two opposing impulses, his survival instinct to run is politely subdued by his manly desire to project a suave and debonair decorum. When Diana is not looking, he steps into the bathroom and pours most of his beer down the sink.

"Diana, sweetheart, I have to run. My wife will be calling the house soon. Once the football game is over, it will take a little time to fight the crowd and the traffic, but after they find a restaurant, she will be on the pay phone."

Trying to be nonchalant as he grabs his dark brown leather jacket, he heads for the old wooden door and says, "You can keep the cooler of beer, and I will see you Monday morning in class."

That night, propped against a huge reading-pillow in her bedroom, Diana carefully records the name, date, location, and the number of climaxes she gave to her nineteenth tryst. Her new stereo system is playing an eight-track Elvis Presley tape. She pauses from her writing and begins to sing with the music while savoring the words from her all-time favorite song.

> You fooled me with your kisses, you cheated and you schemed, heaven knows how you lied to me, you're not the way you seemed.

> You look like an angel, walk like an angel, talk like an angel, but I got wise, you're the devil in disguise, Oh, yes, you are, the devil in disguise.

Her record book indicates that nineteen men and three women have fallen for her alluring, provocative wicked ways. After high school graduation, she moves into her own apartment on the Westside of Kearney and immediately begins to explore her bisexual urges. These fantasies have been silently raging in her mind since she was twelve years old and going to the lake for two-week Bible camps. Every year, starting in junior high, her parents have mandated that she attend their church-sponsored camp never realizing that whenever Diana goes into the girls' shower room, her eyes feast on the naked bodies of her fellow campers. Like a hungry vulture patiently waiting for her next meal, Diana learns to linger in the shower room and stare at the girls without being too obvious.

Diana continues to sing her theme song as Elvis' voice, projected by state-of-the-art quadraphonic speakers, fills the room.

"I thought that I was in heaven, but I was sure surprised, heaven help me, I didn't see the devil in your eyes."

With a wily smile, Diana adds a brief footnote after the teacher's name: "Heaven can't help you, Professor Johnston, your soul belongs to me now, and this illegal rendezvous secured an A for my fall semester algebra class—what a fun way to study math!"

Less than two miles away, in a small, modest one-bedroom brick house, Dr. Gaylon Johnston is praying for help. His prayers are not seeking forgiveness. He does not regret cheating. After all, this is not the first time he has stepped out behind his wife's back. Tonight, his prayers ignore all the temporal issues of this world. Tonight, he is praying for the salvation of his eternal soul.

Fear grips his stomach and his mind. He spends three hours in silence trying to make sense of it all. Now he knows! He is sure of it.

When Diana is on top of him, she has a second climax, her moans and groans signaling deep pleasure. At that very moment, Gaylon looks directly into her eyes. He is surprised. Looking through the window to her soul, he expects to see a carefree happiness wrapped within a young flower of innocence. Instead, he sees dark cruelty with intense hate—and something else. It takes him a while to carefully reflect upon that unknown ingredient. But now, alone in his living room, he is able to identify that mysterious look. With the advantage of hindsight, he is sure he has looked into the young eyes of evil.

Gaylon prays for God's help. He is convinced that he spent the afternoon in bed, face-to-face with a devil in disguise!

Two weeks later, on a clear, windy Saturday afternoon, Diana strolls confidently along lower Third Street in downtown Kearney. This is the old section of town that once rocked with nonstop parties and the vibrancy of an economy fueled by the railroad industry. Seventy-five years ago, Kearney was a major hub for three railroad Companies: the Union Pacific; the Chicago, Burlington and Quincy; and the Nebraska, Wyoming, and Western. With one of the largest switching yards in the Midwest, Kearney hosted an east-west railroad system that bustled with activity twenty-four hours per day, seven days per week.

Today, however, the diesel-powered trains soar through town without stopping. The old-glory days of Third Street are a faded memory. The aged saloons, hotels, and restaurants have become the modern home of dreary pawnshops, tattoo parlors, a few shady beer parlors, several vacant lots covered with weeds, broken beer bottles, and windblown trash.

On this crisp fall day, Diana is in search of a tattoo artist. Not just any artist. She wants someone who can draw and color a beautiful oriental red dragon. As she walks down the sidewalk, her panties are wet with sexual excitement. The idea of sitting naked in front of a total stranger has become a complete aphrodisiac. Carefully, she explores three parlors before she finds the one. After all, she wants the artist's work space to be warm and private because she plans to completely undress and verbally tease the artist while she supervises the placement of her new tattoo on the lower, inside edge of her tight ass.

Since seducing her algebra teacher, she has toyed with the idea for this special tattoo. She remembers the exciting tone of his words in the middle of their love-session. She is on top and moving with the rhythm of his hips, Gaylon pulls her tight just before he climaxes and seductively whispers into her ear, "You have the perfect pussy, and it is like a hungry, red-hot dragon! Dear God, you are my beautiful little red dragon lady!"

The analogy sticks in her mind and the memory gives her a sense of power that always prompts sexual arousal. Many times at night, in her private moments before going to sleep, she replays his words a hundred times as she fantasizes about an elegant hotel room with three men who are there to serve as her sexual slaves. One night, after a few drinks, she boasts to her girlfriends that she is going to get a tattoo. They all think the dragon idea is unique and very cool. After all, dragons are an ancient symbol of mysterious power and good luck. But Diana has to be sure that the tattoo's size and location cannot be seen by her parents when she goes to their summer lake house and swims in her bikini. Instinctively, she knows her dad would explode with anger and severely reduce her monthly allowance if he ever discovers a tattoo on her young body.

———◈◈◈———

It takes Diana five years to complete her college degree. As a junior, she barely qualifies for the Teacher Education Program. After two and a half years, her student teaching application and transcript show a cumulative GPA of 2.196 at the end of her sophomore year. Flashing a red miniskirt, she manages to charm the program director with her flirty ways. Giving her the benefit of his personal attention, he rounds up in order to achieve the 2.2 GPA entrance requirement. Majoring in social science with an emphasis in American history, she finally receives her Nebraska teaching certificate after completing her student teaching assignment with a marginal performance.

On May 17, 1976, she walks across the stage and accepts her Bachelor of Arts degree while her parents cheer from the audience. Publically, she tells everyone about her dream to teach high school history, but privately, she knows the high school scene is not for her. Her student teaching experience in Cambridge has been a dismal disappointment from everyone's perspective. After walking out of the Cambridge High School building, she never looks back and refuses to interview for any additional high school teaching assignments.

That summer, as an unemployed college graduate, her dad becomes angry one afternoon because she is spending most of her time sunbathing in the backyard. Mustering his best patience and parental diplomacy, he says to his favorite daughter, "Honey, are you going to start looking for a teaching job, or do you plan to goof around and spend your entire future beside this swimming pool?"

"You know, Daddy, I have been thinking about graduate school. I may go after a master's degree." Diana carefully selects her words and raises her voice at the end of the sentence, trying to change her declarative statement into a question.

Completely astounded, Mr. Everett replies, "You've got to be kidding! Where in the hell did you get that harebrained idea?"

"Daddy, I have given this a lot of thought. Graduate school is my new dream, my new goal. Besides, they say it is best to start your graduate degree program while all your undergraduate studies are fresh in your mind. You know, before you start to forget the important stuff!"

Still in shock, and now regretting that he initiated this conversation, Mr. Everett realizes that his spoiled little girl is going to hit him for the money to cover all her graduate school expenses.

"And just where do you plan to enroll for this master's degree?"

"Well, I was thinking about Lincoln. You know I have several old classmates living there now, and I could probably save you a lot of money if I shared an apartment with one of my girlfriends."

Diana gives her dad a big smile and a quick kiss on his cheek. She learned many years ago how to roll her eyes and perk her head in order to get whatever she wants from her daddy.

In less than two months, this Kearney State College party girl is on her way to becoming a full-time graduate student on Big Red's campus in Lincoln, Nebraska.

3

The Clarion Call

The evil of the world is made possible by
nothing but the sanction you give it.

—Ayn Rand, 1905–1982

August 1974
Floyd University

Boiling with anger, breaking his pencil, and brandishing his
hands, Buzz nervously hits the desk with his fist. A rude gesture
starting in high school as a display of assertiveness, it eventually
becomes an unconscious, discourteous habit frequently used to
express his dissatisfaction.

It is a beautiful August day in the fall of 1974. Buzz sits at his
desk in a small office on the third floor of Sheldon Hall at Floyd
University. Wilber George Granger feels mixed emotions. Joy
races through his thoughts because today is his first day on campus
as a newly hired assistant professor. At the same time, anger swells
deep in his heart. Someone, presumably the department's frumpy

secretary, has posted his full name on the hallway marquee along with the room number for his office location.

Gazing out the window that faces east and overlooks the trash dumpsters next to the power plant, Buzz reflectively thinks about his lifetime struggle with his name. Generally, he feels a sense of pride whenever he recalls his grandmother's stories about Wade George Granger. After all, Buzz is named in honor of the family's war hero. Nevertheless, he hates his name, and he has never forgiven his parents for using Wilber. He wants a macho name—something that sounds virile and dominating. He always chastises them for not selecting a manlier name for his birth certificate.

Since his young days on the playground, Wilber has demanded to be called Buzz. Tall and large during his youthful years, Buzz learns the art of bullying during school recess. As he gets older and grows to the height of six feet four inches, no one is brave enough to even whisper his real name. And so, Buzz finishes high school and college and only has to tolerate the use of his real name when they print it on his diploma.

There is a knock on the door.

Trying to sound and look professional, Buzz quickly clears his throat and says, "Come in."

The door opens, and the department chair, Dr. Sue Barton, says, "Welcome to Floyd University, Buzz. We are sure glad you have joined us!"

Buzz dutifully stands in the presence of a lady and replies, "I am delighted to be here, but…" His voice trails off into silence.

Dr. Barton, sensing something is wrong, says, "Is there anything I can do to help?"

Buzz ignites with a flash of anger that surprises Dr. Barton. "Yes, there is something—something I demand be corrected today! I want my name changed on the downstairs marquee. No one has permission to ever list my name as Wilber George."

Shocked by this unusual outburst of assertiveness, Dr. Barton quickly responds, "I am so sorry, Buzz. I had no idea you would have this concern. There is no need to get upset. Of course, we can change the marquee. We were just following our traditional protocol."

After a brief exchange of forced pleasantries, Dr. Barton feels awkward in Buzz's presence. She quickly departs with a sense of unease. Puzzled by the primitive tone in his voice, Dr. Barton walks as fast as possible and tries to prepare for a difficult budget discussion. As she rushes across the campus, she anticipates that this monthly meeting with the dean will be ugly.

With his door closed, again alone with his private thoughts, Buzz pops two Tums in his mouth. He tilts back in his wooden chair, places one foot on the top of his old desk, and savors this moment of victory.

Without thinking, he reaches into his left shirt pocket and immediately lights one of his favorite Camel cigarettes. As he deeply inhales, the smoke slowly swirls upward. A beam of sunlight arches across his desk, and the trail of smoke seems to dance through the light toward the dingy ceiling. Buzz feels the nicotine rush to his brain.

He begins to regain his sense of composure. He mentally celebrates his first outburst of anger as a new assistant professor. From a very early age, Buzz has learned to get his way by displaying his temper. Once again, his haughty technique has worked! He feels like this job is going to be a good fit for him. In his mind, he hears the clarion call of a life dedicated to teaching. On this memorable day, stimulated by adrenaline and nicotine, his sense of self-importance hits an all-time new high.

He quickly reaches into his briefcase and grabs his small portable mirror. He checks his hair to ensure everything is in place. With a rapidly receding hairline, he always parts on the left and combs the longest section of black hair back over his crown. It is a feeble, determined attempt to cover a rapidly emerging bald spot.

With a dark suntan and a muscular build, Buzz has just turned twenty-six years old on August 13. As he gazes at his face, he smiles and reflects that it is like a great prophecy when his high school senior class votes him "the one most likely to succeed in life." To be sure, he is walking that predetermined path, and is convinced that he is destined to achieve greatness, regardless of the cost.

After a few minutes of self-admiration, he crushes his cigarette in the ashtray. As he continues to gaze into the mirror, he mutters, "My God, you are one handsome son of a b——! No wonder the women want to jump into bed with you. Look out, Floyd University! Here I come!"

———*◊◊◊*———

Floyd University is a modern, three-hundred-acre campus nestled on the bluffs of the Missouri River. Established in 1901 as a state normal school, the campus has humble beginnings with two buildings on the edge of a cornfield north of Springview, Nebraska. Now, seventy-three years later, the thriving community of 12,500 residents has grown around the campus. Only the northern bluffs on the river's edge prevent developers from designing a municipal golf course that would completely envelop the original boundaries of the campus.

During the first fifty years of development, Floyd University experiences three major name changes. Its original normal school charter transforms in 1924 when the state legislature renames the campus Springview State College and funds its expansion of curriculum. Subsequently, in 1951, the legislature decides to honor a long-serving state senator from Northeast Nebraska by changing the name to Floyd State College. This name prevails until 1969.

When the campus enrollment exceeds four thousand students, everyone wants to capture the prestige of university status. Local leaders, accordingly, petition state officials for another new campus name. Party politics prevail in the legislature. Governor Tiemann, consequently, travels to Springview on September 21. The event is carefully scheduled to commemorate the twentieth anniversary of Senator Floyd's untimely death. After an emotionally charged speech, in the presence of a platform party of distinguished guests, the governor signs the naming legislation and officially declares the historic grounds as Floyd University.

By the time Buzz arrives, the campus has evolved into a comprehensive regional university. Offering more than ninety-five majors and minors, the university is authorized to award associate, baccalaureate and master's degree programs. With more than 500 employees and 4,800 students, Floyd University has become not only the dominant economic engine for the city and Turtle County but also the driving cultural and intellectual force for the entire northeast corner of the state.

At about ten thirty in the morning, Buzz decides to walk over to the student center and buy a fresh cup of coffee. When he was on campus previously for his interview, he stopped at the student center bookstore, so he knows the location of the cafeteria on the second floor. As he moves through the line with his tray, the inviting aroma of fresh cinnamon rolls wafts through the dining room and catches his attention so he decides to try one with his coffee.

A young short, heavy-set lady with curly brown hair politely follows him through the line. As he selects a table near the east window, she establishes eye contact and boldly asks if she can join him.

"Certainly, you are welcome to sit at this table with me. Let me introduce myself. My name is Buzz Granger."

With a friendly smile showcasing perfect white teeth, she responds, "Hi, I am Carol Nodland. Today is my first official day on the job. Actually, I was here last week, but not on the payroll. I needed some extra time to slowly move into my office. It took me seven trips with my car to haul all my favorite books to campus. A few months ago, I was hired as the new biology professor."

"That's great! What a coincidence! Today is also my first day on the job. I was hired last June as the new social science Professor."

Their conversation moves briskly and seamlessly. In some ways, it seems like they have been friends for a long time. Now into his third cup of coffee, Buzz says, "Hey Carol, given your first day on the job, what are you most impressed with here at Floyd University?"

"Well, I grew up on the east coast in southern Virginia. People here in the Midwest seem much more friendly and outgoing, and that really impresses me. I must confess that I am somewhat overwhelmed with all the cornfields. When I drove into town last week, I was thinking that I sure miss the trees of Virginia. How about you? What impresses you the most?"

"I am from the Midwest, so the people and countryside seem very familiar to me. Everything on this campus seems so picturesque with colorful flower beds and neatly trimmed grass. There is a beauty and tranquil peace about this campus. Maybe that atmosphere is true for all campuses, but I feel intellectually alive walking around here, like I really belong."

Carol smiles and nods with concurrence.

"I agree with you, Buzz. There is an ambiance about this campus that is different from my alma mater. I went to school in DC and finished all three degrees at Georgetown. That campus has a busy, dirty, crowded feeling just like the city of DC. How about you? Where did you finish your PhD?"

"Well, I finished my MA degree at Vermillion, South Dakota, and decided to table my PhD program so I could get married and make some money. I hope to go back and complete my PhD after I am eligible to receive a sabbatical leave from here."

"I think that is a great plan. Does your wife hope to work here on campus?"

"Oh no, she is a music teacher and plans to teach piano from our home. She loves little kids and likes to teach beginning piano."

"Hey, Buzz, you asked me about first impressions a few minutes ago. Is there anything about this campus that strikes you as odd or disappointing?"

"Well, no, nothing comes to mind. But, since I have a grand total of three hours on the job, I am not an expert by any means. You are the senior veteran here with much more time on campus than me. Do you have a concern?"

"For sure, I have a strong concern. I spent three days last week walking this campus doing a self-guided tour of every building. I wanted to learn the layout and location of all the classrooms with labs. I am frankly amazed at all the God and church stuff that is posted on the bulletin boards. We seem to have a very active campus ministry here, and they are busy boys peddling all their propaganda!"

"Truthfully, I have not noticed any bulletin board messages. But I already had my first battle this morning over the marquee in Sheldon Hall where they post our faculty names and office locations."

"Buzz, I will tell you without any reservation that I am an unabashed atheist. I believe in science, not God! I purposely found a job at a *public* university to escape the propaganda of religion. Those Catholics at Georgetown almost killed me with their church crap. My parents forced me to go there. Since they were paying the tab, I had to cooperate in order to graduate, if you know what I mean?"

Buzz nods with a reflective gaze of concurrence. "Oh yes, I understand. Are your parents Catholic?"

"Dear God, are they Catholic? Is the pope Catholic? My parents left Italy at the end of World War II and immigrated to New York City. They are old-time, dyed-in-the-wool Italian Catholic! Before I was born in 1949, they moved to Richmond, Virginia, because my dad got a banking job there. I grew up with nuns and priests all around me. My mom made me go with her to mass every day! Needless to say, after high school, I refused to attend any of their convents. So we had a family compromise, and I packed my suitcase and headed for Georgetown."

Carol's comment about Virginia triggers Buzz's memory. For just a few moments, Buzz recalls his grandmother's famous story about her father's immigration to America. Buzz hears this history many times whenever the family assembles for the holidays or other special occasions.

"Well, my family roots go back to Oslo, Norway. According to my grandma, her father sailed across the Atlantic in 1854. He was a young brick mason looking for work. Supposedly, they were originally scheduled to dock in New York City, but an unusual summer storm prompted the captain of the ship to redirect their landing to Norfolk, Virginia. So I guess we share some old family connections with Virginia."

"Do you still have family in Virginia?"

"No, my great-grandfather joined the Confederate Army when he was about thirty-one years old and fought until the Civil War was over. Our family legend says he was some kind of hero at the battle of Gettysburg and eventually made the rank of brigadier general before the war ended. After that, he drifted unemployed for a couple of years. It was a long journey from the battlefields of the Civil War to the Dakota plains. Eventually, however, he ended up as a poor farmer on the eastern edge of the harsh, dry land presently known as the South Dakota Badlands."

"What an amazing story. You must consider working in this part of Nebraska as a chance to be close to your family's roots."

Buzz smiles, looks at his watch, and realizes it is time for him to get back to his office.

"You know, Carol, I must excuse myself and run. I really admire your independent spirit. We must do this again. Would you like to have coffee tomorrow? Same time, same place? Maybe we can plot our strategies to take this place by storm. I want to get involved in the faculty senate, and I think you should join me. You would be a great senator for your department. Maybe, if we work together, we can neutralize all the church activity on this campus. I must admit, now that I think about it, a public university should not harbor or promote any kind of church program."

"Hey, it was a pleasure to meet you, Buzz. I look forward to our next coffee break together. I realize that I am the new kid on this block, but I will tell you that I do not like the idea of being surrounded here with holier-than-thou church boys and girls. It may take me some time, but I plan to do whatever I can to eliminate all the trappings and symbols of Christian shit that hang around this campus."

"I can certainly see your point. Consider me as one of your cheerleaders. My wife drags me to the Lutheran Church every Sunday. I go just to keep her happy, but to tell you the truth, I am a committed skeptic and do not buy into all that religious hocus-pocus. Actually, I would rather go hunting and drink whiskey than go to church and listen to the preacher's hell-and-brimstone sermons! But my wife, she lives every day looking forward to Wednesday night Bible study and Sunday morning worship service. As you might guess, as a music teacher, she is big in the church choir and serves as the first alternate whenever they need someone to play the organ."

Later that afternoon, as Buzz leaves his office and walks across the campus to his car, no one realizes the malicious role this young man is going to play in the future life of campus politics. Moreover, neither he nor Carol realize that their coffee break will forge a secret alliance that they will use for many years to advance their personal agendas.

That evening, Sue Barton calls her best girlfriend, Vicki Thornbee. Vicki is an aerobics teacher at the community center. Dr. Barton explains the unusual outburst of temper displayed by her newly hired assistant professor. While they talk, Sue Barton never dreams there is an emerging twist of fate threatening her future livelihood.

"You know, Vicki, I was caught off guard. He really surprised me. Such an explosive temper over such a minor thing. As we talked, for the first time, I realized his dark brown eyes are kind of spooky. They seem to be hiding a deep reservoir of anger. Do you think I made a mistake when I hired him?"

"Relax, Sue. You had a long, difficult day that culminated with your supervisor dumping all his budget problems on you. Personally, I think your old dean is just impossible, and everyone will be better off when he retires! Don't sweat the small stuff. This Buzz guy is just another young farm boy who needs to improve his manners."

Vicki's response is very casual, and she quickly transitions to her favorite subject—the clothing bargains advertised in Sunday's paper for the upcoming Labor Day sale at Herberger's.

Dr. Barton's intuition is correct. But she dismisses the warning signals and immediately becomes engrossed in a conversation about new sweaters, blouses, and holiday bargain sales. She cannot imagine that in just a few years, Buzz will emerge as the author of many scandals while he orchestrates the ruin of numerous careers in pursuit of the coveted ring of corrupt political power.

The hands of Father Time move with a relentless pace. Once the great shuttle starts weaving, the thread of causes is spinning across the campus, arranging and governing the circumstances of power. With the advantage of hindsight, Dr. Barton's colleagues will reflect that it took about seventy-five years of dedicated work by three generations to establish Floyd University with a stellar reputation as a premier institution of higher education. But it will take Buzz only a few decades to carve his destructive legacy into the private face of this public university.

The chronicles within the great book of deeds will suggest that Buzz was like the Greek God Poseidon. His malicious actions stirred the waves of gossip into storms while he deliberately slandered the character of many good people and maliciously destroyed their professional reputations.

4

The Wheel of Fortune

Out of suffering have emerged the strongest souls;
The most massive characters are seared with scars.

—Kahlil Gibran, 1883–1931

December 2010
Flying into Omaha

Reflections in the window cause him to remember the past. Recognizing the role of evil. Recoiling in fear, JP quickly buckles his seatbelt.

Kissed by the desert wind—this powerful yet brief phrase has rambled through JP's thoughts for almost twenty years. The plane is in its final approach. The pilot just announced they were twenty minutes out from landing at Eppley Airfield. The young lady serving as the plane's attendant reminds all the passengers to turn off their electronic devices, place their trays in the upright position, and ensure that their seatbelts are securely fastened.

With a full moon off the tip of the plane's wing, JP sits alone in dark solitude. The sounds of silence, wrapped within the drone of two Boeing jet engines, give him a rare opportunity for contemplation. Lost amid a cascade of private thoughts, he gazes out the window. In the final moments of the plane's descent, JP recalls the many unplanned, turbulent events that changed his life after his soul had been kissed by the desert wind. He is keenly aware of this ancient phenomenon. Centuries ago, the Desert Fathers observed that the timeless blast from the desert's furnace inevitably transforms the yearnings of one's soul. Since his wartime experience in the desert, JP's life has been unfolding like a stone in the hands of a master sculptor.

Today is the anniversary of that unexpected beginning. On this day, December first, twenty years ago, JP steps onto a treadmill of life-changing events. He is just forty-one years old back in 1990.

Joseph Patrick O'Bryan is a confident, healthy, and optimistic Irish Catholic. After graduating from St. Benedict's Catholic High School, he spends a semester enrolled at the pontifical seminary in Ohio. His eight years of elementary education are under the guidance of Franciscan nuns who teach the entire curriculum within the context of Catholic values. When he is in the fourth grade, he is inspired by a visiting missionary to join the priesthood, but that vocation seems too limited for his own personal aspirations after he celebrates his nineteenth birthday.

Now married, JP is pursuing life's timeless attractions—to become powerful, relevant, and wealthy. He is about twenty-five pounds overweight, but many judge him to be a handsome, young-looking sixty-year-old. His hair has not grayed, his boyish grin still charms, and he has grown accustomed to others thinking he is ten years younger than his actual age.

Raised on a small, 320-acre farm, JP's ancestry includes five consecutive generations of crop farmers. As the oldest son, he is the first generation to leave the family farm in pursuit of a college education and dreams that do not include cows or plows.

He quickly learns a strong, farm-based work ethic. At the age of five, he is milking cows by hand and helping his dad with the chores. Many individuals, including his wife, believe he is a true workaholic. Eighty hours of work each week is JP's normal routine. Idealistic to a fault, he believes human nature is inherently good, and he constantly professes to his subordinates at work that everyone wants to understand the big picture and have the chance to make a contribution to the organization's greater cause.

The fiber of JP's leadership style is interwoven with humanistic values. He leads by example, demands excellence, and is dedicated to a process that fosters teamwork among colleagues. He is convinced that the majority of professional people want to be part of something enduring, part of a successful team and organization that they can be proud of. He believes people inherently want to invest their time and energy in support of a meaningful goal.

It is hard for JP to believe that twenty years have passed since that fateful, late-night telephone call that changed his life forever. After four decades of life filled with work, joy, fun, and peace, it is a shock to answer the phone and be bluntly asked if he is ready to go to war. JP responds with bravado—a default-like confidence that shows his naivety and signals his desire to do the right thing. He quickly accepts the challenge from his brigade commander with relatively little reflection or understanding of the magnitude of the hardships he would endure. Less than forty-eight hours after that auspicious phone conversation, JP assumes command of an Army National Guard unit that is mobilized and deployed to the Gulf War.

Hindsight frequently lifts the fog of uncertainty and yields a clear perspective. As the plane's landing gear hits the runway, the moon's subtle glow of light across the landscape creates reflections in the window that seemed to transcend decades of time.

JP clearly remembers the turmoil brought about by these life-changing events. Like a raging river flowing out of its banks, unforeseen global and national circumstances converge and launch his expedition to the other side of the world. For JP, it is a bold walk into the unknown. This journey rapidly takes him from the cornfields of Nebraska into the desert sands of northern Saudi Arabia, where his world begins anew.

—⚬⚬⚬—

After a successful landing, the plane completes its taxi to the terminal. Hundreds of nearby streetlights dance and glitter against the dark horizon like the flicker of summertime fireflies in the backyard. JP notices the tarmac has a few standing puddles left over from a brief late-afternoon thundershower.

The passengers deplane quickly. JP immediately observes the bright, clean decorum of the terminal's gate area as he moves down the hallway. While walking directly to baggage claim number 3, he listens to the background music, a catchy, classical-piano version of "Killing Me Softly," Roberta Flack's 1972 hit.

As he waits for his luggage, JP activates his cell phone, checks the time, and calls his wife. The face on the phone flashes 9:10 p.m., December 1, 2010.

"Hi, baby. Just made it to Omaha."

"Great, how about your suitcase?" Jennifer replies.

"I am not sure. We are all waiting for the conveyor belt to activate. Cross your fingers!"

Nervous and worried, Jenn says, "I hope you don't have problems. You need that new suit for tomorrow's interview."

"For sure, with a little luck, it should be here in a few minutes. The first bag just now hit the carousel."

"Have you got the rental car yet?"

"No, that will be my next project. Hey, I see my suitcase coming around the corner of the carousel! What a relief!"

"Your plane was more than thirty minutes late. I am worried about your drive to Springview. What time do you plan to get there?"

"I am guessing it will take at least three hours to drive. I should be there shortly after midnight," JP responded.

"You have got to get some sleep so you will be fresh in the morning. You have a long day scheduled on campus."

"I know. But it is exciting. This is the chance we have been praying for. Just think—my first interview for a president's job. Wow, baby, I hope the bottle of moss is working tomorrow." JP briefly reflects on their family tradition of using the mythical bottle of Irish moss as a good-luck charm.

Jennifer realizes the pressure of this situation. JP's work as the provost has become an ordeal. Each year, his soul becomes tattooed with more battle scars. Now, after the faculty union fails to obtain their demands for a 5 percent salary increase, they declare war on JP's character. He becomes their central target, and every day he faces lies, grievances, incivility, and mean-spirited gossip. "Honey, just be yourself, and you will do great. I believe God has a plan to help us get away from all these evil people."

With a reflective tone, JP says, "I just hope we have a chance for a fresh start and the opportunity to work within a good-natured campus community."

In less than thirty minutes, JP is moving down the highway in the rental car. His spirits are high. Filled with optimism, he catches himself whistling with the music as the radio plays "Bette Davis Eyes," Kim Carne's classic hit, within a series of five uninterrupted golden oldies.

JP marvels at the night sky filled with a million sparkling stars. The bright moonlight shines across the highway making his headlights superfluous. It reminds him of nights on the farm driving the tractor under the harvest moon.

As the miles roll by, his mind is racing with multiple scenarios that could unfold in the near future. He mentally anticipates questions that might be asked during the interview, he wonders about the pay and time line to be negotiated with a potential job offer, and he thinks about the logistics of a possible move and the hard work required for another cross-country U-Haul truck adventure.

Lost in thought, the mile markers blur like unnoticed passing strangers on a crowded street. The time flies.

"Good morning, mid-America. It's 12 o'clock midnight," the radio blares!

"This is Sam Henry, your favorite midnight DJ coming right at you, riding the giant waves of WNAX! Yankton, South Dakota's powerhouse reaching across the Great Plains of the USA! For the next five hours, I will be punching all your favorites and bringing you the best of the '60s, '70s, and '80s!

"Tonight, ladies and gentlemen, I am going to start the beat rolling with that incredible, all-time classic, "Bridge over Troubled Water." This was the record of the year in 1970 by Simon and Garfunkel."

JP listens to the music with mixed emotions. He reaches for the dial, turns the volume up, and sings with the radio. As the song ends, he mutes the radio, picks up the cell phone, and calls his wife.

"Hi, sweetheart, how are you? Did I wake you?"

"No, I am fine. Just watching TV and waiting for your call. Are you there now?"

"Not yet. Just passed a sign that said forty-five miles to Springview."

"Wow," Jenn exclaims. "It is going to be almost 1:00 a.m. when you get there. Why so late?"

"Well, about thirty miles back, huge storm clouds moved in with heavy rain. I was forced to slow down. I am barely doing 45 mph, and the wipers can't keep up with this downpour. Fortunately, the temperature is hanging in the midforties, and this stuff is not freezing."

"Damn, I was hoping you would get a good night's rest before you face tomorrow."

"I will be fine, Jenn. Hey, I want to ask you something. I have been thinking a lot." JP pauses and proceeds with caution.

"Do you think I am doing the right thing? I mean, working at a university? Or do you think I should have stayed on the farm and continued our family tradition?"

Sensing JP's nervous tone, Jenn tries to humor him. She knows she is married to a man with conflicting dreams of happiness. This is a timeworn topic of conversation in their marriage, and it seems to surface at very odd times.

"JP, that new gray suit would not look too good after you spend the day driving the tractor through a corn field."

"Come on, Jenn! I am serious! You know what I mean! Sometimes I feel like I don't fit, like I don't belong. Tonight I have been thinking about Cartwright's Alamo and wondering if I am on the right career path. Maybe I should have stayed on the farm and followed my dad's footsteps. Sometimes I wish we could turn the clock back to 1970. Do you remember?"

Yes, she remembers. 1970 is their wedding year. JP has just returned from his tour in South Korea, with an honorable discharge after completing his two-year enlistment. Drafted right after leaving the seminary, JP completes his basic and AIT at Fort Ord, California. He expects orders for Vietnam. But his record-setting performance on the 81 millimeter mortar changes his anticipated destination. He can set, level, sight, fire, and hit the target faster than any other soldier in his infantry training brigade. As the "top gun of the 81 mike/mike," he is selected for a critical mortar assignment on the South Korean DMZ.

JP returns home from Korea with his pockets full of money. Most of his army pay has accumulated in the bank while he is stationed on the DMZ's northwest quadrant. He begs Jenn to marry him, and she accepts his proposal. They have been dating since their sophomore year in high school. He often says, "July 14, 1970 was the luckiest day of my life."

"Honey, all your dreams are on their way. If you need a friend, I'm sailing right behind you. I want to ease your mind."

JP recognizes the "Troubled Water" lyrics. This song has become a private Morse code for their communication, almost a spiritual-like connection between two soul mates.

"Jenn, I am basically a simple guy who wants to live a good life. I hate conflict, and I despise mean-spirited people. Give me an old, loyal cow or trusted horse any day, and I'm happy."

"Sweetheart, you are tired and nervous about tomorrow. I believe in you, and I know you are a capable leader. You have invested your total career to prepare for a presidency. I know you will do great. When times get rough, I'm on your side."

JP tries to get a grip on his emotions. Ever since being drafted, his entire life has felt like it is in constant turmoil. He is always looking for the "bridge" to get over his "troubled waters."

"You are right, Jenn."

With renewed confidence and a sense of determination, JP promises to call when he arrives at the motel.

"Love you, baby. Talk to you as soon as I get there."

Unbeknownst to him, this same evening in the governor's mansion, the great wheel of fortune is turning. Vintage Silver Oak Cabernet Sauvignon flows freely during a five-course meal that features a prime fourteen-ounce filet mignon, cooked to perfection. Around the table, a select group of men toast the governor and each other as they celebrate their anticipated rise to power and the projected downfall of several good leaders.

In the true spirit of Machiavellianism, with the desire to seize every opportunity while acquiring power for its own sake, Governor "Abe" Turner stands at the head of the table and delivers closing remarks after everyone finishes their caramel crème brulee dessert. He has saved the best part of the meal for last. Hoping to accentuate his speech with a grand toast, every guest receives a beautiful crystal goblet filled with a 1976 Baron de Lustrac. As he raises his glass in the air, silence falls across the room. The governor clears his throat and says,

"Gentlemen, my good friends and colleagues, we are intelligent, resourceful, and gifted men. As our very distinguished guest, Mr. Ace, always says, we must be ready to seize opportunities and use our leadership power. And if I may share a thought from that great book, *The Prince*, always remember that it is better to be feared than to be loved. You know, the Lord helps him who helps himself! Strong measures are needed to accomplish great goals, and it always helps if you go into battle wrapped in the arms of a great brandy!"

Everyone cheers. They raise their glass with a grand gesture of camaraderie and begin to enjoy this amazing, full-bodied after-dinner drink. The creamy texture glides across everyone's palate and signals the perfect ending to a wonderful evening filled with great food, fellowship, and frivolity.

As the governor moves around the room to shake hands and bid each man a good night, he notices that his chief of staff is unusually jaunty and animated. He also notices an eerie spark or glint in his eyes that is highlighted by his facial roseola. If ever there is a man drunk with the euphoria of authority, tonight his trusted chief has overdosed. On this special occasion, the governor's faithful hunting buddy and long-serving assistant is like a man overcome with the passion of finding a new religion. For the first time, the chief of staff crosses beyond the threshold of reality becoming lost within a grandiose sense of self-importance. Like an uncontrollable zealot infused with the energy from abusive political power, he soars past the point of no return.

At about one thirty in the morning, JP crawls into bed—totally exhausted, both emotionally and physically. After moving his luggage into the motel room, he calls Jenn to let her know that he has arrived safely. She reminds him to hang his new suit, shirt, and tie in the closet with the hope that some of the wrinkles might disappear by morning. Then he quickly shines his shoes and sets the alarm for 5:45 a.m. As he surrenders to a deep sleep, his final thoughts repeat the words from his favorite St. Jude novena prayer, requesting help for all his spiritual and temporal needs.

Without JP's knowledge, the second order implications from the governor's dinner would ripple through time and change his destiny. The incoming tide of karma begins to push and align the long-term variables that will, ultimately, chart the trajectory of his career. The hand of Fate carefully weaves the outline of yet another timeless masterpiece. Meticulously, the threads of human life begin to crisscross through countless silent nights filled with full moons.

Since 1974, Lady Fate has been busy tracing a mystic pattern at Floyd University with a cast of characters who have established their roots, comfort zone and malicious thought patterns. JP's journey into this complex mosaic will be like the ship that sailed directly into an unexpected hurricane. As JP confidently walks into his presidential interview, he does not realize the road he has chosen will become a gauntlet of sorrow laced with unfulfilled dreams. As the new University President, he will not be able to change the color of thread used by the hand of Fate. During the next five years, JP's moral compass will be like a small candle flickering against a strong wind. He will learn, eventually, why the winds die.

PART II

Give a Dog a Bad Name and Hang Him

Nonresistance to evil which takes the form of paying no attention to it is a way of promoting it. The desire of an individual to keep his own conscience stainless by standing aloof from badness may be a sure means of causing evil and thus of creating personal responsibility for it.

—John Dewey, *Human Nature and Conduct*, 1922

5

Renaissance Man

Progress is impossible without change, and those who
cannot change their minds, cannot change anything.

—George Bernard Shaw, 1856–1950

August 1983
Springview, Nebraska

On this beautiful August day, filled with abundant sunshine, the
Nebraska cornfields have never looked better. The old-timers
remark during their morning coffee break at the corner café
that you can hear the corn popping as it grows toward maturity.
This is corn country! For many generations, Turtle County has
been the home base for farmers who are proud to be dedicated
cornhuskers. Generally, the community's morale rises or falls
based upon local crop reports and the future corn prices with the
Chicago Board of Trade.

A tall, slender man stands on the cracked cement less than
fifty feet from Highway 81. More than six decades of time are

taking their toll on his strength and vitality. Today he feels old. His private thoughts are focused upon the application process for social security. The boiling summertime heat is relentless as he inhales diesel fumes and listens to the roar of the Greyhound bus engine. Hot or cold, rain, snow or sunshine, he has stood on this same piece of broken cement seven days each week, twice each day for the past twenty-one years. Everyone in town knows him simply as Mr. Greyhound. He frequently tells his wife that his official job title is "The Chief, Head Cook, and Bottle Washer" because he is expected to answer the telephone, sell the tickets, handle the luggage, deliver the freight, and be the janitor at closing time.

The Springview bus depot is a modest building. Once the community's proud Mobil gas station, the famous red-winged horse still towers above the front driveway on the south side of the property. The badly faded sign signals a bygone era when cars and trucks were less sophisticated. This 1930s vintage station is remodeled in 1959 becoming the bus depot, and the logo of the racing Greyhound dog is nailed to the front of the building. Two weatherworn barrels stand like century guards adjacent to the front door. Both are filled with yellow daises, colorful marigolds, Canterbury bells, and red blooming Irish moss. Every day, after finishing his cleaning duties, Mr. Greyhound waters and cares for the old flower barrels with the skill of a self-trained horticulturist.

The Omaha bus rolls to a stop. Mr. Greyhound immediately goes to work unloading the passengers' luggage, and today there are several boxes of freight. Once again, the bus is late—almost twenty minutes late today. Springview is the last stop in Nebraska before this bus crosses the mighty Missouri River and heads for Yankton, South Dakota. This evening, at around 7:30 p.m., the bus would arrive in Sioux City, Iowa. The driver parks it overnight, and the next morning, a different driver reverses its route and pulls back into Springview at about 10:30 a.m.

Inside the depot, three young teenage boys insert their dime into the vending machine and, while making their selection, debate the pros and cons of the all-time best candy bar. They have identified three possible options for this chocolate award—Snickers, Milky Way, and 3 Musketeers. Their bikes are parked in the shade of a huge cottonwood tree, next to the old oil shed. Once serving as the "Gents" and "Ladies" outhouse, this dilapidated building had been converted years ago into a storage area when indoor plumbing was installed within the station.

After the bus is parked and the loud engine is turned off, the young boys move outside into the extreme heat. They hurriedly eat their candy before the chocolate melts in their hands. Anxious to begin, they politely wait for the old man to unload their bundles of newspapers. Luggage first, freight second and newspaper bundles last—that is Mr. Greyhound's rule. Six days each week, they wait for the bus so they can begin delivering the *Norfolk Daily News* to their paper customers. Generally, they are not in a hurry to begin their paper route. But today is different. The sooner they start, the sooner they finish because today they have agreed to meet at the city's swimming pool. It is a race to see who finishes first. The anticipation of the pool's cool water beckons them to hurry so they can escape the sun's scorching heat.

"Pardon me, dear chap. Would you please direct me to the nearest hotel?"

The old clerk is stunned. This is not the typical accent or tone of conversation usually heard in the Springview bus depot. Smiling, the Greyhound agent responds, "Well, our one and only motel is across town, about two miles from here."

"I say, be a good lad and call me a cab," Samuel says.

Smiling profusely, standing perfectly erect, and stepping through the door, Samuel B. Boswell arrives with poise and flare. Dressed in a silver pin-striped three-piece suit, accented with a red bow-tie, he creates quite a stir of stares and whispers as he secures his suitcases and climbs into the taxi.

In many ways, Dr. Boswell is a complex soul. He has a brilliant mind, frail body, and the personality of an old eighteenth-century British gentleman. He is twenty-five years of age when he steps off the Greyhound Bus in downtown Springview. A newly minted PhD from SIU-Carbondale, Samuel is quickly labeled by many as an odd bird. From his very first day on campus, his colleagues believe Samuel's eccentric eighteenth-century spirit has been lost in a time warp and mistakenly reincarnated two centuries later.

Many joke about his love for high tea and the hint of a British accent in his speech. Samuel is a bit of an anomaly being born and raised in the British Virgin Islands. His friends consider him somewhat of a renaissance man, a cultured individual who has acquired knowledge in several diverse fields of study. And yet, this inquiring mind with boundless intellectual energy finds himself in rural Nebraska rather than on an Ivy League campus. In the fall semester of 1983, Samuel follows in his father's footsteps and begins teaching English composition and literature classes at Floyd University.

For his undergraduate degree, he majors in psychology and minors in philosophy. While in graduate school, Samuel changes his focus of study and elects to major in European literature. He loves Shakespeare but writes his dissertation on John Donne. From an early age, while in elementary school, Samuel falls in love with books. His six-foot willowy stature is neither athletic nor attractive. And so, while others play high school football and go to dances, Samuel devotes three hours every day to reading and some time every night to writing in his diary.

By the time he arrives at Floyd University as a new assistant professor, Samuel's diary has become an established habit and his primary passion. Each evening, before going to sleep, Samuel seeks the privacy of his bedroom and finds solace in his writing. He tries to understand the challenges of life and make sense out of the difficulties he encounters. As a general rule, his diary helps him connect ideas, achieve synthesis, discover new insights regarding the purpose of his life, and occasionally, find a sense of intellectual peace. All his worries, fears, and secrets are recorded in his diary.

—*∿∿*—

One October morning in 1987, the junior faculty coffee club is meeting in the student center, and Samuel learns about the underground movement against the new VPAA, Dr. Kelley.

"They say some of our senior professors are out to destroy Dr. Kelley," Emmy says with a hushed tone in her voice.

Dr. Ellen Marie Martinez is an inveterate hard charger within the art department. As a junior assistant professor, many consider her a dedicated work alcoholic. She stands at five two with piercing brown eyes and long, shimmering black hair that elegantly stops in the middle of her back. Dr. Martinez is always smiling and very fun-loving. Twelve months out of the year, her dark, soft skin gives her a stunning suntanned look. Her perfect white teeth gleam against the contrast of her skin. She is incredibly thin, only weighing ninety-five pounds. Most people attribute her lack of weight to her boundless energy and devoted work habits. Always smartly dressed, she is a very attractive single lady. All her friends at work affectionately call her Emmy.

Samuel responds with disbelief, "Surely, you are kidding. She is the most progressive and talented academic leader I have ever encountered."

"Nonetheless," Pete Harrison chimes in, "some people do not like change, and she is pushing hard to change several things. Damn, I am not surprised that she has enemies."

Samuel is astounded. Dr. Kelley is a visionary, a brilliant change agent. She has inspired more people with new ideas than Samuel can begin to count. She is respected, admired, and truly valued by the vast majority of the faculty.

He glances around the room to ensure they had reasonable privacy. "Who do you think is leading this mean-spirited effort?"

Emmy responds with great certainty in her voice, "I heard from a very trusted friend that Buzz Granger started this ball rolling."

Several in the group nod affirmation supporting Emmy's assertion.

Samuel's diary that night includes an extensive reflection about those who resist change. He notes that some people have never met a new idea that they liked. He also comments about man's haunting ability to use corrupt power.

———꠸꠸꠸———

As the 1988 fall semester begins, Samuel enters his fifth year of teaching at Floyd University. He is nervous, more nervous than he can ever remember. He is approaching the time to start his tenure review process, and he feels insecure and intimidated, and he often questions his professional worth. Ever since his friend Marsha Ann was denied tenure, Samuel has wondered if he would be approved.

Four years ago, Samuel initiated a Thursday afternoon tradition at Bonnie's Brew. The scuttlebutt rumor among his friends suggests that he has been a trust fund baby since the age of eighteen; as the sole heir of his mother's sugar cane plantation in Tortola, money has never been an object of concern. Throughout the academic year, once per week at precisely 4:00 p.m., he hosts a table filled with delightful finger foods and sinful sweets. Samuel insists upon a dress code of "smart casual," and he always wears a dark sports coat with a dapper bow tie. All his friends have a standing invitation, and the assembly usually numbers between fifteen and twenty people.

Almost exclusively junior faculty, the group frequently finds themselves discussing the harsh mysteries behind the tenure process. Occasionally, Coach Moore confides some of the inner workings of this demanding process. For the past three years, Mark Moore has served as the recording secretary for the faculty senate's tenure review committee, and consequently, he has all the inside details regarding the strengths and weaknesses of every recently submitted packet.

Floyd University's faculty handbook outlines three major criteria that must be demonstrated within a tenure packet: successful teaching within an assigned discipline, a scholarship within a designated discipline as evidenced by publications, and demonstrated service to the campus and community. A successful packet has to achieve outstanding scores in two out of three and at least an excellent rating in the third criteria. Mark repeatedly comments that the key to a successful tenure application seems to hinge upon the two most important criteria. First, a successful teaching record that includes positive student evaluations, and second, three published articles or one published book that confirms scholarship within one's specific academic field. Samuel is a fervent writer. He dedicates almost an hour every day to his diary. But, his academic scholarship is less than stellar. His list of published essays in professional journals is somewhat sparse. He has two articles pending review, but the journal editors do not seem very enthusiastic about his submissions. And yet, he continues to hope for publication success.

Campus colleagues such as Buzz Granger have no idea that Samuel's diary chronicles their antics and mean-spirited deeds. Unbeknownst to most, the vast majority of his diary entries are inspired by the drama of their university life.

One winter evening as the cold wind howled, Samuel makes a brief observation about Buzz in the final section of his diary entry. The notation suggests that old Baldy frequently acts like a sick narcissist, a true emotional vampire with no empathy for others. Samuel closes his last sentence with these words: "There seems to be no limit or boundaries for Buzz's cruelty."

6

Dancing with the Red Dragon

Lord almighty, I feel my temperature rising. Higher,
and higher, it's burning through to my soul. Girl,
girl, girl, you gonna set me on fire. My brain is
flaming; I don't know which way to go.

—Elvis Presley, "Burning Love," 1972

May 1985
Diana Dawson's Apartment

"Oh, Ted, that was the best screw of my life. You are such a huge stud. I am impressed! You are better in bed than you are on the football field! I love the way you drop into my pocket!"

Once again, Diana lies. She chuckles to herself and continues to praise her new boy toy. "After that performance of manly prowess, I may tell my friends that you are my all-time best research assistant!"

"Holy shit, professor! That was a hell of a ride. Honestly, I never expected you to be so good in the sack."

Diana laughs with a sly hint of evil disguised within her voice.

"Well, Ted, as Elvis would say, I'm just a hunk of burning love! Besides, practice does make perfect, and I have to admit that I have had a few more years than you to practice. But I have decided that we must schedule one more 'practice session' for you. After all, I want to go the extra mile to get you ready for your graduation."

While she reaches for her cigarettes, she looks directly at her new conquest and continues, "How does that sound to you, sweet boy?"

"Great, hell yes. You just name the time and the place, and I will be there!"

"By the way, Ted, I am going to change our bedtime rules a little. Next time, I want you to bring your best friend, Jake, with you. I hope you don't mind sharing? Trust me, there is enough of me for the two of you!"

She pauses and gives him a coy look with a flirty wink.

Ted is surprised but more than willing to include his best friend. He knows Jake gets horny every time she brushes against him during her American Civil War lectures. In fact, Jake has confessed that he gets a royal boner just smelling the scent of her perfume.

"Sure, just tell us when you want to jump our bones in bed."

"Well, that is part of my surprise graduation present for you. We are not going to tumble into bed. Next Tuesday night, at midnight under the full moon, I want both of you to meet me on the fifty-yard line in the middle of the football field. We are going to tumble on the coach's precious grass!"

"Oh my God, how wild and crazy. This will be awesome! But wait! What if we get caught?"

"That is part of the excitement, big boy! The risk will increase your adrenaline. I want both of you at the same time on the fifty-yard line. This will be my special treat for you. Trust me, I will give you a great memory to climax your football career!"

They both laugh as Diana pulls two cans of beer out of the refrigerator. It pleases her that Ted has caught her sexual play on words.

"Here is the plan. Park your cars in the auditorium's parking lot and walk across campus to the north gate of the field. I have a key to that gate, and I will leave it open for you."

"Wow, so cool! This is going to be awesome!"

Ted smiles as he chugs his Michelob Light and asks for another.

"Sure, help yourself." Diana pauses while he grabs another beer out of the refrigerator. When he returns to the bedroom, she continues. "I will be waiting on a silk sheet in the middle of the field! Don't be late. I want both of you to dance with my red dragon!"

Diana Dawson arrives at Floyd University in the fall semester of 1984. Earlier, during the spring semester, she walked into Dr. Barton's office and completely impressed her during their two-hour conversation and interview. Before the end of that day, Diana leaves the campus with her first job offer as a university assistant professor. Finally, her master's degree lands her the kind of job that her parents expected. That summer, her father, Mr. Everett, organizes a family reunion and a big celebration to commemorate their family's new university professor.

During her first two years on campus, she becomes deeply involved with the faculty senate and other university committees. She also establishes a routine procedure with the head football coach that provides her with the opportunity to carefully screen and select a football player every semester to serve as her exclusive research assistant. Dr. Barton has approved this part-time research position as part of Diana's contract negotiation. This fifteen-hours-per-week job is financially supported by the university's work-study program.

Late that night, when Diana is alone in the privacy of her bedroom, she pulls her black notebook from the nightstand and carefully follows her established routine. She records Ted's name with the date, location, and the number of climaxes she gave him.

She finishes her entry with the following thought: *Ted, Ted, Ted, you gonna set me on fire under the light of a silver moon! Just think, the university is paying you to do the research that will light my fire!*

7

Forging a Lethal Alliance

A person may cause evil to others not only by his
action, but by his inaction, and in either case he
is justly accountable to them for the injury.

—John Stuart Mill, 1806–1873

September 1985
Floyd University

After eleven years of teaching experience, Buzz has learned to be politically correct and somewhat assertive among his colleagues. Last summer, after Dr. Martin's retirement, the vice president for academic affairs position was temporarily vacant. This brief window of time gives the dean of Arts and Sciences the opportunity to ignore all the established equal-opportunity requirements and give his friend a promotion. The dean moves quickly. He does not advertise or search for a new chair. Rather, he unilaterally appoints Buzz to serve as the new social science department chair. This surprised many because Buzz does not have a doctorate degree, and he is junior to five other professors within the department.

Buzz is not surprised, however. In fact, he expects the promotion. It is part of the secret deal he has made with Dean Frank Warton. Only three people know the truth—Buzz, Dean Warton, and the local state senator, W.A. Turner. The previous November 1984, they had hatched the plan while sitting around the campfire after hunting deer. Inspired by Jack Daniel's Old Number 7, they vengefully plot the downfall of the department chair, Dr. Sue Barton.

It takes most of the academic year. Buzz follows the game plan and does as he is told. Without reservation, he repeatedly betrays his mentor and professional coach. The lady who affectionately guides him through a difficult tenure review and politically supports his academic promotion is now completely expendable. Daily, Buzz is on the telephone to someone with a hot, fabricated rumor or a harmful piece of gossip about Dr. Barton.

As a tenured associate professor, Buzz has become very influential on campus. His outward decorum of confidence and diplomacy disguises his true human nature. Few have detected his cutthroat tactics, insipidity of character, or his eye for the young ladies.

True, there are rumors during his tenure review process. But Dr. Barton comes to his rescue. She dispels the gossip and advances his successful application. Regardless of Dr. Barton's assertions, six years later, the rumbles continue to echo around the campus. Supposedly, Buzz has traded grades with two foxy basketball girls for the benefits of some clandestine oral sex.

Buzz sits in his new office, gazing out the window that overlooks the campus quad. From his desk, he can see the south face of the historic clock tower. He pauses from his work as he remembers that cold evening in a deer camp. Buzz convinces his hunting buddies that Dr. Barton is out to get him—to ruin his academic career. Buzz complains of being mistreated and frequently misunderstood. He is convinced Dr. Barton is jealous of his abilities. A master of manipulation and whining, Buzz has spent many years polishing the ability to cover up his evil intentions by loud-voiced protests of virtue. Within the private chamber of his dark thoughts, he covets Dr. Barton's job.

Warmed by the campfire and the spirit of JD's Tennessee Whiskey, the three men forge a lethal alliance. With a sacred oath of secrecy, these three unlikely amigos dub themselves the "Remarkable Trinity" and charter the downfall of a dedicated professional and an exceptionally talented department chair.

Now, as the department's new chair, Buzz scans the room. He admires the beauty of the highly polished dark wood floor and the matching window trim that contrasts against the antique oak furniture. He really likes this private office, and he feels a surge of power rush through his veins. It has been almost too easy to crush Dr. Barton. The trinity's plan has worked in a flawless manner.

———

At the time of their annual fall hunting trip, Senator Turner is serving his third term in elected office. He has emerged as a major powerbroker within the state's Republican Party. Last year, he chaired the legislative subcommittee on appropriations. During the process, he becomes very friendly with the state auditor.

Three days after the Remarkable Trinity plotted their campaign of gossip and rumor against Dr. Barton, Senator Turner calls the state auditor and asks for a confidential favor.

In the milieu of state politics, especially across the heartland of rural America, the coin of the realm is "traded favors." When the senator asks for copies of all expenditures initiated by Dr. Sue Barton, the state auditor does not hesitate to comply because she knows Senator Turner is not only a charming and wealthy man, but also, as one of the senior senators, he is next in line to become the majority whip when the legislature reconvenes.

The research task takes eight evenings of work to accomplish. The state auditor does the work herself because no one else needs to be involved with this confidential request. Two weeks after their deer hunting trip, the senator sits next to Dean Warton during their weekly Rotary luncheon. While the program announcements are being made, he discreetly passes two large sealed envelopes containing copies of more than four years of Dr. Barton's financial vouchers. As the guest speaker moves to the podium, the senator finds a private moment to lean into the old Dean's ear. He quietly says, "Now let the fun begin!"

It takes another week to hit pay dirt. Like old miners panning for nuggets of gold, Buzz and Dean Warton invest many hours of work sifting through hundreds of vouchers and receipts, hoping to find the "silver bullet of dirt" to use against Dr. Barton. Finally, at about midnight on Thursday evening, Buzz finds the bonanza—the mother lode of incriminating evidence.

Armed with the discovery of eighty-eight late-night, long-distance telephone calls spanning almost three months of time, Dean Warton and Buzz start to work the campus grapevine. Soon, the whispers are floating not only across the campus but also downtown in four community coffee groups that include business leaders, city council members, and a number of retired, wealthy farmers.

Dr. Sue Barton is a strikingly beautiful, trim, physically fit fifty-two-year-old lady who lives alone, separated from her husband. When she accepts the assignment at Floyd University, her husband refuses to move, staying in Kansas to work. For several legal and financial reasons, they never divorced. The path of least resistance encourages them to avoid a messy legal battle. Over time, their separation becomes the congenial norm as they move through their middle-aged years with separate careers. Inevitably, their loving relationship deteriorates, and they become nothing more than long-distance friends who share the same last name, file a joint tax return, and obligatorily talk once each week on the telephone.

After fourteen years on the job at Floyd University, Dr. Barton is emerging as a senior department chair. This winter, she is asked to travel as a member of the campus team to Chicago in order to attend the annual accreditation conference sponsored by the North Central Higher Learning Commission. During the conference, she meets an outgoing, good-looking man who is ten years her junior. Their initial conversation is like spontaneous combustion. There seems to be a spark of magic when they are together. The combination of common interests and erotic opportunity escalates a casual, fun afternoon cup of coffee into two consecutive evening dinners with wine at a very romantic restaurant within walking distance from the hotel. Two lonely souls together, untethered from their domestic leashes; it feels like they have been friends for years. Their last night in Chicago is spent together in Sue Barton's bed making passionate love, drinking champagne, and eating chocolate-glazed strawberry cheesecake.

During the next two months, they talk almost daily on the telephone. Eventually, however, the magic fades like the tail of a fleeting comet racing across the sky. Sue senses her young lover losing interest in their relationship. Finally, he calls one evening at about midnight and explains that things have changed with his wife. They have reconciled their differences, and he plans to return and remain faithful to her.

Dr. Barton is heartbroken. Days of depression turn into weeks. At work, she is going through the motions of each task, but she finds it almost impossible to concentrate for any length of time. With no trusted confidants, Sue endures this sadness on her own. Eventually, this debilitating depression begins to subside. She starts to feel better and finds personal solace by focusing on the challenges of her work.

Soon, the spring semester draws to a close. Final exam week is underway, and Dr. Barton is looking forward to the upcoming Saturday morning commencement because this year, coincidentally, her birthday is the same day as the graduation ceremony.

When the vice president for academic affairs summons Dr. Barton to his office on Wednesday morning, it seems a bit unusual to her. She assumes they are going to discuss the first draft of the self-study report she coauthored for the next fall's HLC accreditation visit. As Dr. Barton enters the room, she never expects the university attorney to be seated at the conference table next to the vice president.

Mr. Peter Sedworth has served as the university's legal counsel for almost ten years. He is the epitome of a lazy state bureaucrat. He loves to push papers, delay transactions, feign bravado as he cites the chapter and verse of state policies while intimidating faculty with his brash legal jargon.

It has taken him three attempts to pass the state bar exam. His mom always said, "Third time is a charm!" During law school, he concentrated his studies in the area of estate planning but in the end elected to take the path of least resistance and pursue state employment rather than risk the challenge of private practice.

Over the years, he has become content with his work. He has tabled his devotion for estate planning and concentrates on the legal aspects of university business. Mr. Sedworth believes that all employees are expendable and should be fired whenever they do something that places the reputation of the institution at risk. Privately, the faculty and staff have nicknamed him. Around campus, everyone calls him "Mr. Sledgehammer," because no matter the size of the nail, Peter always uses the big, fifteen-pound sledgehammer to solve every problem.

After a few formal introductory remarks, Mr. Sedworth presents Dr. Barton with a two-page statement of charges. This startling document is overwhelming for Dr. Barton. Her eyes blur as she tries to read these unbelievable statements. Sue Barton has never been more embarrassed. Stunned, shocked, and dismayed, she sits in the vice president's office and listens to the attorney's outrageous proclamations. Three scathing statements are typed with bold letters on page two: "misuse of state funds for personal gain; misuse of the state's telephone equipment, and illegal use of the state's communication system for personal business."

The attorney places copies of more than eighty documents on the conference table. Somehow, this packet of vouchers and receipts has mysteriously and anonymously arrived in the mail with no return address. As it is addressed to the president's office, his administrative assistant immediately asks their legal counsel to work with the vice president to resolve the issue while the president is traveling out of state.

Since the state's communication system randomly records every tenth long-distance call that is initiated after 9:00 p.m., Mr. Sedworth proclaims that some of these telephone conversations contain inappropriate sexual content and the tone seems to be personal messages of love and romance. With a rude, assertive accusation, the attorney suggests that this misbehavior is premeditated, and he emphasizes that three of these telephone recordings recount the vivid details and pleasures of wild sex in a Chicago hotel room that, incidentally, has been paid for by the university because Dr. Barton claimed lodging expenses as part of her reimbursable travel costs.

Thunderstruck, Dr. Barton sits in a daze and stares at the floor. Mr. Sedworth's blitz-like ambush has worked. Sue Barton is in an emotional spiral. She has lost her ability to think clearly. The entire meeting feels surreal. The vice president brings the conversation to a close. Dr. Martin's concluding message is cruel and blunt: "Either resign today, or be fired tomorrow."

As Dr. Barton leaves the vice president's office, her complexion is sheet-white. Her tongue is thick and heavy. Fear grips her throat, and her mouth is dry. It is difficult to walk because her knees feel weak. She is completely speechless when one of her best friends, Ann Spencer, greets her in the hallway. Like a walking zombie, she tries to find the door to get out of the building. The shock and trauma are so severe that a single thought races through her mind: *I must get out of here!*

As she leaves campus and drives home, it is like awakening from a nightmare. She clearly remembers signing the personnel action form while her hand trembled uncontrollably. But for some reason, she is not sure about the effective date of her resignation.

That night, she calls her parents. They are overcome with grief. As she cries, Sue's mom repeatedly says, "This is so unfair. Surely someone with a rational mind will listen to your side of the story. Surely, your friends will stand up for you."

Sue's dad is angry, "This does not make sense. All your dedication, all your outstanding work—your talent is being ignored. What about your tenure rights? This is a classic case where the punishment does not fit the crime."

That night, well after 2:00 a.m., Sue Barton finally drifts to sleep, clinging to her cat and the hope that campus friends and colleagues would speak up on her behalf and come to her rescue.

The next morning, Springview's coffee klatches are buzzing with juicy gossip and wild speculations. Rumors are flying. The daily newspaper has published two short paragraphs on page five in the Local News section. Briefly entitled "University News," the article says:

> Plans continue to develop for Vice President Martin's retirement dinner. Hosted by the president and his wife, this forthcoming event promises to be a gala affair. This evening assembly is scheduled for May 20, 1985, in the country club's banquet hall. Attendance is open to the public. Community members desiring to attend should contact the University Relations Office and make their dinner reservations.
>
> Also, today, Dr. Martin regretfully announced the resignation and immediate departure of Dr. Sue Barton.

"Dr. Barton has been a valuable member of our leadership team, and we will miss her. We wish her the best of success as she pursues her future goals," Dr. Martin said. "I understand Dr. Barton will be returning home to Kentucky in order to be closer to her family and to assist her aging father who is fighting cancer."

Floyd University has three different groups who assemble at the student center each day for coffee and conversation. Most of the mean-spirited rumors skillfully planted by Buzz sprout roots and flourish. People love to talk about other people's dirty laundry. Unfounded facts instantly become valid through proclamation. Many embellish the details and repeat vicious gossip while savoring the chance to be in the loop during these morning gatherings.

One club consists of full professors, and joining this group requires an invitation from the university's senior faculty member. The second club is an assembly of younger faculty members. It is an informal gathering, and the relaxed atmosphere encourages anyone to sit at the table and join the discussion. The members of the third group are very exclusive. Only retired male faculty and staff can join. The chief coordinator, or "quarterback," for this assembly is the retired Joe Harlow, the legendary football coach.

Within the full professor group, Dr. Ann Spencer, professor of chemistry, proclaims she was in the administration building the day before and overheard the VP's secretary talking in the ladies' restroom. Apparently, Dr. Barton was forced to resign because she had used some of the money in the department's budget to purchase personal items such as luggage and a new briefcase.

Across the room on the other side of the cafeteria, a second-year assistant professor, Dr. Mary Beth Glazer, declares that Dr. Barton recently missed several aerobics classes at the community rec center and that lately she's seemed really depressed, almost heartbroken. Three people said they heard that Sue's husband was pressuring her for a divorce. The group concludes it must be true, so apparently she resigned in order to deal with the pending messy divorce issue.

One hour later, the retirees assemble for coffee and take control of the tables previously occupied by the full professors. In less than five minutes, the hot topic of conversation becomes Dr. Barton's unusual departure. The group's "senior member," Joe Harlow, quietly shares with his friends that he has heard from a very reliable source, a vice president who serves on the president's cabinet, the true, confidential reason for this immediate resignation. Everyone leans forward to hear and savor the details.

In a calm, low-pitched voice, old Coach Joe tilts his head to assert his authority, and with a casual hand gesture, he smiles and simply says, "Apparently, the president was recently making the rounds on campus and walked into Dr. Barton's office one afternoon to say hello. He accidentally caught her having sex on the floor with the new Spanish teacher. You know, that young, handsome man from Minnesota who just started teaching in the language department."

As final exams conclude and commencement day arrives, not one friend or colleague elects to speak on behalf of Dr. Barton. The senior department chair and distinguished professor of physics, Dr. Bud Warton, calls a few colleagues and privately questions the proportionality of this harsh punishment. His questions and concerns fall on deaf ears. Everyone chants the wisdom of NIMBY: "not in my backyard." Three different chairs remind him that this issue is not their fight, and it is certainly not in their job description.

The campus community, at large, fails to demonstrate the fundamental aspects of critical thinking that are taught everyday throughout the curriculum. Hasty judgments are made, while many faculty and staff jump to unfounded conclusions. Most of the faculty are perplexed, but they still prefer to stand aloof from the turmoil. The majority of employees are content with the auto response that underscores their culture of silence. After commencement, the entire faculty with nine-month contracts quickly departs the campus for summer break.

Three weeks later, on June 12, a Mayflower moving van is parked in front of Dr. Barton's house.

———✦———

Now the campus clock chimes two! Buzz quickly realizes he has less than thirty minutes to prepare. As the department chair, today is his first meeting with his old hunting buddy, the dean. Suddenly, his secretary calls on the intercom to announce that Ms. Diana Dawson would like to visit with him for a few minutes.

Buzz is privately delighted, but he responds in a condescending manner as he formally instructs his secretary to invite Ms. Dawson into his office.

Buzz smiles as he hears the quick rhythm of stiletto heels clicking into the room.

"Good morning, Diana."

"Hi, sweetheart," Ms. Dawson replies.

Buzz snaps. "How many times have I warned you? Don't call me that when we are on campus!"

"Now, sweetheart, we are alone, your door is closed, and you know that old battle-ax of a secretary is hard of hearing."

After a quick kiss, Buzz melts like butter and wraps his arms around Ms. Dawson. He slowly runs his hands down her perfect curves and grabs her tight ass.

She immediately slides her arms around his neck, leans back against the desk, and wraps her legs around his waist. As she gently licks the inside of his ear, she whispers, "Do you like my new sundress, honey?"

"Yes, I love your new dress, and you are wearing my favorite perfume!"

"Good, I bought this dress just for you, and I want you to know that I am not wearing anything under it. Does that interest you?"

"Hell yes, but your timing could not be worse. I have a meeting in less than twenty minutes."

Buzz still marvels at this hot, sexy blonde. Diana unexpectedly walks into his life, and quickly becomes his dream-come-true sexual playmate.

In less than six weeks, Buzz conquered the girl who has become the talk of the town. Hired by Dr. Barton last August 1984, Diana walked onto the campus and immediately became the center of focus. When she enters a room, all the men find a way to look, hopefully without staring. Her flirty ways, sexy dresses, and youthful curves are known to all; even the security guards have been smitten by her charm.

There are some problems to overcome in the beginning. Since they are both married to other people, they have to hide their undercover romance.

"Honey, why don't you tell your wife you have to work late tonight grading papers so we can have some fun over at my apartment? I promise to fix your favorite lasagna, and I will serve you dessert in my new crimson red outfit from Victoria's Secret!"

"Wow that sounds great. Consider it a date."

Buzz is lost in thought for a minute. How easy this conquest has developed for him. All the circumstances seem to have fallen into place like some great master plan. She wants his support as department chair. She is demanding paid leave to pursue her studies for a doctorate degree. One hot August afternoon during the campus picnic, he disguises his proposal as a joke and casually suggests his endorsement might be possible to arrange if she joins him in bed. And to his surprise, this beautiful twenty-eight-year-old lady quickly smiles, and with the sunlight glistening across her ponytail, enthusiastically says yes.

She is about ten years younger than Buzz, and she truly enjoys the excitement and suspense of an extramarital affair. Standing at five feet seven inches tall, by everyone's standards, she is a perfect 10. Without question, she is the best eye candy in Turtle County. Buzz gives her a 12 whenever she takes him to bed because her slender, agile body knows all the moves for countless sexual rhythms and positions. She always takes him to erotic playgrounds that far exceeds his wildest fantasies.

She convinces Buzz that he is her first tryst. She tells him his charisma is compelling, totally irresistible. But in reality, he is number thirty-one on her coup d'état list. He never dreams that she aspires to add many more names to her small black pocket-sized diary. This sleek little booklet is inscribed on the first page with a beautiful calligraphy that says: "Today's Conquest becomes Tomorrow's Opportunity."

Married to a wealthy man twenty-three years her senior, the flame of love in Diana's marriage died years ago while she was struggling to finish her master's degree. Since her husband lives and works 260 miles away, she is alone most of the time throughout the week. The exception to this rule comes on weekends when she travels home to join her family. Whenever together, their failing marriage suffers through many long hours of silence and mindless television. Their newly built five-thousand-square-foot mansion stands in the middle of Stone Cliff Estates, an exclusive gated development just across Highway 2 near the Niobrara River. They jointly own a half section of land covered with native blue spruce and Scotch pines. Within the confines of exorbitant luxury, weekends are a time for Diana to holler at their two kids and fight with her semiretired husband. Every Sunday evening, she looks forward to her return drive to Springview. Monday through Friday, within the privacy of her two-bedroom rental home, she lives a lifestyle of uninhibited sexual freedom.

8

Partners in Crime

What the ancients called a clever fighter is one who
not only wins, but excels in winning with ease.

—Sun Tzu, 600 BC

November 1985
Floyd University

"Thanks for this hot tea. Do you by chance have any sugar?" It is a rhetorical question. Marsha instinctively knows her friend Emmy has some sugar in her desk drawer.

"Oh, absolutely! My apologies. I should have offered some sugar to you when I gave you the tea. I also have creamer if you want some." Emmy reaches into the large bottom drawer on the left side of her massive oak desk.

"No, thanks! I just need a little sugar. You know, Samuel has spoiled us with his extravagant layouts for high tea. I really enjoy those gatherings out at Bonnie's."

They both laugh. Emmy nods in agreement as she looks across at Marsha Ann. It is clear that Marsha's decorum matches the troubled look that is written all over her face.

For several minutes, both ladies sit in silence, sipping their steaming tea. With their hands wrapped around the Styrofoam cups, they stare into the golden liquid as if searching for a glimpse of understanding that would disclose the meaning of life. Emmy senses that something is wrong, but she hesitates to pry. Their friendship is warm but casual. Their offices are across the hall from each other, so they share a collegial bond as neighbors within the same hallway. Emmy does not want to push the boundaries of this conversation too far. Besides, this is a rare occasion. Normally, Marsha is one of the most positive, upbeat persons on campus. But today, she is in a reflective, subdued mood.

With a pensive gaze out the window, Marsha says, "Have you ever thought about the dark side of human nature and the way it influences our life here on campus?"

Emmy hesitates. Truthfully, as a young assistant professor in the art department, she has not spent much time analyzing the organizational culture of their university. She wants to be a good listener, so she says, "Marsha, you have more years of teaching here than me, so I feel like I may not have enough experience to answer your question. Did you have something specific in mind?"

"Yes, several things come to mind. Generally, I like to think about the positive side of life. You know, like love and peace and joy and a willingness to help others. I always trust people to do the right thing, and my poetry tries to convey those feelings and values."

Marsha halts briefly and looks directly at Emmy. She wants to level with her colleague, but she wonders if Emmy is willing to engage in a serious conversation about this topic. Marsha continues. "My intuition tells me that I will be denied tenure. I believe there is a dark side to the human heart, and unfortunately, we have several influential people on campus who go through each day guided by a value system that fosters evil and harm to others."

Emmy gasps. She is so shocked about Marsha's tenure statement that she fails to hear or comprehend the rest of Marsha's observation about the unabashed evil on their campus.

"Whatever gave you the idea that you will not be approved for tenure? I can't think of anyone else more deserving. Oh my gosh! If you don't make it, the rest of us are doomed!"

"How well do you know Diana Dawson and Buzz Granger?"

Emmy responds, "Really not that well. Since they both office in a different building across campus, I don't see them often. Why do you ask?"

"If you had to guess, what do you think about their relationship? I mean, specifically between us girls, do you think Buzz is screwing her?"

Smiling profusely, Emmy bubbles with the enthusiasm that comes when you share a good tidbit of gossip. "Well, since you asked, I would say…hell yes! But actually, I hear more rumors about Buzz sleeping with female student athletes than I hear about him screwing Diana."

Marsha presses for more details. "And why do you suppose they call Diana the Red Dragon Lady?"

"That is a really good question. I first overheard two football players using that phrase after one of my freshmen art classes. At first, I had no idea who they were talking about. I assumed they were discussing another female student who was hot in bed. Their voices were hushed like two young fraternity boys talking about their secret handshake or sacred password. A few weeks later, Samuel told me they were probably talking about Diana. I was shocked!"

"Well, Diana reminds me of a certain beautiful flower—the angel's trumpet. Have you ever seen one, Emmy?"

"No, I am not familiar with that flower. Where does it grow?"

"Last year, my husband took me to the botanical gardens in St. Louis. They have several species growing there in the outdoor courtyard next to a huge fountain. In some tropical parts of the world, these shrubs grow wild and bloom all year. I was so impressed with their shape, color, and beautiful scent. However, like Diana, they are beautiful to look at, but totally poisonous."

Emmy's gaze returns back into her cup of tea. Her trance-like focus signals someone lost in an ocean of deep thought. Again, both ladies become momentarily silent.

Finishing her tea, Marsha starts to gather her books as she prepares to leave. "Emmy, have you ever been in Buzz Granger's office and looked at that weird Chinese war slogan on his wall?"

Puzzled, but responding to the question with friendly body language, Emmy answers, "No, what does it say?"

"Emmy, I think it speaks volumes about the attitudes and dirty politics that seem to permeate the organizational culture of our campus. I grow weary every time I hear about these hoodlums and all their ruthless stunts. The joy of teaching here has been tarnished by their dark energy and mean-spirited ways."

Marsha stops. She manages to smile, but there is deep sadness in her eyes. "Hey, I don't mean to be so preachy. Guess I better run, or I will be late for my afternoon class. Thanks again for the hot tea. See you later, my friend."

As a young college professor, Buzz has become enamored with the ancient text *The Art of War* by Sun Tzu. Over the years, beginning on the playground as a bully, Buzz has become hooked on the sense of authority he feels whenever he coerces someone to comply with his demands. Like a man constantly looking for his next emotional high, Buzz feels euphoria every time he goes to "war" against an opponent.

During this past decade, he has managed to cultivate a network of colleagues on campus who relentlessly maneuver to get whatever Buzz wants. In his own way, he practices the classic art of "an indirect attack" investing countless hours developing intricate plans that prompt his friends to admire the clever ways he manages to get things done.

Frequently, it is difficult for Buzz to find anyone at the student center coffee nook willing to discuss Sun Tzu's concepts. Several times during coffee conversations, Buzz flaunts his knowledge about the Chinese art of warfare, but someone in the group always finds a way to change the subject back to a topic more relevant to university life.

Privately, many of the other department chairs feel Buzz carries most of his warfare conversations too far. After all, the Vietnam War is over, and the peace and tranquility of their rural campus hardly seems to fit the context for Buzz's military pontifications. To his surprise, very few visitors ever notice his favorite warfare sign that he proudly displays in his office.

In 1974, after starting his new teaching job, he promises his wife a real vacation. She is thinking perhaps of Disneyland. He is thinking about something less expensive and somewhere close, within driving distance. They finally compromise and drive six hundred miles to Medora, North Dakota, to visit the Badlands and the Theodore Roosevelt National Park.

While there, Buzz finds an artist who has mastered Chinese calligraphy working in downtown Medora at the corner gift shop. Buzz pays him a premium fee of $25 to convert his favorite Sun Tzu saying into a framed calligraphy print suitable for hanging. Ever since returning from vacation, this sign has been hanging in Buzz's office as a bold signal of his professional philosophy. The ancient *Art of War* slogan says,

Opportunities multiply as they are seized.

With some reflective thought, Buzz concludes that this ancient slogan encourages audacious initiative, and the great Chinese master is suggesting that the ends always justify the means.

Like a little old woman, Buzz loves to hear gossip. Moreover, he is skilled at fabricating and planting believable rumors. After all, Sun Tzu says, "All warfare is based on deception." This inclination toward dishonesty, plus his admiration for Sun Tzu's other deception strategies, converges over time motivating Buzz to foster and utilize a network of spies whenever possible.

Occasionally, his friend Diana listens to his Sun Tzu ramblings. At times, he thinks she is just humoring him, but sometimes her interest seems genuine. There are a few conversations where Diana actually seems to share a small degree of interest regarding Buzz's knowledge of Sun Tzu. From time to time, she uses Sun Tzu concepts in her civil war class.

One afternoon, during coffee at Bonnie's Brew, Buzz leans across the table and confides in Diana, "You know, I am convinced my office is bugged."

"What a crazy idea, Buzz! Whatever prompted you to think that?"

"Diana, there have been a couple of times when the vice president for finance has repeated some of the words almost verbatim that I have said in the privacy of my office. You know he chairs the facilities committee, and I am attending those meetings as the faculty senate representative. It is uncanny the way he knows what I have said about his crazy construction proposals."

Very skeptical and puzzled, Diana says, "Surely you are kidding. How could your office be bugged? Buzz, you sound kind of paranoid. I don't think it would be technically possible to plant a bug in your office. Maybe you have been watching too many James Bond movies!"

"Look, I did the research. There are small audio receivers about the size of a dime that will transmit normal conversations to approximately two hundred yards. Yesterday, I tried to act casual while I walked across campus, but I paced the distance from my office over to the VP's office in the administration building. By my measurements, it is about 180 yards. So, he could sit in his office and listen to everything I say during the day!"

"Buzz, I certainly hope you are kidding. Why would the VP for finance want to sit around all day and listen to you belch, fart, and talk on the telephone?"

"Well, I am worried. This is serious, Diana. Yesterday, I used the pay phone at the student center and placed an order for one of those magic wands that you can get out of that home security catalog. The description says this battery-operated stick is guaranteed to detect any electronic device that transmits for more than two consecutive minutes."

Diana hesitates. A frown creeps across her forehead as she attempts to continue the conversation. She wonders if Buzz is starting to lose his grip on reality. Casually, she looks out the window and says, "Well, let me know if you find anything. We better curtail our sexual comments the next time you call me for a date and talk about another blowjob fantasy."

Desperately wanting to change the subject so she can address her primary agenda, Diana says, "Sweetheart, with all your knowledge about warfare, how would you quickly crush someone you absolutely hate?"

Buzz lights up like a bright high-intensity bulb. Now she wants to talk about one of his favorite topics.

"Well that depends upon the situation, Diana. As a general rule, Sun Tzu would say you must move swift as the wind, quiet as the forest, and conquer like fire." Buzz hits the table with his fist while chanting the words from one of his favorite verses.

"I really like that approach! I have someone in mind, and I propose you and I swiftly crush her, but we must be quiet like a mouse when we do it!"

"Come on, Diana, quiet as a f-o-r-e-s-t, not a mouse! There is nothing manly about the image of a mouse!"

"Okay, okay, I want you to be my ally and help me destroy Marsha Ann Montgomery! No questions asked!"

Silence fell across the table. Buzz was astounded.

"Marsha? But why? She is such a great teacher. I think she seems to be well-liked on campus."

Sensing his reservations, Diana's voice and demeanor immediately becomes harsh and assertive. "Hey, sweetheart, I said no questions. You are going to do this because you like to take me to bed. I am looking for a trusted partner in crime! On the other hand, if you lack the courage to follow all those Sun Tzu's slogans, then this conversation is over and you will never touch my pussy again. And who knows, your wife might accidently find some surprising information in her mailbox when you least expect it!"

Marsha Ann Montgomery is a bright star within the university's crown of academic talent. She has her act together. She is a great teacher and published author; her last book of poetry was translated into three languages and published in fourteen different countries. Her PhD transcript from Northwestern University showcases an impeccable 4.0 GPA.

Born on a northeast Iowa farm, raised as the third child among seven children, Marsha emerges from her teenage years as a "very old soul." When questioned and teased by her family, she jokingly says her old soul was genetic. She begins writing poetry at the age of twelve and by the time she finishes high school, her writing has become a daily habit.

She gets married while in graduate school; her husband is an engineer who does not want kids. Eight years ago, he was transferred by the State Department of Transportation to Springview as the regional highway manager. During the first two years in Springview, Marsha works on campus as an adjunct professor. And then by chance, in the summer of 1980, there is an unexpected retirement and subsequent opening in the English department.

During the last six years, her teaching record has been stellar. She is involved with the faculty senate, and her campus service record with student organizations is outstanding. With several published journal articles and three successful books, her scholarship is unquestioned. To be sure, she is emerging as one of the most published scholars in the history of the university. Just recently, she signed a book contract with Brick Road Poetry Press, a major publishing house headquartered in Columbus, Georgia. This publisher has global marketing outlets and plans to translate her next poetry book and sell it throughout Asia.

By all established standards, Marsha is a shoo-in for tenure. Everyone expects her tenure packet to be readily approved. A few of her aerobics friends are secretly planning a surprise party for her once the announcement becomes public. But late one Thursday afternoon, in the spring of 1986, the campus community is stunned when Marsha is denied tenure.

Once the tenure committee vote is formally endorsed by the board, the outcome of the tenure proceedings becomes public knowledge. Marsha Ann is devastated. It is one of the greatest injustices she has encountered during her forty-one years of life. After that fateful day, she stops attending Samuel's high teas, and is never seen again at the student center or the campus bookstore. She immediately becomes reclusive and withdraws from all campus committees and activities. She continues to teach her classes and maintains her mandatory ten office hours per week. However, following the May graduation ceremony, to everyone's great surprise and disappointment, she quietly transferred to Chadron State College with a new teaching contract that started during the next fall semester. About six months later, her husband's request for a job transfer is approved, and he joins her in Chadron.

—ɷ—

"Do you think anyone knows about out private coup d'état?"

Diana whispers into Buzz's left ear as they are lining up for the 1986 fall semester opening convocation.

He is cautious and reluctant to respond in such a public setting. Undaunted, Diana continues to flaunt her prowess. "Don't you think old Sun Tzu would be proud of us?"

After all, like a great battle captain, Diana coerced Buzz to use his campus influence in a magnificent way. Subsequently, he forced Coach Moore to alter the outcome of the committee's tenure vote. The entire process is flawless! And the best part— only three people know the inside story and the dirty details. Buzz smiles and winks at his partner in crime. "Yes, I think the ancient master would be very proud of us! We were swift as the wind and quiet as a forest."

They both laugh as they move into their assigned positions for the convocation march into the auditorium.

Diana wants the last word, so she turns and brazenly says, "You know, I think this will be a great academic year! We are off to a wonderful beginning."

9

Rowing through a Turbulent Storm

The real evil with which we have to contend is not
the physical evil…but the moral evil of the selfish,
perverse, and turbulent character of the people.

—Charles Trevelyan, 1807–1886

April 1987
Bonnie's Brew

After almost three years of tradition, today's high tea event goes on record as one of the best-ever Thursday afternoon gatherings. Samuel's weekly party has become very popular among the junior faculty. Everyone has had a great time, and the conversations are upbeat and delightful. Samuel is pleased. Every now and then, the group's chemistry is just right, and today a crowd of about twenty-five shower words of appreciation upon Samuel as they depart Bonnie's Brew. The beautiful spring weather seems to accent Samuel's hospitality, and this winning combination produces a smashing afternoon success.

"Emmy, did you have fun this afternoon?"

"Oh, for sure, Samuel, I think your party today was one of the best we have ever experienced."

"Hey, we are the last two dogs to leave. How about joining me on my back deck and I will grill a couple of steaks? Are you hungry, Emmy?"

Emmy smiles. Her stormy eyes flash with delight. "That really sounds wonderful. Let me make one stop downtown to pick up my prescription refill and run by the house to walk my little dog, Dannyboy. I will join you at your house in about an hour."

Samuel is pleased. His friendship with Emmy has grown this past eighteen months. About two years ago, Samuel courted Emmy's friendship with romantic designs. Through his love struck eyes, she was the perfect doppelganger for his first girlfriend, Patty, back in the Missouri Bootheel. He adored Emmy and hoped she felt the same about him. Finally, one evening, Samuel pushed very hard to get a commitment from her. He had been shopping for a diamond ring and wanted a signal from her that his feelings were reciprocated. Under pressure, Emmy decided to level with him. So that evening, they had a serious talk that lasted until almost midnight. Yes, she loved him but she loved him like a brother, not a husband.

Samuel still remembers the conversation like it was yesterday. In a thousand years, he would have never guessed that Emmy was a closet lesbian. He was completely speechless when she told him that she preferred other women for her sexual encounters. After she confided in him, Samuel's ego was hurt. For weeks, he was embarrassed about his shopping excursions for an engagement ring. After a few months, however, he came to terms with Emmy's sexual preferences. For Samuel, Emmy was his *la douleur exquise*! From that point forward, their platonic love and trust grew. Their friendship was like an aged wine that became enriched with the passing of time.

"Samuel, you know I am currently sleeping with an older woman who lives in Sioux City, don't you?"

"Yes, Emmy. You told me that a few months ago."

Well, last weekend, she told me a tale that completely blew my mind."

Carefully pouring a nice Italian Pinot Noir into Emmy's wine goblet, Samuel responds, "Really, what did she say?"

"Well, her ex-lover, who happens to still be her friend and business colleague, is somewhat of a power lesbian. A few weeks ago, they had coffee together. During their visit, this classy lady confided that while she was having a Sapphic slump, she started cheating and had a brief fling about two years ago with Diana Dawson."

"Good Lord! What the hell is a Sapphic slump? And surely you don't mean our Diana Dawson, do you?"

"Samuel, Samuel, what am I going to do with you?" Emmy smiles as she prepares to broaden his sexual knowledge and liberate his old-fashioned paradigms.

"Yes, I am sure of it. How many Diana Dawson's do you know from Springview that work here at our university? And by the way, a Sapphic slump is a low-point in a lesbian relationship when the two ladies are not getting along."

Samuel stops pouring the wine giving Emmy his complete attention.

"Anyway, one night, they were together in bed. During their pillow talk after sex, Diana was drinking and let her hair down. According to my friend's old lover, Diana talked nonstop about a beautiful lady here on campus who had become the loathe of her life after she totally rejected Diana's sexual advances. My friend clearly remembers because the lady from the university was married and older than Diana. Her name was Marsha Ann something."

"I say, dear Emmy, do you think it was Marsha Ann Montgomery?"

"Well, I am not sure, but deductive reasoning would indicate that it was probably Dr. Montgomery. Who else could it be?"

Samuel's brain is in a fog of confusion. His thought process jumps to several possible conclusions, and he feels somewhat besieged. He desperately wants to understand, but his mind is sorting conflicting facts. Trying to adjudicate these disconnects, he begins to logically sequence these circumstances.

"Emmy, we both know Diana and Marsha are married and living with their husbands. I have always thought Diana was cheating on her husband and taking old baldy, Buzz Granger, to bed, but this homosexual thing confuses me. How could this be?"

Emmy smiles. She never ceases to be surprised at Samuel's school-boy innocence and old-fashioned naivety.

"Come on, Samuel, you need to get with it. Step into the twentieth century and liberalize your paradigms! For God's sakes, you should know this is the age when bisexual women double-dip! They actively seek dual relationships."

Samuel quickly raises his glass of wine and chugs it like a man looking for courage in the bottom of the glass.

"You know, Samuel, I have given this some thought. I clearly remember Diana aggressively flirting with Marsha at the rec center. But at the time, I just thought she was, like, over-the-top friendly. I frequently saw them together because they always enrolled in the same aerobics class at the gym. Hey, did you ever see Marsha in her sleek black spandex?"

"My God, no, Emmy! You know I would not be caught dead at that community gym. I hate the thought of exercise. And I hate to sweat! I can honestly and proudly say that I have never stepped foot in our famous rec center."

"Well, trust me. Marsha was really built. She had a gorgeous body. She was a looker, for sure. Great curves and a body shaped like she was about twenty-five years old. I certainly understand Diana's possible interests if she really is bisexual. To be perfectly honest, I frequently found myself turned on by Marsha's beauty and charm. In my world, she was hot!"

Still trying to sort the facts and understand the scenario, Samuel excuses himself and goes out on the deck to get the steaks. In a few minutes, he returns to the kitchen with a wooden platter that holds two perfectly cooked filet mignons.

"Samuel, since we are on this topic, I assume you have heard about Diana's exploits with her students?" Emmy coyly smiles as she begins to cut her steak.

Pensively, Samuel looks across the table. "No, Emmy, I can't say that I have ever heard any gossip about that topic, but tell me more. This seems like a good time to hear the rest of the story, as Paul Harvey would say!"

"Well, I can say with reasonable confidence that Diana's sexual exploits are legendary with some of our football players. Did you ever notice how Diana handpicks her student workers and they always seem to be young, good-looking football players? Trust me, this is not a coincidence."

"Truly amazing! Doesn't she realize those sexual trysts could get her fired? And if those guys are minors, she could go to jail!"

Emmy pauses from her meal to enjoy the wine.

"Actually, I don't think she ever worries about that. She is so bold, so arrogant. She acts like one of those gangsters from the 1930s who called themselves The Untouchables. After all, she is above the law, and the rules don't apply to her."

Samuel quickly reflects upon Emmy's description of Diana. There is merit within Emmy's words. Over the years, Samuel has learned to value her ability to observe and describe people.

Silence lingers across the wooden table and stands like an invisible bridge between two friends who are comfortable together in silence. Finally, Samuel poses a serious question that he must get off his chest.

"Emmy, do you think Diana had something to do with Marsha Ann Montgomery's failure to get tenure?"

"Samuel, you read my mind! I have thought that for more than a year. For several months, the rumor mill on campus suggested Diana and Buzz had something going against Dr. Montgomery. You know my department shares office space with the music, theater, and English departments within Neihardt Hall. The huge consensus in our building believes the tenure vote had to be rigged."

"Emmy, Emmy, how could this be? The tenure procedure is like a sacred tradition. The process is centuries old and has to be respected. My God, we are doomed if our senior colleagues can't be trusted."

"Well, Samuel, you know the old saying about a woman scorned! I believe Diana would be totally ruthless if she was the scorned lady in a failed relationship."

"I say, dear God! All this moral corruption overwhelms me. It is too much! Sometimes I feel like we are continually rowing through a turbulent storm of dirty politics. Emmy, do you ever become weary of all this selfish, abusive power that seems to thrive on our campus? Whatever happened to our sense of fairness, decency, respect, and kindness?"

"Samuel, I want to tell you one more thing. Promise you will keep it confidential?"

"Yes, you have my word!"

"One afternoon before the tenure vote was announced, Marsha Ann stopped in my office for a quick hot tea. She said the tea would give her a badly needed surge of energy. She was really down and wanted to talk. It was like she had some kind of premonition about the vote because she feared that her tenure packet was denied. Can you believe it?"

"Absolutely, yes I believe that some people have a gift, a kind of intuition that signals upcoming problems or pending disappointments. Perhaps Marsha had been given a clue or tip that all was not going well with the review process. Who knows?"

"You know, Samuel, I have thought about that conversation many times. If we had more time, I think Marsha really wanted to bare her soul, and for some reason, she selected me as her confidante. Anyway, she seemed angry and worried about our campus culture and the many corrupt souls who were doing cruel things to others."

Samuel is deeply touched by Emmy's words. The magnitude of these egregious facts stuns him into silence. He tries to avoid any additional conversation by concentrating on his glass of wine.

Emmy fears that she has just sent a ten-ton truck over a five-ton bridge and her dear friend is overwhelmed by her message and their topic of conversation. She tries to become lighthearted and manages to playfully change the subject.

After completing their meal and finishing the bottle of wine, Emmy thanks her dear friend for a wonderful day. She drives directly home because the next day is Friday and she has to teach an early Introduction to Art class that starts at 7:50 a.m.

10

The Scorpion's Hidden Sting

There is an appointed time for everything,
And a time for every affair under the heavens...
A time to love, and a time to hate; a time of war,
and a time of peace.

—Ecclesiastes 3:8

August 1987
Floyd University

In 1987, the world is a vibrant place as the late summer sounds of evening cicadas announce the arrival of autumn colors. The chronicles of American history are filled with headline news about the Iran-Contra hearing and President Ronald Regan's negotiations with Russian leaders to control the proliferation of nuclear missiles. The Minnesota Twins and the St. Louis Cardinals are locked on a collision path to battle each other in the World Series. *Les Miserables* opens on Broadway and launches a performance record that eventually becomes one of the top five longest-running shows in Broadway history. And Paul Simon's album *Graceland* is on a trajectory to win the Grammy Award as the best record of the year.

And on August 30, 1987, the space shuttle *Discovery* is launched for a six-day mission that includes the deployment of a relay satellite and a number of classified scientific experiments. As the shuttle soars into space, millions of people around the world sit with their eyes fixed to their television.

Diana Dawson, however, could care less about space exploration, baseball, or politics. Late that morning, she drove to campus to work in her office to complete the final edits for her fall semester course syllabi.

Outside, the sun is blazing as the temperature races toward another hundred-degree afternoon. In keeping with the weather forecast, Diana is wearing a new red, very sheer sundress that gives the casual viewer a distinct outline of all her curves and her red Victoria-Secret lace bra. The telephone rings. Diana answers and finds herself talking directly to the vice president for academic affairs.

The conversation only lasts a few minutes, but Diana does not like the message. In less than sixty seconds, she loses control of her temper and completely explodes. "If you think I am going to accept this decision, you have a lot to learn. You bitch! Who do you think you are? I will make you dread this very day! For as long as you continue to work here, I will make you pay for this outrageous decision."

Diana is red-hot. Her temper matches her new dress. As she slams the phone down, she cusses like a drunken sailor. Ever since her elementary school years, Diana has always found a way to get what she wants, and she never accepts no for an answer.

The vice president is stunned as she hangs up the phone, blazing cusswords echoing in her ear. She is not accustomed to such rude verbal abuse from a subordinate. She expects faculty members to be polite and professional regardless of the circumstances. This expectation was especially true since she was talking with a junior faculty member who was asking for a favor. Actually, there was very little to discuss. The faculty handbook is very clear on the matter. Individuals seeking extended professional development leave have to complete seven years of service with the university before they are eligible for a paid sabbatical. There is a formal application process that must to be followed, and, if approved for a sabbatical, the individual can elect one of two options. Paid sabbaticals are defined as either one academic year with half pay or a single semester with full pay.

Fifteen minutes after slamming the phone down, Diana walks across the campus and finds her friend Buzz drinking coffee at the student center. She carefully hints to him that they need to talk. Buzz looks at his buddies, excuses himself, and departs with the pretense that they have some faculty senate work to complete before the upcoming September organizational meeting.

Buzz escorts Diana back to his office. She remains silent as she walks with a very brisk pace. Buzz realizes that she is super mad. Once his office door is closed, Diana turns her back to his window, casually slides out of her sundress, and drops it on the floor.

Buzz is momentarily stunned by her fearless exhibition. The miniblinds on the office window are completely open. He quickly moves over to the door and turns the lock. This is not a good time for his secretary to walk in with a phone message.

Diana is wearing red satin panties, a skimpy see-through bra, and red designer sandals. As she sits on top of the oak desk, she crosses her legs and commands, "Buzz, I need a drink, and it has to be something stronger than coffee."

In the corner of the office, there is a badly worn, government-surplus file cabinet that looks terrible but has a perfectly functional lock system. Buzz moves like a graceful pro. He unlocks the cabinet and reaches into the bottom drawer. In less than three minutes, he hands Diana a plastic glass filled with Kentucky's finest whiskey bottled by Jim Beam.

Buzz tries to start the conversation. "Sorry, I can't offer you any ice. I hope you like it straight because I don't have anything on hand to mix with it." Trying to be cute, he adds, "Besides, it is made to cure what ails you."

Diana turns with anger and gestures toward the administration building. "That bitch! She thinks I am outrageous! She believes my request is unfair and violates the established policy. Just because I only have four years of teaching service, she wants me to wait three more years before I get a paid sabbatical. Imagine! She had the nerve to decline my request! She does not want to set a new precedent that others might abuse!"

Diana points her finger at Buzz as she downs her glass of bourbon and asks for a refill. "Buzz, this is war. That royal bitch has to go! I am telling you, make it happen. Get rid of her. Nobody says no to me and survives without paying the price."

Buzz tries to be diplomatic. He struggles for words. "Diana, try to calm down. Let's think this through."

Diana explodes like a cork popping out of a wine bottle.

"Shit, Buzz, I am done talking. There is nothing more to debate. This is a time to hate and a time for war. That haughty bitch has to go now."

Diana pauses and Buzz notices her nipples are erect.

"Let me put it to you in plain English, Buzz. I am telling you that if you ever want your hard cock to touch this pussy of mine again, you *will* find a way to make this happen. Start pulling some of your political strings today."

With a draconian demeanor, Diana is a spoiled little girl who wants to get her way regardless of the cost to others.

In a flash of movement and with agile fingers and soft hands, Diana grabs the zipper on Buzz's grey Dockers. Quickly, she undoes his belt, and his slacks fall down around his ankles. His cock is throbbing after watching her guzzle bourbon like it was water as she moved around the office in her red underwear.

Diana looks directly into his eyes.

"Buzz, the rumor around the girl's locker room says you like a good blowjob. Is that true, sweetheart?" The tone in her voice has changed. Like flipping a switch, she is no longer angry. Now she sounds like a sweet little schoolgirl who wants to play.

"Hell, yes!" Buzz replies as he enjoys the slow stroking movement of her satin-like hands against his cock.

"Well, since you are going to be a good boy and help me get my revenge, I am going to make you stand in front of your office window while I give you a nice reward for your good behavior. You watch your friends go down the sidewalk, honey, and I will give you a blowjob that you will always remember."

In less than five minutes, Diana finishes her task at hand. She savors every drop and playfully kisses his balls while helping Buzz pull his slacks back up. He slowly fastens his belt as he watches her get dressed.

Diana smiles as she climbs into her sundress. She stuffs her bra into the side pocket of her purse and politely says, "I could use another refill on my bourbon, sweetheart. Think of it as a chaser!"

With his eyes transfixed on Diana's low-cut, braless look, Buzz delightfully complies and pours the last of his fine Jim Beam into her glass.

Playfully, Diana looks at Buzz, smiles, and pauses like she is pondering a profound thought. "Honey, there is no time like the present. I expect you to start the ball rolling right now. I want that son of a b—— vice president to suffer."

Buzz goes to the phone and dutifully dials the only number he knows he can trust behind the serene veil where unabashed power prevails. He pauses briefly after hitting the second number in the five-digit campus sequence. For just a few seconds, he feels an unusual blend of emotions.

For sure, there is the feeling of pleasure from the afterglow of an incredible blowjob.

But also, there is a sense of shock, like a man realizing he has just been hit by the scorpion's hidden sting. And there is a sense of regret because he is being forced to start an unexpected battle. Plus, there is a tinge of fear like a man haunted when he has been pushed down a long, slippery slope into the shadows of a dragon's chamber.

The phone rings three times. A male voice with a friendly tone answers.

"Good afternoon, this is Dean Warton. How can I help you?"

11

Assassinate the Vice President

> Slander is a kind of murder, for we have three lives: the spiritual, the physical and the social...Sin deprives us of the first, death takes away the second, and slander robs us of the third...Slander is the true bane of our society.
>
> —Saint Francis de Sales, 1608

September 1987
Floyd University

"Shit! We can do this!" Buzz says.

"Are you sure?" Dean Warton snaps.

Visibly irritated and quick to anger, Buzz answers. "Hell yes! It worked last time, and it will work again. She has to go."

It has been almost three years since Buzz and his two hunting buddies launched their battle plan to depose Dr. Barton. The success of that experience has fueled Buzz's sense of power and importance. He feels invincible! And more importantly, he wants to please his girlfriend, the little red dragon.

Now Buzz has declared war on a new foe—Dr. Mary Jane Kelley. On the inside, he is boiling with rage as his blood pressure escalates. Outwardly, his face is bright red, his eyes are squinted, and he is pacing the floor like a man overcome with agitation. Clearly, his short fuse has ignited an uncontrollable reservoir of anger, and he is ready to muster all available resources to teach her a lesson.

Three years ago, in mid-August 1985, Mary Jane Kelley walked on the campus as the new vice president for academic affairs. The first female in the history of the school to ever serve at the rank of vice president, she was not well received. Too many new ideas! She met a wall of resistance. None of the department chairs wanted to change anything. After all, they were working in their comfort zone, and they liked their daily routines.

"How much support do we have across the campus?" the dean asks.

Buzz knows he is on solid footing. "I can assure you at least ten of our twenty-one chairs will help us. And the rest, well, they can be persuaded to either go along or stay the hell out of the way." Buzz spoke with arrogance. He has transformed his bully childhood techniques from the playground to the hallways of campus. After all, practice does make perfect. Consequently, Buzz has become a very sophisticated bully. He is simultaneously subtle and bizarre. Many privately fear his wrath, especially the custodial staff.

During the last several months, Buzz has used his underground network of friends to develop and circulate a three-page statement of accusations against the VPAA. Most of the complaints are unfounded gripes and exaggerated rumors. But that does not deter Buzz. He is determined to assassinate the vice president's character with a major campaign of slander, and he expects the dean to join the cause.

With a haughty sense of confidence, Buzz says, "I will be in Omaha next weekend, and I plan to anonymously mail a copy of our charges to the board chairman. So I need you to carefully watch for signals from the board and president. We need to know if they are going to act upon our complaints."

Dean Warton is uncomfortable. He says, "Let's check with Senator Abe and see what he thinks before you mail the packet."

Buzz agrees. Then he smugly reminds the dean that he has a secret weapon that they can use. "Don't forget my wife is very good friends with the president's wife. They get together for coffee every week after they finish choir practice at the church."

"Going after a vice president is risky. I don't want to jeopardize my position as dean and hurt my retirement plans."

Buzz cunningly tries to give the dean some confidence. "Remember, the Remarkable Trinity is an unbeatable team. And I can always ask Maggie to probe with a few questions. She always digs up hot poop whenever I need the inside scoop."

Senator Abe never fails to reach into his treasure chest of tricks to come up with a winning strategy. This time he decides to use his friendship with the newspaper editor to place that haughty VPAA under the microscope of public scrutiny.

The senator wisely suggests the main avenue of attack should come from someone off campus. This approach would disguise their intent while protecting the dean and his undercover cohort, Buzz. And from the sidelines, they would be free to work the campus grapevine while they stay behind the scenes.

The next day, the senator invites the editor, Ronald Harvey Kronberg, to lunch at the country club. Everyone in town just calls him Harvey. After living in Springview for more than twenty years, he is well known and his weekly editorial is widely read. Every Sunday, his OPED appears, and the readers know Harvey always finds the glass at least half-empty, regardless of the topic. Many times his viewpoint is controversial, and most of the time, his target is either the mayor or the city council.

During lunch, the two men spend most of their time discussing a variety of rumors about the VPAA. With a false pretense of innocence, the senator remarks that the newspaper might want to request copies of the VP's travel expenses, especially, the Atlanta trip that happened two months ago.

Harvey is quick to support the senator's suspicions. Many times in the past, he has served as a stenographer for the senator's political power. He returns to his office after lunch and composes a formal FOIA, or freedom of information act, request for the VP's travel expenses from the last two years.

Two weeks later, after several late-night discussions at the senator's house with creative brainstorming sessions fueled by good whiskey, the final plan emerges. The senator calls Harvey almost daily in order to "give" him suggestions.

The next Sunday morning, to everyone's surprise, the residents of Springview awake to find this headline across the front page of the paper: "Vice President Kelley Squanders Taxpayer's Money."

The article contains very few facts, but lots of opinion. The reporter has slanted the numbers and discusses them out of context. It is a standard writing approach taught in every journalism curriculum: sensationalism. For more than four hundred years, entrepreneurs have used the printing press to spread gossip and make money. Carefully coached by Harvey and his assistant editor, Jolee McBride, the young reporter crafts a textbook perfect example of yellow journalism. Around the newsroom, Harvey repeatedly says, "Come on, folks. Let's make hay while the sun shines." Every evening, Jolee thrives on the opportunity to compose a number of inflammatory headlines that quickly stimulate a 20 percent increase in newsstand sales.

While Harvey wants to please his hometown senator, he secretly hopes to generate some excitement in order to increase the sales of his newspaper. For the last two years, his net income has shown red-ink numbers. The deficit has been so drastic within his last quarterly financial summary that he has had to take a second mortgage on his home in order to generate cash flow for his monthly payroll.

This past year, the university's strategic plan was updated, and the VPAA inherited the new goal to foster student success and improve both retention and graduation rates. Consequently, the vice president organizes a team of six senior faculty and staff and takes them to Atlanta to attend the annual National Student Success Conference. The third evening of the conference is open for participants to enjoy the sights of Atlanta. Vice President Kelley invites her colleagues to dinner with the hope of fostering their sense of teamwork and to begin a conversation about ways to transfer ideas from the conference back to the campus in the form of action plans.

The restaurant is not high-end, but evening dinners in downtown Atlanta are expensive. They have a four-course meal: soup, salad, main entrée, and dessert with coffee. During the meal, they enjoy three bottles of red wine. The VP could have asked for individual tickets, but as the host she pays the bill and turns the receipt into the business office along with her other travel expenses. She documents all the meal receipts following university policy and state auditor guidelines. And she uses her personal money to pay for the wine. The total cost for the evening meal exceeds $1,000—$160 per person. Seven people plus gratuity totals almost $1,300.

In rural Nebraska, the average citizen is conservative and quick to join any uproar that involves taxpayers' money. Few residents of Springview have ever been to Atlanta, and most of the outspoken critics have never considered the rising cost of food in a major urban city. Besides, no one wants to examine the facts or use reflective thinking skills. A mob-fever mentality sweeps through the community, and the VPAA is guilty until proven innocent.

After the lead story, Harvey follows the next day with a scathing editorial that fills half a page. The newspaper's hotline accumulates burning, inflammatory statements as well as rumors and gossip about the vice president. Most of the anonymous accusations have nothing to do with the topic of travel expenses. The ultraconservatives use this opportunity to bash state government in general and no-good, liberal intellectuals in particular.

The third day of turmoil witnesses a quantum leap of frenzied accusations when the state's taxpayers association circulates an outrageous newsletter and the *Omaha World Herald*, the only newspaper with statewide distribution, elects to run a front-page, top-fold story that basically repeats the AP content from the initial story in the *Springview Press*.

By the fourth day, this wildfire of slander has consumed, figuratively, the university president's desk. His telephone never stops ringing with calls from irate taxpayers; some of these calls are from people who live on the other side of the state, more than four hundred miles away.

The situation escalates from bad to worse when Springview's hometown pride-and-joy, Mr. Craig Jacobson, uses his syndicated weekly column to chastise Dr. Kelley for her "unconscionable extravagance." As a hometown boy, Mr. Jacobson was an honor-roll student throughout his high school years and the only graduate from Springview to ever attend Harvard. After completing four years at Harvard and graduating with honors, he is nominated to be a Rhodes scholar. As a semifinalist, he is invited to New York City for an interview. Unfortunately, the committee does not select him, and he has spent the last twenty years of his adult life lamenting the cavalier way he answered some of their interview questions.

When the news breaks that he was not approved by the Rhodes selection committee, his father suggests he take some time and get away for a respite. Consequently, he roams around Europe and parties for almost two years. Finally, with his parents' money exhausted, he is forced to return home but quickly moves to Sioux City, Iowa, where he finds a job and begins hosting a radio talk show every Monday through Friday. As a bitter, lonely, overweight man, the tone of his daily talk show increasingly becomes cynical and negative toward most human endeavors, especially anything involving higher education.

After a full week of derogatory publicity, the firestorm forces the university's governing board to take action. In a television interview that is part of the 10:00 p.m. news, the board chairman announces that she is calling a special board meeting for the following Monday. She has received a three-page packet in the mail with anonymously written complaints against the vice president. Now, this horrific travel voucher scandal demands the board's immediate attention. She expects that most of the meeting will be a closed session totally devoted to a review of the vice president's job performance. While Dr. Kelley has submitted a formal request to attend this meeting and speak with the board, the chair privately tells the president that Dr. Kelley is not welcome and is not to be permitted in the room while the board deliberates.

The next morning, Harvey proudly circulates his newspaper with a front-page article speculating that the president has already demanded the vice president's resignation.

That Saturday evening, the senator grills three king-sized T-bone steaks on his patio in the backyard. When his guests are halfway through their meal, he raises his glass of Jack Daniel's best and toasts their great victory.

"To the Remarkable Trinity and the end of that bitch's career! Gentlemen, I can assure you our university will be looking for a new vice president after the board meets."

Buzz and Dean Warton smile. Buzz asks, "How can you be so positive, senator?"

"Because the vice chair of the board is my goddamn banker! He works for me!" Everyone laughs.

It is common knowledge that the senator owns controlling interest in three banks, including Springview's West Gate Bank Center.

"I called him today and persuaded him to dump that arrogant whore. We don't need her kind working at our university! This community will be better the day she leaves."

Once again, the Remarkable Trinity has achieved its goal. Once again, a planned campaign of devious slander has destroyed a talented professional's career. Once again, the senator has designed the perfect blueprint. And, once again, Buzz feels the surge of power and the satisfaction that only comes when someone is able to assert harmful means to get their way while they crush their opponent. As he savors his Jack Daniel's whiskey, he cannot wait to share this good news with Diana. More than anything, he wants to please her.

On this beautiful spring night in April 1988, the evening twilight yields to a clear sky filled with a full moon and a million bright stars. Neither the senator nor the dean realize the significance of their celebration. Like launching a rocket into space, they have lost control of their friend's orbit but do not realize it. The "student of slander and smear" is about to become the master. The senator, unknowingly, has created a monster. He has coached and mentored a super-ego that one day, in the future, even he would not be able to control.

PART III

Washing Hands of All Guilt

He took water and washed his hands before the multitude,
saying, "I am innocent of the blood of this just person."

—Matthew 27:24, KJV
Pontius Pilate, Governor, 30 AD

Washing one's hands of the guilt of others
is a way of sharing guilt so far as it encourages
in others a vicious way of action.

—John Dewey, *Human Nature and Conduct*, 1922

When the silent majority remains silent, the vocal minority
becomes empowered to control the podium, the microphone,
and the message that is conveyed. A culture of silence
nurtures and fosters the growth of unabashed evil deeds.

12

Rocky

Now every gambler knows the secret to survivin' is knowin' what to throw away, and knowin' what to keep. Cause every hand's a winner, and every hand's a loser, and the best that you can hope for is to die in your sleep.

—Kenny Rogers, "The Gambler," 1978

November 1987
Floyd University

Mark looks worried. He seems distracted from his coaching duties. His thoughts primarily are focused upon the bad weather and the predicted overnight sleet and ice storm. To him, it is absolutely critical that he be able to leave early in the morning to catch his flight out of Omaha.

Today, he is working with the junior varsity women's basketball team. The team is trying to practice four new offensive plays that pivot around their 6'6" freshman center, Marsha Hertz. The practice is not going well.

After six consecutive wins during the annual Platte River Tournament, the player's rhythm seems out of step, and their enthusiasm is very flat. Everyone, especially Mark, is glad this upcoming weekend has an open date with no regular conference games scheduled for another nine days. It is getting late and close to shower time. Mark blows his whistle and calls a time-out.

The old gym has seen its better days. Built in 1952, the overhead lights and air handling system both represent a bygone era of technology. The pull-out bleachers give the gym a seating capacity of four thousand, but the thriving enrollment at Floyd University has outgrown this facility. Most events attract an audience that exceeds available seating and the state fire marshal has recently issued two formal capacity warnings against the university's president. Many in the community lament this seating constraint, but there is no clear indication that financial support can be obtained for an expansion, and a major gym renovation has been prioritized as the number six project on the master plan for campus facilities.

On this second day of November, the furnace runs in high gear trying to keep up with the frigid Nebraska winter temperatures. A forty-mph northern wind blasts the community creating a fifteen below-zero wind chill.

Originally identified on the campus map as the college gym, it is renamed the Paul Cunningham Athletic Center in 1978 to honor Mr. Cunningham's outstanding coaching career. After eighteen years of incredible success with twelve conference championships, the head coach for men's basketball is diagnosed with lung cancer and quickly dies four months later at the age of forty-seven.

Today, this gym proudly boasts newly installed dark oak flooring with a fierce blue panther in the center of the court. Every day, it serves as the home facility for the men's and women's basketball teams and their nationally ranked wrestling team. With these three indoor sports actively practicing and competing against their opponents, the musty scent of sweat and dirty gym bags always faintly lingers in the air whenever you initially enter the building.

———⟨⟩———

"Hey, coach, I need another Q," Samantha whispers as she reaches for the water bottle.

That is the team's code word for one of two illegal drugs that the assistant basketball coach routinely sells to the players. After all, he reasons they are like a family. And the coach wants to help whenever his players need that extra boost of energy or that quick surge of adrenaline to push through the exhaustion that plagues every athlete during the last period of the contest.

Assistant Coach Mark Moore is young, energetic, and immersed in the game of basketball. But, more than anything else, he loves to gamble in Las Vegas. At the age of twenty-nine, he is hooked. Very few people know about his addiction. The coach lives a Dr. Jekyll and Mr. Hyde lifestyle. His secret desires fuel a compelling habit that propels the dark side of his life. He flies to Vegas once each month for a three-day weekend. It is a thrill for him; truly life in the fast lane. But his good looks do not transfer into good luck when he rolls the dice and plays black jack. In fact, during the last two years, he has made twenty-five trips to Vegas and has lost the value of his entire annual income to the dealers at the green felt tables.

He has IOUs at three major casinos, and these debts have compounding interest rates that grow weekly. All his credit cards are maxed out, and he is living on a shoestring. He is two months behind with his apartment rent and three months with his car payment. Six months ago, his car insurance lapses because of his failure to pay the premium. Mark has pawned all his furniture and sleeps on the floor in a sleeping bag in an empty living room. He works on campus, appears to have no social life, and when not on the basketball court, he lives each day planning his next trip to the bright lights and felt tables of Vegas.

Mark's life hangs on a slender financial thread. The cash from his drug sales to students keeps him going and pays for his plane tickets. Fortunately, the volume of drug sales has gradually increased during the last three years. This little side business provides the cash to maintain his raison d'être, his only true purpose in life. He always feels an adrenaline rush when he walks across the casino floor and the dealers call him by his favorite nickname, "Rocky"; that tag stands for the "The Rock." He has earned that label because of his fearless but foolish courage at the tables. He gambles with a stoic persona. Like a rock, his body language is frozen as he repeatedly bets "the dime" or "the dollar" against the long odds and risks hazardous uncertainty.

"I can give you one Vitamin C and two Q10s for an even twenty," the coach responds as he cautiously scans the practice floor.

Samantha quickly speaks in a hushed voice, "It's a deal. Put it on my tab."

In less than one minute, hidden by the quick exchange of a towel, the coach has passed a small packet with three pills—one white and two red.

He smiles as he mentally calculates his profit for the day. It really pleases Coach Moore that this young, vibrant blonde has emerged as his all-time best customer. He privately thinks, *And she is just a junior. I can't wait until she starts her senior year.*

Floyd University has more than six hundred student athletes enrolled to play on sixteen teams—eight men and eight women team sports. As a long-standing member of the National Association of Intercollegiate Athletics (NAIA), the Floyd University Panthers have a winning tradition in almost every sport. Year after year, everyone who follows college sports knows the Panthers. Their winning records are legendary. Their teams are always in the hunt for the conference championship. In many ways, this competitive spirit propels Mark's drug business and gives faculty like Buzz Granger the opportunity to pressure student athletes for personal sexual favors.

Since drug testing is optional for all NAIA Schools, Floyd University has elected to save money and forgo the lab expenses. The budget is tight, and each year, travel costs escalate beyond anyone's projections. So the coaches try to save money by neglecting to start a drug testing program. Once, during the previous season, the athletic director hears a locker-room rumor about drugs being used by the ladies basketball team. He approaches the head coach with questions. After a strong, honest rebuttal from her, the AD drops the subject and considers the rumors to be idle gossip with no substance or truth.

———

The Las Vegas International Airport is conveniently located just off Interstate 215, about a fifteen-minute taxi ride from the main casino strip on Flamingo Road. Inside the terminal, the evening sunsets of November quickly disappear behind the Spring Mountain range, but the early morning sunrises cheerfully linger throughout the boarding areas. The bright rays of sunlight are completely unimpeded by the skyline of modest buildings facing east toward Henderson.

In the airport's terminal 1, level 2 concourse, a visibly troubled, unshaven, sleep-deprived young man is sitting in the warm sun with a small cup of black coffee. Mark is oblivious to the beauty of the sunrise sweeping across the black padded seats at Gate C-8. He looks as white as a ghost. Lost in his private thoughts, he blankly stares at a nearby wall lined with Lucky 7 slot machines. His chin grimaces from the pain of two broken fingers, and his hands tremble from the bone-deep fear that permeates his entire body. To most onlookers, he is just another poor, unlucky gambler leaving the city totally broke.

As the boarding for American Airlines Flight 2583 begins, Mark struggles to collect his thoughts. He is desperately trying to think of a way to quickly come up with $10,000. His journey home will take him from Las Vegas to Dallas and then into

Omaha. After landing in Omaha, he will have to drive about three hours to get home. Fortunately, he has left his car at the airport with a full tank of fuel, and there is a twenty-dollar bill tucked inside the ashtray to pay for the weekend parking fee.

Tomorrow is Monday. When the bank opens, Mark plans to beg the loan officer for a short-term, six-month loan. Since he has no collateral and a deplorable credit rating, he is nervous about the loan request and doubtful about its approval. Just a few hours ago, in the basement of the Palace Casino, he bartered for his life with the "merchant of death." Big John, the casino's debt collector, straps him to a chair. Using number 10 Vise-Grip straight jaw locking pliers, he methodically breaks two fingers on Mark's right hand. Tortured with excruciating pain, Mark admits that he cannot immediately pay his bad debt, so Big John threatens to jam his entire right hand into a large, commercial-sized food blender. Stricken with total fear, Mark pisses his pants and screams for mercy. Mark begs him for the chance to live one more day in order to apply for a bank loan. With sobbing cries, he pleads for the chance to get his hands on some money so he can make a good-faith payment against his debt. Big John reluctantly agrees to give him forty-eight hours to make good on his promise.

On Monday evening, Mark paces the floor in his living room like a caged, hungry lion. His loan request has been denied by the bank. Mark is lost in an ocean of worry. Haunted by a gut-wrenching fear, Mark's cavalier confidence is badly shaken. The combination of pain and fear causes his hands to tremble.

His small portable radio is tuned to the classic rock station located in Sioux City, Iowa. By chance, the DJ is playing one of Mark's favorite songs, Kenny Rogers' great 1978 hit, "The Gambler"! As the song's lyrics flow across the airwaves ("You've got to know when to hold 'em, know when to fold 'em, know when to walk away, and know when to run), a casual knock and a friendly voice at the front door said, "Pizza delivery!"

Mark smiles. He is hungry and the thought of hot pizza gives him temporary relief from the throbbing pain in his hand. The last few years, he becomes established and distinguished as the community's best customer at Big Red's Pizza Barn. Periodically, as a demonstration of appreciation, the owner, Papa Louie, sends him a complimentary pizza whenever they have an unclaimed carryout order on the delivery shelf at closing time.

Hurriedly walking across the room, Mark opens the front door, expecting to greet a familiar college student delivering the pizza. That is the last decision Mark makes before feeling a burning needle go into his arm. Quickly, Mark collapses in the living room. Three men storm into his apartment and pin him on the floor. The men move rapidly like skilled professionals. With a precision rhythm, they tie his hands and carry him outside to a black van with Illinois license plates. In less than three minutes, the van leaves the poorly lit parking lot with Mark's crumpled and unconscious body in the back cargo area amidst a bunch of construction tools.

Two hours later, Mark is brutally forced to climb out of a drug-induced sleep. As he becomes conscious, he frantically tries to scream because of the pain radiating up his arms and into his chest. When he opens his eyes, he sees an unfamiliar young man smiling with pride like someone who has successfully completed a difficult task. While Mark is still unconscious, this guy uses a twenty-pound sledgehammer to crush both of Mark's hands.

Confused and out of his mind with pain, Mark struggles to understand his circumstances. The last thing he vaguely remembers is hitting his head on the living room floor when he fell in his apartment. Now he feels cold, very cold. He has a severe headache. He is bewildered, and he feels excruciating pain in his arms and hands as well as in his legs. A few seconds later, as he regains full consciousness, he realizes that there is duct tape across his mouth. He looks up. The night sky is clear, the moon is almost full, and a million stars dance against the dark horizon.

Mark struggles to no avail. He is tightly staked on the ground. His arms and legs are outstretched and secured in a spread-eagle position. Mark starts to shiver. The snow on the ground makes his hands and bare feet numb. Confused and filled with fear, he tries to scream, but the tape over his mouth makes his voice inconsequential.

A tall, heavyset man in a dark top coat approaches Mark from his right side. He stands silently for several minutes and gazes directly into Mark's fear-struck eyes. He is wearing a Chicago White Sox baseball cap with dark sunglasses. Finally, the man speaks with a heavy European accent and stilted politeness.

"Mark, allow me to introduce myself. People know me as the Exterminator. I do special work for very special people. You need to know that Big John is goddamn disappointed. You missed another payment deadline."

Mark struggles to talk. His muffled voice emits garbled words. His plea is incoherent. He wants to beg for more time, but his words are lost under the tape over his mouth.

The man interrupts Mark's gibberish and calmly says, "Now, now, Mark, no more excuses. No more time. You have had your last chance."

The man pauses, turns his head and reflectively looks up at the sky. "Listen Mark, what the shit do you hear?"

Helplessly, Mark twists against the tight ropes. Despite the cold temperatures, Mark's forehead is covered with fear-induced sweat. There is just enough moonlight for Mark to see a faint tattoo of a medieval sword on the man's neck as he faces away and stares at the distant sky.

Then he speaks again. "Mark, listen carefully. What the hell do you hear?"

Mark looks through eyes filled with terror. He strains to listen, but there is nothing to hear except the sounds of nighttime silence and the timeless howl from the gusting wind blowing across the open field. Another few minutes of moonlit silence pass, but to Mark, this brief lapse of time seemed like an eternity.

The man finally waves his hand in the air, like he is hailing a taxi in the middle of rush hour. With panic, Mark looks left and right. He sees nothing except snow piled next to both sides of his head. As the man breaks into a big smile, the silence is broken.

Mark hears the sputtering of two motors trying to start. At first, he does not recognize the sound because both motors stall out. For a brief second, the noise kind of reminds him of his old lawn mower. Several more seconds pass, and a blast of wind lashes snow across his face, and a stray cornstalk lodges against his left foot. Terror sweeps through Mark's body. He feels a wave of nausea in his stomach as he realizes the renewed sound is coming from two chain saws that are slowly accelerating into high speed.

Two young, brutish men slowly walk from the van to Mark's body. Each one carrying a chain saw. Their light jackets, bare heads, and hunched posture clearly indicate that they are miserably cold. The blustery wind continues to drift corn stalks against Mark's legs. With the motors running on idle, they place both chain saws on the ground next to Mark's ears. The popping motor noise is deafening! Both men look toward the Exterminator, carefully awaiting his signal. An eternity of fleeting seconds pass. Fear and trembling consume Mark's body as he shits his pants. With a slight nod of his head and a quick hand gesture, the Exterminator smiles like a well-paid man who enjoys his work. Tonight, he just earned a five-thousand-dollar bounty.

Mark screams in anguish. His final thoughts and muffled voice are lost in the dark silence of a deserted, snow-covered cornfield. The big man starts to walk away, pauses with a backward glance, waves his baseball cap, and casually speaks above the background noise, "Hey Mark, Big John sends his regards!"

It is a beautiful, crisp morning on November 24, 1987. Ten consecutive days in the mid-fifties have melted most of the snow. The community's dedicated walkers and joggers are enjoying this reprieve from Old Man Winter's wrath.

Unexpectedly, Coach Moore fails to show for his physical education class. He has an exceptional teaching record and good student evaluations, and he is dependable—always on time for class. Everyone jumps to the conclusion that he must be sick. After several failed attempts to reach him by telephone, the AD drives across town and gains access into his apartment. Two shock waves simultaneously hit the AD as he enters through Mark's front door. First, the Spartan-like, empty apartment is appalling. Trash is piled in every corner, and empty pizza boxes are everywhere. Second, there is no trace of Mark Moore.

As the day proceeds, anxiety grows, and finally, campus officials report Mark missing. The county sheriff immediately enlists the help of the highway patrol. Days turn into weeks. At first, some speculate that Mark has jumped the gun to start an early Thanksgiving break, but as the sense of foul play grows, the town mystery escalates and becomes the number one topic of conversation across campus, in the local coffee shops, and throughout the community.

Nothing of this magnitude has ever happened in Springview. Finally, after five weeks of suspense, there is a break in the case. The Chicago police find Mark's car parked along an obscure side street in East Chicago, not far from one of the city's largest warehouse districts. But the car offers no clues, and the case goes cold again. Months go by, the holidays pass, and the New Year arrives without any new clues.

On April 10, 1988, a Friday morning, the residents of Springview awake to shocking news. The newspaper headline reads, "Coach Moore's Body Found." The coroner's report is not released, but word quickly spreads like wildfire. The volunteer ambulance crew has been talking. There is no mystery regarding the cause of death. His body is found staked to the ground. He is gagged, and someone has used a chain saw to cut off both arms and both legs.

The unusual cold winter and heavy snow has frozen and covered his body. He has lain there for almost five months; just four miles west of town, in the middle of a three-hundred-acre cornfield. Mark's body is found in a small gully by Jake Fisher. Old Mr. Fisher, seventy-six, has farmed that land all his life. This year, the long winter has delayed his chance to get into the field. During a nice break in the weather, he has been running his tractor in full-throttle gear, hoping to complete his spring plowing before income tax day.

"They say Mr. Fisher was hospitalized for shock after he called 911," Diana says.

Buzz answers, "Well, I am not surprised. I bet Mark's body was a haunting sight."

"Now all the speculation is over, and thank God our secrets are safe. Remember, a dead man can't talk!"

Buzz sits back to ponder Diana's comment. "Do you think Mark left any records that can be found?"

"I doubt it. You know all the papers from his office and apartment were seized by the police. Relax, Buzz. There is nothing to worry about. If they had found anything, trust me, we would know by now because we would be in trouble. Besides, I heard the cops are totally focused on the drugs they found."

Diana pauses, remembering Ben Franklin's old saying about keeping secrets. "Hey, Buzz, let's go for coffee."

"Wow, I need more than coffee today!"

Reflectively thinking about the tormenting pain inflicted upon Mark, Buzz continues. "You know, they say all the bones in Mark's two hands were crushed before they cut his arms off at the shoulder!"

Diana shudders and quickly tries to change the subject. "That's super strange. Why would they take the time to break his fingers and then chop off his arms? Come on, honey, we need to get away from the campus. Let's blow this place. Today is my treat."

Not counting a McDonald's out on Highway 81, there are only three places in town to go for coffee. And Bonnie's Brew is the only option if you want to have a private conversation.

"Okay," Buzz says, "but I want that corner table at Bonnie's."

"Great. I am dying for a latte! I will meet you there in fifteen minutes."

To avoid as much gossip as possible, they always travel in separate cars ever since Buzz's wife has become suspicious. About six months ago, she heard some rumors after choir practice regarding a possible affair between her husband and one of the secretaries on campus. Buzz gracefully denies this affair and finds a marginal degree of solace with the fact that he is not sleeping with any secretaries. Since then, however, Buzz has become extra cautious and always tries to cover his tracks.

The telephone rings five times. Buzz grows impatient. He mutters to himself, "Dammit, why does this shitty time and temp number take so long!"

The recording clicks. "The time is 7:32 a.m. Today is Saturday, April 18, 1988. The expected high for today will be 62 degrees. Tonight's low will be 38."

Buzz lights a Camel—already his fifth cigarette this morning. The ceiling fan quickly disperses smoke all over the room. He glances into the mirror hanging on the closet door. "Goddammit, that bald spot keeps growing!"

Today is special; his sixteenth wedding anniversary. Tonight he has promised to take his wife out to dinner at the country club. She is excited about the occasion; he is not. He better order flowers!

Buzz gazes out the window. It has been eight days since the coach's body was found. His mind races with worry. He hopes his dark secrets stay buried with the coach! In the privacy of his office, he begins to talk to himself. "Shit! What if the sheriff discovers my hidden skeletons? It will end my career, and the felony charges will probably send me to jail."

"What if the university president finds out that I rigged that tenure vote? Even though I am tenured, he most likely would fire me. And holy Christ, what if my wife finds out I have been sleeping with students, young girls half my age? She would surely file for a divorce and take everything."

Buzz coughs twice. Again, he inhales his cigarette, savoring the taste, and waiting for that slight nicotine boost to hit him.

"Damn, I could sure use a blow job right now!"

He reaches for his telephone and dials his wife's favorite flower shop on Third Avenue. He orders a dozen roses with a helium balloon that says "Happy Anniversary."

After placing the obligatory order for the flowers, he pauses and stares at the telephone. For a few minutes, he thinks about calling his good friend, the old senator. But, their last conversation did not go well, so Buzz dismisses the idea. Last night, at about ten o'clock, Buzz called the senator to fish for information about the ongoing investigation into the coach's death. The senator seemed very irritated. Perhaps it was the late hour. However, Buzz was offended when the senator accused him of being an insecure, paranoid man who never stopped worrying.

Buzz reaches into his pocket and quickly lights a fresh cigarette. Even though he is very distracted, he begins to work on a draft agenda for next Monday's department meeting. But his mind sprints down a path of countless fears and speculations. He wonders if the sheriff ultimately might knock on his door with an arrest warrant.

The seasons of the year march with a relentless pace. The unforgiving hand of fate quickly turns the calendar as months become shadows of time and years roll by like mile markers on the interstate. Unbeknownst to Buzz, at this very moment, more than a thousand miles away, there is a quickly scrawled letter in a USPS semitruck moving down the highway. When the mailman eventually delivers this letter, it will make an impact that will ripple for decades. The letter's long-term implications will go in directions Buzz cannot possibly predict.

13

Bitter Pill to Swallow

> Great spirits have always encountered violent
> opposition from mediocre minds.
>
> —Albert Einstein, 1879–1955

May 1988
Central State University

"Do you really think we can try to sweep this problem under the rug?" JP is incredulous. He speaks assertively, and signals his irritation with unsettled body language.

The registrar, Susan Miller, quickly pleads, "Please, Dr. O'Bryan, don't try to press charges on this one. I happen to know the union is looking for the chance to have a big fight with you."

"Susan, this is a huge breach of protocol and a moral dilemma for our university. Your transcript analyst has been changing grades and forging false transcripts for money—for personal gain. How long do you think she has been doing this?"

"Well, I am not sure. At least eight years, maybe longer. Our new PeopleSoft database makes it almost impossible to trace prior to 1980."

—ɷɷɷ—

In the spring of 1986, JP and Jenn move from Norfolk, Virginia, to Montpelier, Vermont. JP has accepted a job offer that promises to be a significant promotion. Together, they load a big U-Haul truck. With their compass set on north, they launch another new adventure filled with optimism and high spirits. The seven-hundred-mile journey takes three long days of travel because the truck's universal joint breaks at 10:30 p.m. while they are south of New York City on I-95. After they arrive and unload the truck, JP reports to the Central State University campus and joins the president's cabinet for their weekly Monday-morning coordination meeting.

Central State University is a historic campus with approximately 210 acres completely surrounded by commercial development and residential homes. With a strong liberal arts program, CSU was established in 1841 as one of the nation's first state normal schools. Now approaching its 150th Anniversary, it has evolved into the state's premier, undergraduate campus. By most standards, CSU is second only to UVM, the land-grant university that most everyone fondly knows by its Latin nickname, the University of the Green Mount.

As a modern, progressive, residential campus, CSU boasts its open-admissions policy and its student-centered focus as points of distinction. It consistently enrolls about ten thousand students every fall semester and maintains a nationally competitive basketball team within the NCAA D-II program. There is a healthy town-and-gown relationship because Montpelier's city fathers realize the university is a major driving force within the community's economy.

Now in his second year as the associate provost at CSU, JP's daily work revolves around the boundaries, personalities, and diplomatic mediation required to implement three different collective bargaining agreements. The faculty, professional staff, and clerical staff have their own respective unions with an elected steward on campus who is paid by the union to orchestrate all formal grievances. Across the state of Vermont, all public university employees belong to one of the many unions that include most of the state's workforce. Collectively, these labor unions speak with a formidable voice on every political issue that captures the attention of their union leadership.

———❧———

"Wow, eight years. How much do you think she embezzled during that time?"

Susan pauses, reflects, and responds with caution.

"That question is difficult to answer. I can tell you Maria was charging $500 for every A that she inserted and $300 for every B that was fraudulently posted. Most of her customers were trying to get into out-of-state graduate programs, so they probably needed at least a 3.2 or maybe a 3.5 overall GPA on their transcript. Depending upon their final GPA after they finished with us, she may have changed several letter grades per transcript in order to mathematically get the required cumulative GPA that the student was requesting."

"Oh my God, Susan! We are talking thousands and thousands of dollars. This is more than an academic integrity issue for us; it is also an IRS violation for Maria's annual income."

JP pauses, looks out the window, and then asks, "Susan, how many customers used Maria's personal transcript service?"

"Again, that is hard to say. She has worked here for twenty-one years. She became our primary transcript analyst twelve years ago. At first, I think this was a rare thing that only happened once in a blue moon. You know, an occasional favor to help a friend.

But with practice it became easier to do, and her clandestine willingness to help our graduates surely seemed to travel by word of mouth. I think the last few years she probably helped six or seven students every year."

With a calm and firm resolve in his voice, JP says, "Susan, please continue your research. Keep this topic very confidential. Try to discover as much as you can without signaling that we know about this travesty. I plan to share all these details with the provost later this afternoon when I have my routine coordination meeting with her."

At 2:00 p.m., JP arrives at the provost's office. The secretary greets him and asks for his patience because the provost is running behind schedule. Currently, she is on the telephone with one of the board members.

Finally, after a twenty-minute delay, JP is invited to enter the provost's office. Dr. Hazel Schmidt is a warm, intelligent, feisty lady in the twilight years of her career. With more than four decades of experience in higher education, she has spent the last ten years at CSU as the provost.

"Welcome, JP. Sorry I am running late. Come in, have a chair. Would you like a coffee or cold water?"

"Thanks, coffee would be great. I need to increase my daily quota of vitamin 'C'—caffeine, that is."

Dr. Schmidt smiles and asks her secretary to bring two coffees. JP senses the provost's unusual decorum. She seems distracted and upset, but she is trying desperately to hide it. Ever since third grade, JP has used his "radar" to read people. He starts with Sister Leonina, his teacher, and progresses over the years to the point where, as an adult, everyone in JP's presence conveys nonverbal messages to him. His family frequently teases him about his "sixth sense." He generally brushes this skill aside and only occasionally talks about reading vibes from other people.

As the conversation begins, JP proceeds with caution given the provost's mood.

"Dr. Schmidt, we have a problem in the registrar's office. I want to define the issue as best I can, but we still have much research to accomplish before I can determine the full magnitude of this situation."

JP carefully explains all the details as he knows them. The more he talks, the more visibly agitated the provost becomes. At times, he wonders if she is listening because he catches her gazing out the window with a look that indicates she is a hundred miles away. When he finishes sharing the complete story, the provost leans across the table and aggressively says, "Just what do you propose we do? What is your recommendation regarding this mess?"

"I believe we have to finish our research and be prepared to make a full disclosure. There is a good chance this will hit the news if one of Maria's customers brag to the wrong person at the wrong time. It may be just a matter of time before this becomes headline news. I think we should be proactive and up front with people. Somehow we have to preserve the public's trust and demonstrate a willingness to admit our mistake as we try to correct this situation."

"And just what do you think Maria's union will do?"

Given the tone in Dr. Schmidt's voice, JP knows he is facing a hostile audience. For the first time, his CSU boss is upset with him. He is surprised. Of all the people he has worked for, he thinks the provost is synchronized with his values and they are on the same page.

Before he can answer the provost's rhetorical question, she loses her temper and explodes.

"JP, I know you want to press formal charges against Maria because you think it is the right thing to do. But I am telling you that we can't go there. Not now! For God's sake, not at this time! For the good of the institution, we have to keep this under wraps. I know you. And this is a bitter pill to swallow, but you must follow my directive."

Stunned, JP hesitates, and then he finds the courage to ask, "Okay, I understand your position. May I ask *why* you want to ignore this problem?"

"Look, don't try to put words in my mouth! I did not tell you to ignore this problem. I told you to keep it under wraps! Get with legal counsel and begin negotiating an early retirement for Maria. She has to go! But it must appear to others that she has elected to leave on her own initiative, and she must sign a confidentiality agreement." The provost's anger now permeates the entire room.

"And furthermore, I want you to remember that we both work for the president, and he works for the board, and they work for the governor. Have you forgotten this is an election year? The governor has made it very clear to everyone that he does not want any union problems while he runs for reelection. I think Maria's union steward is 'cruising this campus' and just looking for the chance to have a big public fight with you."

JP is silent. He never dreamed Dr. Schmidt would react this way. For some reason, her entire decision-making process is now guided by the governor's political agenda.

Given the decorum in the room, JP elects to bring his remarks to a close. He hoped to discuss some budget concerns, but today does not seem like the right time to examine numbers and red-ink budget problems.

Driven by a burning curiosity, JP asserts, "May I ask one more question before I leave?"

"Of course. What is it?"

"Why are you so sure that the union steward is hoping to pick a fight with me? Earlier today, Susan used almost the same words that you used. Both of you seem convinced that the union is mad at me."

"Look, JP, you have accomplished more during the last two years than most people get done during their entire career. You have inspired many changes. You encourage people to excel.

You always promote best practices. Don't you see why the union is mad?"

"No, I really do not see why they have a bone to pick with me. We are all working to support the same goals—to make this university a better place."

"Oh my God! JP, you can be so naïve! Not everyone wants to excel. For some, okay is good enough. Excellent or outstanding requires extra work. Not everyone wants to move from good to great! From the union's perspective, they want to be paid extra for this extra work. Don't you see? They are looking for a way to bring you down because you are ruining their comfort zone!"

JP remains silent as he gazes at the conference table. Sadness and anger simultaneously rush through his mind.

"JP, three weeks ago I had lunch with the president. He told me the union grapevine is buzzing. They are getting their strategy ready for the next bargaining session. We are back at the table next year to negotiate another three-year agreement. We anticipate they will propose new language that will establish a bonus clause. Supposedly, whenever administration asks their membership to implement best practice standards, they want bonus pay. You see, for some, average is really good. Average is okay when you don't want to change. Not everyone is driven to achieve excellence like you. Your aspirational way of thinking is foreign to many of them. They oppose the extra work required to achieve standards of excellence. That is why they don't support your goals."

Overwhelmed, JP feels like his boss has just pulled the rug out from under him. He gathers his notebook and starts to leave the room. Lost for words, he tries to politely smile as he thanks her for the coffee and today's meeting.

Dr. Schmidt snaps, "JP, close the door and sit back down. I have more to say!"

There is a long silence in the room. Neither person is ready to say anything. JP realizes that he is the subordinate and she is the superior, so he politely waits for her to begin. He expects some kind of reprimand.

"You know, the first thing I want to do is apologize for my frame of mind and my sharp comments. JP, there is more going on than you could ever imagine. I want to talk with you, but I insist that you will promise me the strictest confidence. You cannot say a word of this to anyone, not even your wife. Do you understand?"

JP nods and non-verbally signals his agreement.

"Today, I had lunch with the board chairman. We are facing a major leadership crisis, and the board is actively working to contain the pending explosion—both the chair and vice chair have been talking with the governor, trying to exercise damage control."

At this point, JP begins to realize that he is not the problem or the cause for the provost's anger. Dr. Schmidt continues.

"Last night, our president was stopped by the highway patrol. He has been charged with drunk driving, and he spent about five hours in jail before posting bail. We anticipate the story will break tonight with NBC's six o'clock news."

Speechless, JP ponders this unimaginable turn of events.

Dr. Schmidt gestures with four fingers raised on her right hand.

"The board has multiple options. They can continue to support his presidency and weather the storm, or they can place him on administrative leave and suspend him until these charges move through the formal court process, or they can ask him to plan an early retirement, or they can move quickly and terminate his employment with some kind of contract buyout."

"What does this mean for you?" JP realizes that Dr. Schmidt is number two in the chain of command.

"I am not sure, and it may be next week before we know. At lunch today, the chair gave me fair warning that I may be asked to quickly step in as the acting president and serve until they can sort things out. If they do a national search, I may become the interim president for most of the next academic year. I believe sometime tomorrow, the board will announce a special meeting that will convene next Wednesday."

The provost abruptly stops talking. She again looks out the window like someone hoping to find something that has been lost. Out of respect, JP remains silent. With a deep sigh, Dr. Schmidt turns her chair, stands, and slowly walks toward her office door.

"JP, I expect we will know more in a few days. I am counting on your help as we move through this terrible ordeal. Remember, not a word to anyone!"

14

The Four Horsemen

Riders on the Storm, Riders on the Storm,
Into this house we're born, into this world we're thrown.
If ya give this man a ride, sweet memory will die,
Make him understand,
The world on you depends, our life will never end.
Like a dog without a bone,
An actor out alone, Riders on the Storm.

—The Doors, "Riders on the Storm," 1971

October 1988
Floyd University

Dr. Raymond Thomas Wheelwright is a mathematician par excellence. He is also a beer-drinking, tobacco-chewing, eccentric kind of a guy who loves to curse and always says, after his third beer, that he is "meaner than a junkyard dog." Every afternoon by four o'clock, six days each week, Ray homesteads the corner bar stool at Bogner's downtown bar and grill. Married and divorced four times, he lives a meager life in a sparse one-room, semifurnished rental apartment because most of his monthly salary is under court order to pay multiple alimony settlements.

There is a quality about his mathematical ability that arrests attention. In his younger years, when his thoughts were clear and not under the influence of alcohol, he frequently displayed a magnificent mind, especially during his calculus and statistics lectures. However, as he enters the twilight of his career, his mental acuity has noticeably declined. Days and months turn into years as Ray systematically drinks gallons of beer methodically killing millions of brain cells.

This fall semester is the beginning of Ray's fortieth year at Floyd University. Four decades ago, he arrived in Springview with two badly worn, brown Samsonite suitcases and less than a hundred dollars in his pocket. During WWII, he attends Stanford University with a special "math and science" draft deferment that exempts him from military duty. After completing his MA and PhD degrees in calculus with a magna cum laude distinction, he receives a postdoctoral research position at Stanford working on one of the university's classified defense contracts. His career trajectory is bright and promising until he starts going to work under the influence of alcohol. Finally, after two DUI convictions and a poor annual performance evaluation, the project manager does not renew his employment contract in the summer of 1947.

As a tenured, full professor at Floyd University, he routinely flaunts his independence and lack of respect for basic policies and rules. Among private circles of conversation on campus, it is a standing joke that Ray performs his weekly required ten office hours in the afternoon at the downtown pool hall. After four decades, he has emerged with the employment distinction of being the senior faculty member. For the first time, next May, he will have the honor of carrying the university's ceremonial mace during the annual commencement ceremony. Last month, as a demonstration of respect for his longevity, the faculty senate unanimously elected him as the president of the senate for the current academic year. Diana Dawson was elected as the vice president, Carol Nodland as the treasurer, and Buzz Granger was reelected for another term as secretary.

Collectively, according to the bylaws, these four positions serve as the senate's executive committee. With forty-eight hours advance written notice to the membership, the executive committee is empowered to meet and discuss potential agenda topics with the stipulation that the senate president must give the full senate a brief oral report during their next regularly scheduled monthly meeting.

On this windy Thursday afternoon, colorful maple leaves are blowing across the street in patterns similar to the swirls of drifting snow. The month of October has been dreary and unusually cold as the fall season wanes and Old Man Winter waxes. Today, with winds gusting over forty miles per hour, the sun shines intermittently as vertically developed cumulus clouds race across the horizon. With the afternoon high of forty-two degrees, it is sweater-and-jacket weather in Springview as the executive committee drives across town and assembles at the back table of Bonnie's Brew.

After some lighthearted bantering, the group is seated with their favorite cup of Bonnie's best caffeinated elixir. Ray is noticeably irritable, and there is a faint hint of beer on his breath. Abruptly, he takes the initiative to formally begin their discussion.

"Well, shit, let's get started. I have another appointment with a friend in less than two hours over at Bogner's, so I want to start and finish this discussion with no more than an hour of conversation. Can you all live with that?"

With chuckles of agreement, the group nonverbally consents to Ray's imposed time limit. Everyone knows the details regarding Ray's unspoken commitment to meet his friend, Bud. Ray never misses the opportunity to enjoy at least a six-pack of Budweiser during happy hour at Bogner's.

"You know, this is my last year on the faculty senate. My two-year term expires next May, and while I have not declared any official retirement plans, I am thinking this could be my last year of teaching. Damn, I want to raise some hell! I want to use this year as a chance to stick a hot poker in the president's eye. I want to make him and his haughty little cabinet squirm. I am still pissed from two years ago when President Gill laughed at me after I presented that signed parking petition. You will recall we collected more than three hundred signatures requesting a designated parking space on Campus Drive for every faculty member. Furthermore, when I was in his office, I told him every full professor with more than twenty years of tenure expected to be given a private space with their name on a mounted sign."

Buzz interrupts. "Hell, Ray, that idea is a stretch. Even the president himself foregoes a designated space for his university car. Many times, I have seen him park across the campus near the gym and walk to his office."

Ray does not like to be interrupted.

"You know, Buzz, I don't give a rip where the president parks his ass. But I will never forget that he had the nerve to rebut my argument. He said that if Campus Drive were to become marked with reserved parking rather than open parking, he would be more inclined to designate the parking spaces for our students rather than our faculty because the students are the reason we all work here."

Everyone listens attentively and gives him unspoken signals of empathy. Ray continues.

"Dammit, I want to find some way to get even. I want to watch him struggle before I hang it up and blow this two-bit town." Ray pauses and looks across the table. "Buzz, what do you think? You seem to carry a big stick around this campus. You got any ideas?"

"Well, one thing is for sure. The old president has egg on his face after last year's debacle with Vice President Kelley. And I have good reason to suspect that our friend Harvey would love another juicy story on the front page of his newspaper. The time might be ripe for us to cram a big, rotten tomato down the president's throat. One thing is for sure, Sun Tzu would say, 'Move swiftly and act where your enemy does not expect you'!"

Diana radiates a condescending smile. She looks at Ray for moral support as he grimaces and says, "Goddamn, spare me the Sun Tzu crap!"

Carol immediately speaks up. She is leaning on the edge of her chair and having a hard time containing her enthusiasm.

"Well, Ray, I could not agree more. I think there is a long line of faculty waiting for the chance to kick the old president in the ass. All we have to do is take the initiative, and the silent majority will slither into the shadows like sheep and let us do our thing. You all know how I feel about this Christian bullshit that surrounds us every day. Four years ago, when I was elected for my first term on the senate, I tried to get everyone to support a resolution to cancel that hideous benediction prayer that is inflicted upon us during every commencement ceremony. But my idea died for lack of interest. I always will remember that goody-two-shoes Marsha Ann Montgomery speaking against me. Maybe this year, the time is right to revisit my old proposal. After all, we are a *public* university, not some goddamn church!"

With passionate concurrence, Diana quickly asserts, "I am with you, Carol. My blood boils every time the ugly face of Christianity surfaces on this campus. I absolutely hate the mental slavery of religion!"

Ray is enthusiastic and also supportive of Carol. "Holy shit, Carol! I think you may have the perfect topic. What makes a nice Catholic girl like you so anti-Jesus?"

Carol places both hands over her ears and looks up at the ceiling. "Don't go there, Ray. You know we had this discussion a few years ago over a case of Budweiser! Just the thought of that night makes my head hurt! You are more close-minded than a clay brick!"

Ray smiles with self-righteous pride.

Diana wants to add fuel to the fire, so she quickly tries to tease Carol.

"Now, Ray, you know how much Carol loves to see our big-time Christian, tippy-toes vice president glad-hand all those preachers whenever they have their campus ministry meetings at the student center."

Everyone laughs at Carol's expense, and she gestures with her fist waving in the air and her index finger flashing the bird. "That little wimp! I hear he is super light in the loafers, and my Baptist friends say he is headed for hell. I would pay big money to have the chance to run this fist up the old deacon's ass and listen as he begs for help from the Lord!"

Ray quickly responds, "Shit, I want to sell admission tickets for that event! We will make a fortune!"

The group continues to laugh with carefree spirit. Feeling creative, Buzz takes the initiative to speak. He is very impressed with his colleagues, and it is fun to hear them openly talk against the campus administration. He has not had this much fun since the Remarkable Trinity's last night in deer camp when they finished drinking the remaining few bottles of Jack Daniel's Single Barrel.

"I think there is a story somewhere in Chinese warfare literature about the four horsemen who rode around the kingdom together and wreaked havoc upon the good guys. Maybe we could nickname ourselves the "Four Horsemen" as we ride across the campus and tear a new asshole in the president!"

Diana flinches her eyes at Carol and smiles. "Buzz, you are so full of bullshit. Everyone knows the four horsemen are in the Bible, not some damn Chinese warfare book!"

Laughter abounds around the table. Even Buzz finds Diana's criticism funny. Carol speaks as she finishes laughing. "That's right, Diana. And as I recall, each horse was a different color and symbolized some kind of problem. The colors were white, red, black, and pale. I think the pale horse represented death, as in the old grim reaper. I think that horse would be you, Buzz! It is a perfect match for the pale bald spot on top of your head!"

Diana roars with uncontrollable laughter and says, "Well, I don't know what the red horse stands for, but red is my favorite color, so the red horse is mine!"

Holding her hand in the air like a student volunteering to say something, Carol says, "Hey, if we are claiming colors, I want the white horse because it represents conquest, and I am out to conquer those preachy ministers who force us to pray during our public commencement ceremony."

Ray is delighted. In less than an hour, the group has achieved agreement and a sense of cohesion regarding a major project for the year. He says "Goddamn perfect! That leaves me with the black horse, and black is my favorite color. Visualize this: when we assemble for next month's senate meeting, I could ride into the room on my black horse swinging a meat cleaver over my head."

Buzz interrupts again. "That will be a sight for sore eyes! Hell, someone will probably panic and call campus security!"

Ray continues with an assertive tone in his voice, "I believe the essential, primary quality for an effective senate president is to be a good butcher. And from my viewpoint, the meat to be carved is the president's ass."

Diana quickly speaks, "During my undergraduate years, I once read some of Thomas Hobbes, and he said there are two cardinal virtues in war—force and fraud. I think we should declare war, wear the garments of malice every day, follow the advice of Hobbes, and pull out all the stops!"

Ray follows Diana's train of thought. "I totally agree! Before we leave this table, let's have a pledge that we are a modern-day version of the four horsemen dedicated to ride roughshod over the president as we pillage his goals and plunder his sacred little benediction ceremony! Do I have your support?"

With more laughter, a boisterous cheer from Buzz, and handshakes all around the table, the group gives their full endorsement to Ray's proclamation.

So the Four Horsemen of Floyd University launch their campaign on the wings of a blustery October wind. Like riders on the storm, the four horsemen take control of the microphone and the message. With some help from the local newspaper, the facts regarding nondenominational prayer are ignored, and the gossip mill runs rampant with slander and false accusations against the president and the campus ministry program.

At first, the university president tries to reason with the senate as he explains the merits of nondenominational prayer. He attends their December meeting and gives them several examples of prayers that have been approved in Washington DC by the Supreme Court. During his remarks, he appeals to their humanistic connection with students and talks about the university's long-standing tradition of caring deeply about each student, their sense of belonging, and their ability to enthusiastically launch a successful career after graduation. He suggests that the benediction prayer is a kind gesture, similar to one saying good-bye to dear friends who have been guests in your home. You always want to wish them all the best as they depart. He also suggests the benediction prayer is a thoughtful encouragement for each graduate to move into the future with a sense of optimism as they join the ranks of active alumni.

After the holiday break, President Gill asks the university attorney, Mr. Sedworth, to reinforce his remarks to the senate by sending a letter to all full-time faculty outlining the value, history, and tradition of a benediction prayer. Mr. Sedworth's explanation also includes several examples of closing benedictions crafted as nondenominational prayer that are in complete compliance with the Supreme Court's guidelines.

However, for six consecutive weeks, Buzz uses his most aggressive bully techniques to target the senators who are the most vulnerable. Additionally, Buzz and Diana use the well-established underground network of daily telephone calls to coerce and manipulate the senators who initially resist their proposal. After three months of turmoil across the campus, Ray places a carefully written resolution on the senate's agenda.

The atmosphere during the senate's meeting is very tense. Throughout the discussion, the opposition voice is unusually silent, and it is clear to many that several members of the senate have been bullied prior to this meeting. Buzz and Diana provide articulate words of support for the proposed ban. With premeditated malice, Ray has invited a local reporter from the *Springview Press*, and many are reluctant to speak because they do not want to be quoted in the daily newspaper. Carol has been programmed by Ray to "call the question" after relatively little discussion. Ray quickly responds to Carol's request. He indicates there is no need for a confidential ballot. Hoping for peer pressure to sway a few undecided senators, he stipulates that he will accept a show of hands as a time-saving technique to record the votes.

The proposal passes with a simple majority; specifically, twenty-six say yes, eighteen say no, five senators abstain, and two are absent. That evening the Four Horsemen assemble at Bogner's for happy hour, and Ray asks the bartender to run a tab because they have a serious celebration to enjoy.

The next day, this vote against prayer garners front-page headlines. When the newspaper reporter asks President Gill for a comment, he says that he is embarrassed and very disappointed. However, he knows the board expects him to keep the peace and avoid another situation that might escalate into national news. Consequently, he feels forced to capitulate and endorse the senate's ban on future benedictions.

In May, Carol Nodland is seated across from Diana Dawson during the commencement ceremony. She raises four fingers on her right hand as she winks, smiles, and privately signals their unholy pact as the Four Horsemen. Instinctively, as she savors the moment, Diana knows this is a significant victory for her colleagues!

While carrying the ceremonial mace, Ray proudly approaches the podium and declares the commencement ceremony closed. He beams as he leads the faculty processional out of the auditorium. As the band plays the traditional march music, many parents and guests seated in the audience silently wonder why there is no traditional benediction prayer to conclude the commencement ceremony. They depart feeling like this long-awaited celebration has been somewhat incomplete, and there should be a more reverent way to close this special occasion.

With a sense of sadness, President Gill leaves the front platform and walks directly across campus to the public reception. He leaves the auditorium knowing today's ceremony has been tarnished by a few mean-spirited faculty who worked with a capricious agenda. In hindsight, he is surprised that the silent majority of faculty permitted such an outrageous campaign in a community where the Chamber of Commerce proudly boasts they are a Christian-oriented city with more than forty active churches. Intuitively, he believes the senate has walked a path that cannot be retraced for many years, perhaps at least two generations. And unfortunately, it is probably just a matter of time before the memory of public prayer dies at Floyd University.

15

Cartwright's Alamo

The ultimate measure of a man is not where he stands
in moments of comfort and convenience, but where
he stands at times of challenge and controversy.

—Martin Luther King, Jr., 1929–1968

October 1988
Central State University

The newspaper headline publicly signals a jet stream of turmoil at the university: "Fired President Pleads Guilty!" After six weeks of turbulence and senior leadership confusion, the fall semester is underway with a precarious launch. The newly appointed interim president, Dr. Hazel Schmidt, tries to restore the university's sense of balance. The end of the summer witnesses an unprecedented level of gossip and commotion that finally culminates with the brutal removal of their long-serving beloved president, Alex Demos. After he is formally charged with drunken driving, the board votes unanimously to terminate his contract.

Realizing the need for stability within the two senior leadership positions, the board uses significant financial incentives to coax the former provost out of retirement and ask him to serve for a year while they conduct a national search for a new president. Dr. Schmidt requests "retreat rights" and negotiates arrangements to return to her provost assignment once the new president is hired. She hopes to remain in that position until she elects to take retirement in about three years.

On a bright, crisp Friday afternoon in October, Dr. Schmidt grabs her office telephone and calls JP.

"Hey, JP, this is Hazel Schmidt. If you can break away for a few minutes, please come down to my office for a visit. I have a fresh pot of coffee ready, and I will join you if coffee sounds like a good idea this late in the day."

"Absolutely, I will be right down, and you know I am always ready for fresh coffee. See you in about five minutes."

JP is reviewing the fall semester enrollment numbers that have just come from the registrar. At first glance, the numbers seem to be down, but he needs more time for analysis in order to determine the impact upon cash flow. He quickly closes his reference folder and tells his secretary that he is on the way to meet with the president. Within a few minutes, JP is seated in Dr. Schmidt's office, and she is serving him coffee.

"JP, I assume you aspire to someday advance your career and move into a provost's job and perhaps eventually a president's position. Is that correct?"

Surprised by this direct question, JP is not sure if this is a hypothetical question probing his long-term aspirations, or another signal that more turbulence and yet another rotation is pending within the top two administrative positions.

With caution, JP responds, "It has been awhile since we last talked about my future career. My hopes and dreams still continue with the thought that if I work hard enough and accomplish positive goals that advance our institution, I will someday earn a promotion."

Dr. Schmidt smiles and privately marvels at JP's old-fashioned commitment to a meritocracy. She reaches across a large, wooden coffee table and hands JP a four-page, glossy brochure. The front cover catches JP's eyes, and he immediately recognizes the logo for the American Council on Education.

Dr. Schmidt says, "JP, you know I presently serve on the board of directors for ACE. During our last meeting in DC, the board decided to sponsor a new senior leadership seminar that will help prepare young professionals such as you for future senior leadership assignments. I want to nominate you for this inaugural class of participants, but I need you to review the requirements and assure me that you truly aspire to a future leadership assignment either as a provost or president."

"Hey, Dr. Schmidt, this is a wonderful surprise on a Friday afternoon. Yes, I am interested in this seminar, and yes, I remain hopeful that someday, my career will include senior assignments."

"Okay, take this brochure home over the weekend and talk with your wife. Participation will require you to travel and attend four different workshops over a period of eighteen months. We will use professional development funds from my budget to cover your travel costs. There will be extensive advance reading assignments for each workshop, and you will have to write a ten-page application essay that outlines your educational and leadership philosophy as well as your career aspirations."

Six months later, JP is accepted into the ACE Senior Leadership Program. In preparation for the first seminar, he packs his suitcase, flies to San Antonio, Texas, and eagerly joins twenty-three other participants at a downtown hotel for a three-day meeting. The program schedule is intense. Every morning starts with a 7:00 a.m. breakfast and a structured round-table discussion.

At the conclusion of the seminar's second day, JP accepts a spontaneous dinner invitation from the conference facilitator, Dr.

John Moorehouse. On the first day of the seminar, JP immediately feels a professional connection with Dr. Moorehouse. He hopes the dinner invitation signals that perhaps these feelings are mutual. For many years, JP has hoped to find someone to become not only a career mentor and guide but also a professional friend willing to listen and offer a few helpful thoughts whenever JP encounters a major decision point at work.

Their evening conversation departs from casual topics after the salad is served. John quickly focuses his questions upon the first book each participant is to read before arriving. At times, JP feels like he is taking an oral exam over the reading assignment as John cross-examines JP's conclusions. The book, entitled *Leadership Crises in American Universities*, provides the reader with five case studies where established university presidents are abruptly fired by their governing boards. Each case study includes interviews from the departing presidents along with a detailed analysis of the organizational aftershocks. With the advantage of retrospect, the author interviews many key stakeholders. The narrative explains the extreme institutional chaos that always unfolds after the president's abrupt termination. Sometimes, the campus turmoil prevails for more than two years because the board elects to implement a vicious leadership transition rather than a humane rotation. Whenever possible, the book also addresses the media's coverage of the termination and the severe impact this negative news has upon the institution's public image. In some cases, the damage to the institution's reputation tarnishes public perceptions for many years.

As Dr. Moorehouse outlines the five top reasons university presidents are fired, he senses JP's naivety regarding the political landscape of public higher education. Hoping to probe JP's thoughts, Dr. Moorehouse asks, "JP, do you think our reading assignment outlined presidents who deserved to be fired because they did something wrong or presidents who were fired because mean-spirited board members elected to use their political power in an abusive manner?"

Surprised by the blunt nature of the question, JP pauses and slowly drinks some of his dinner wine. After a minute of reflection, JP responds, "As I recall, all five Presidents were brutally fired over minor incidents that seem to pale in comparison with the major accomplishments they had completed. I will confess that I found these case studies very unsettling. The board's decision to terminate these presidents seemed harsh and unfair and demonstrated a lack of reflective thought. If you are asking me for my opinion, I think these board decisions were an abuse of their power."

John wants to probe deeper, so he says, "JP, do you believe university presidents are always treated fairly by their employer and given the courtesy of a fair-minded dialogue?"

"Well, I would certainly hope so. After all, I believe the culture of higher education is certainly different from the dog-eat-dog climate in the corporate world. If ever there was a place in our society where critical thinking should prevail, it is in the oversight of our universities! Among the social institutions that serve humanity, our universities and our churches stand out as special organizations because they help us clarify our values and inspire our thoughts while encouraging us to practice what we teach."

John counters, "That is an admirable thought, very idealistic, but I am not sure it is congruent with reality. Why do you expect the average citizen serving on a university governing board to effectively use critical thinking?"

"You know, John, your question cuts deep into my core values. I believe people are inherently good, and generally, they try to do the right thing. Like old Saint Augustine said, I believe an all-powerful and supremely good God created mankind in his own likeness, and therefore, our goodness is an inherent part of our makeup. It is embedded within the software of the brain; it is part of our DNA, so to speak! Yes, our ability to be good can be corrupted by evil, but our default nature is guided by a conscience that governs our sense of morality. This inner light seems to be a universal phenomenon that always tries to highlight the right thing to do. It's Plato's white horse pulling the chariot guided by the charioteer, our sense of reason. I also believe educated, accomplished citizens who serve on governing boards recognize that life is full of complexities, and there is always more than one side to any situation. Therefore, as they deliberate, they will take the time to examine the facts and consciously try to look holistically at the big picture. Reflective thinking behaviors such as open-mindedness, suspended judgment, and respect should be the norm for any policy-making governing board."

John smiles as he raises his glass of wine and swallows the last trace of a Mottington Napa Valley Merlot. Looking directly at JP, he asks, "What do you think is the most important leadership characteristic for a university president?"

"Well, if I had more time, I would like to give that question some serious thought; perhaps it would be optimism." JP pauses and then quickly continues "Or it could be perseverance."

John nods his head to signal agreement. "Both those traits are critical, but after many years of experience, I think public university presidents must have a boundless reservoir of courage." John reflectively hesitates and then continues, "JP, I am not talking about the personal courage that is fueled by adrenaline and gives a man the motivation to charge a machine gun. I am talking about an unseen, bone-deep, abiding sense of courage that is active 24-7. Every day, presidents stand in an open arena surrounded by a covey of lightning rods. They never know when storm clouds will bring an unexpected bolt of lightning. The unannounced crisis could be an athletic violation, or a secretary embezzling petty cash, or a faculty member sleeping with a student, or a tragic suicide, or a young student diagnosed with contagious TB, or a residence hall filled with an outbreak of bedbugs after spring break, or a deranged individual who failed an exam going across campus on a shooting spree with an automatic rifle. The list of potential problems is almost endless. Each volatile event can instantly become headline news. Like a bolt of lightning hitting a large tree, the damage to the institution can be significant. Occasionally, when this flash of lightning strikes a university, its energy ripples in unexpected ways and may kill the president's career. Presidents must be willing to always stand in harm's way with a calm decorum while conveying a contagious sense of optimism as they encourage others to advance the institution's mission."

John glances around the restaurant and realizes most of the guests have departed and their tables are empty. He says, "Let's move into the lobby area somewhere near the fountain and find a couple of soft chairs. If you have some time, I want to tell you a story about my old friend, Woodrow Cartwright. Have you ever heard about Cartwright's Alamo?"

Puzzled, but happy to stretch his legs and move into the lobby, JP says, "No, but I look forward to learning more about your friend. Is he still working as a president?"

With a deep sigh that indicates sadness, John says, "No, he is not working. Unfortunately, he unexpectedly died in a car accident a few years ago. He was a good friend, and I still miss him today."

Once they are seated in two overstuffed comfortable chairs in a quiet corner of the lobby, John begins to tell the tale about Woodrow Cartwright's Alamo.

"In the summer of 1978, my old friend Woodrow accepted his first presidency at a small regional state university in Oklahoma. He and his wife, Ashley, gave their heart and soul to that job, and after about two years, they had earned the respect and friendship from many internal and external stakeholders. As gracious hosts and diplomatic ambassadors, Woodrow and his wife worked tirelessly to foster goodwill and organizational progress. I believe Woodrow hoped to stay and make a difference in the life of the institution and the community. Privately, he told me he wanted to spend the next ten years trying to make a contribution. He was driven to enhance and build his university's programs, facilities, and public reputation.

"In many respects, he was a change agent seeking to promote a progressive spirit and hoping to make a leadership contribution that inspired others to advance the educational goals of the institution. He frequently said that he wanted to leave the university in a better condition than the circumstances he inherited when he arrived. If you are familiar with Robert Greenleaf's concept of servant leadership, then you will understand Woodrow's leadership style. He cared deeply for people and the institution.

"By all standards, JP, I would say Woodrow accomplished more in three years than most presidents accomplish in ten. His track record earned him the admiration of many, and observers would say he demonstrated a great deal of ability and talent. Using your meritocracy paradigm, he certainly earned the right to keep his job or advance his career by moving to a larger university. However, as they say in Oklahoma, it is a short trip from the castle to the outhouse, and a mountain of merit can be overlooked or erased when you have abusive political animals out to get you.

"Regrettably, public higher education seems to have more than our fair share of those individuals who believe the end always justifies the means. On many campuses, the concepts of fairness and justice remain elusive, idealistic goals that are rarely achieved. I sometimes play golf in a summer league with a retired three-star army general, and he maintains that the lethal politics of the Pentagon pale in comparison to the ruthless politics that unfold behind the ivory tower's public facade.

"Woodrow's problems started on his first day on the job. Perhaps he was doomed before he started. The lady who served as president of the university foundation board, Stevie Harms, opposed Woodrow's application for president. But she was outvoted by the other members on the search committee, and

Woodrow got the job. Once he hit the ground running, Stevie became a master of charades. During public gatherings, her words were smoother than butter, but anger and hate raged within her heart. In private settings, she used every opportunity to circulate unfounded gossip and terrible rumors about Woodrow and his wife. Her campaign of vicious lies and slander was relentless.

"But my friend always stayed on the high ground, and while he privately lamented Stevie's actions, he publicly maintained a positive, professional approach toward her and the foundation. Finally, during his third year, Woodrow encountered a surprise attack from his opponent, Stevie the Tiger! For about two years, like a camouflaged tiger waiting to pounce upon its prey, she had secretly conducted meetings with the foundation's executive committee. According to their bylaws, the university president was a member of the foundation's executive committee, but she always excluded Woodrow by scheduling a meeting without his knowledge. Frequently, she would plan their get-togethers when she knew he would be traveling out of town on university business.

"When he was not present at the meeting, she maliciously told the other officers that he had been invited, but he was too busy to attend. Obviously, she said, the foundation's work was not on his priority list. During these private committee discussions, she convinced the foundation's leadership that they should use their charitable organization 501(c)(3) tax status to build a new residence hall for the university. Under the guise of helping the university, she told the executive committee that it would be a great addition for the university and a nice way to make some money for the foundation. After all, the increased income that would be collected from the students through their housing fees could be used eventually by the foundation to help support a few of the university's ongoing efforts. Without consulting anyone at the university, the foundation developed an independent proposal to receive a low-interest-rate construction loan from the federal government. These funds were channeled through the county's board of commissioners and targeted toward projects designed to foster economic development within the community.

"Woodrow became aware of the foundation's proposal after he read the newspaper article that announced the recipients for the new economic development loans. These federal loans required a 50-50 match with private funds. So, the foundation was actively seeking seven private investors who would each donate a million dollars under the foundation's charitable gift annuity program. The donors would be given an immediate income tax deduction, and the foundation guaranteed each donor an annual income for life with payout rates that would vary between 6.5 percent and 8.0 percent per year. With these donations, the foundation was going to build a fourteen-million-dollar residence hall that would be configured as modern, two-bedroom apartments and located on foundation-owned property about three blocks from the campus.

"The web of lies around this construction project almost defied explanation. For three years, Woodrow had asked the foundation to help the university by increasing the scholarship program. Each time he submitted a scholarship request, he was told the foundation could not afford to give any more money. Then he asked the foundation for a five-year commitment to incrementally expand the number of students enrolled within the university's honors program under the foundation's largest and most prestigious academic scholarship. That proposal was denied. Twice, he asked the foundation to begin collecting funds to support the university's upcoming centennial celebration, and both times Stevie replied that since the centennial was about six years away, it was too early to mobilize alumni and get them involved with any fundraising efforts. During Woodrow's second year, he asked Stevie for some additional funds to help cover the budget deficit that had accumulated in the athletic program's travel account. That year, they had three different teams qualify for their respective national tournaments, and these unexpected travel costs to the tournaments had pushed the athletic program's operating budget into the red. Stevie responded that it would be simply impossible to support any request that was not already within their planned annual budget.

"You know, the mindset of a foundation board generally falls into two distinct camps. One, when the board is dominated by successful entrepreneurs who excel at making money, they frequently are inclined by default to use the foundation's resources to make more money. Consequently, they focus upon goals such as enhancing net assets, or improving the return on cash investments, or increasing the net worth of the foundation's stock market holdings rather than using the money to help the university with its immediate needs. The other camp is rare, in my opinion. It truly takes a special mindset to find a foundation board that feels good about giving money away rather than using money to accumulate more money so that some rainy day in the future there will be funds to give away!

"Stevie repeatedly convinced the board to ignore the president's funding requests, and she constantly talked about the importance of using their fundraising efforts to accumulate more money in order to grow the foundation's net worth. They spent endless hours during their quarterly meetings analyzing the money market trends and the potential rates of interest that could be expected from various investments opportunities. Unfortunately, they never gave more than a few minutes of discussion to any of Woodrow's requests for financial help."

John pauses to wave at one of the conference participants as she walks across the lobby.

Judith immediately comes over and says, "Well, you guys look pretty comfortable in these big chairs!"

John smiles.

"You know, John," Judith continues, "I just finished the reading assignment for tomorrow, and it really touched my heart."

Curious, John responds, "Well, I hope that is good. What part did you like the best?"

Trying to be polite, Judith quickly says, "Hey, gentlemen, I don't want to interrupt your evening conversation. You guys continue where you where before I crashed into your space. Tomorrow I will explain my feelings about the reading assignment. Suffice it to say, my campus is still spinning because last year we had a college dean who was falsely accused of forging part-time enrollment numbers. The news media painted the picture as a big scandal and assassinated his character so badly that he took his rifle and shot himself. It is the greatest travesty of justice I have ever experienced! The handout I just read seems to focus upon a similar case study of social injustice, and it reminded me of the ghosts that presently haunt us at West Virginia University."

As Judith turns to depart, John quickly responds, "I am sorry to hear about your campus tragedy. I hope you are okay. Have a good evening, and we will look forward to your comments during tomorrow's round-table discussion."

JP is stunned by Judith's disclosure. "Wow, a suicide! That is really a sad commentary to consider."

Turing back toward JP, John says, "Yes, it most certainly is very sad, but you must remember the private face of public universities always reflects the fabric of our society. We are nothing more than a cross section of America's social context. Like any other organization, we have people who demonstrate the good, the bad, and the ugly sides of life. As senior leaders, our primary efforts should seek to foster the best in people and focus upon the goodness that can be accomplished through the educational process."

John shifts his position in the chair. "And so, JP, since the hour is late and we start early in the morning, let me move toward the conclusion of this story about my friend, Woodrow. Needless to say, he was cruelly hurled from the castle to the outhouse like someone discarding an empty beer can into the trash.

"Stevie felt scorned by the search committee, and she was seeking revenge by trying to publicly prove that Woodrow was not worthy of his presidential appointment. She is one of those people Confucius described when the old sage discussed individuals who are guided by the profit that is gained through their actions and motivated by egoism and greed.

"Stevie had a sister married to a successful lawyer, Paul Allgood, who served as the vice chair of the university's governing board. Simultaneously, Mr. Allgood provided legal counsel to the foundation under an annual consulting contract that was supposedly designed to safeguard against conflicts of interest. Unbeknownst to Woodrow, Stevie and her sister inherited a significant amount of money when their ninety-five-year-old aunt died. They both received six large cattle ranches located in the Oklahoma panhandle, and every ranch had at least one producing oil well. Stevie's goal to build a new residence hall for the university was motivated by her personal selfish agenda. She and her sister were both looking for a place to serve as tax shelters for some of their inheritance, and Paul Allgood was privately preparing the foundation's blueprint in order to help his wife and sister-in-law with their estate taxes.

"Stevie developed, with the legal help of her brother-in-law, a financial plan to assemble seven donors. Each million-dollar gift would qualify for all the advantages of an immediate tax deduction. Furthermore, the value of their annual payout rates would be renegotiated after five years to ensure a fair-market return based upon the going interest rates. After the initial five years, the gift annuity was guaranteed to never be less than 8 percent per year and could exceed 10 percent per year if the money market conditions warranted.

"Consequently, when Woodrow tried to convince the foundation that a new residence hall located off campus would be detrimental to the existing on-campus residential life program, he unknowingly created a set of battle lines that angered Stevie, her sister, and her sister's husband, Mr. Allgood. Both families eagerly planned to invest a million dollars toward this new apartment complex, and they did not want the old president standing in their way.

"As you know, the university's budget for residence halls is considered an auxiliary account that must self-sustain without the use of public tax dollars. Woodrow inherited a significant bond indebtedness against their dorms when he arrived. Before the original construction debt had been paid, the university refinanced their indebtedness with a second loan in order to have the funds for some remodeling and interior upgrades. So, the residence halls were seriously mortgaged and had to maintain an 85 percent annual occupancy rate in order to maintain cash flow and stay out of the red. Given the bond debt, plus rising operational costs for utilities and custodial care, Woodrow was barely making ends meet within this housing account. The previous year, the state auditor had flagged this account as a potential problem. As the cost for utilities continued to increase, his occupancy rate fell from 87 percent to 85 percent. He knew the foundation's new residence hall would attract students away from existing campus housing and thereby push their residential life program into deficit spending.

"The more Woodrow tried to appeal to the foundation board to table their construction plans, the angrier Stevie became. She used her established community connections and her family's financial influence to wage a private war against the man she originally opposed during the interview process. In many respects, Woodrow found himself defending the university's existing residence hall program for all the right reasons, but he underestimated the unfair tidal wave of cruelty and political clout that would hit him.

"The simultaneous, joint attack from Stevie and her brother-in-law focused upon slanderous accusations regarding Woodrow's lack of vision and his failed relationship with major community donors. They almost completely ignored the proposed construction issue as they spread false rumors about Woodrow. Rather than focus upon the facts, they carefully planned a smear campaign of slander designed to completely assassinate Woodrow's character. I believe, unfortunately, that the earliest form of human conflict was, most assuredly, slander. You can be sure that long before Cain killed Abel, he bad-mouthed his brother to anyone who would listen.

"This attack escalated into headline news when the owner and editor of the local newspaper quickly decided to support his friends who were hometown wealthy power brokers. By coincidence, the editor socialized every Sunday morning with Stevie and her brother-in-law because they all attended the same Methodist church and participated in the after-service fellowship breakfast. Inspired by the opportunity to increase newspaper sales, he composed several inflammatory headlines that graced the front page of his daily paper and fueled the fires of community gossip and hostility.

"Additionally, over a period of six weeks, he wrote three major Sunday editorials that blasted Woodrow's leadership ability and lack of vision. As a master craftsman of slime and slander, the editor ignited the community's emotions. Woodrow became the target for public scorn. The coffee chatter roared as a raging inferno of gossip exploded. He walked a brutal gauntlet as people crushed his character and betrayed his friendship. Even his wife, Ashley, could not go grocery shopping without encountering some kind of insult or verbal attack from people she previously counted as dear friends. Keep in mind that this was a time before caller ID existed. People could say anything over the phone while remaining anonymous. The answering machine on their home telephone was filled daily with crude messages and obscene threats. Sadly, as the general public became more agitated, Woodrow's post office box received several pieces of unsigned hate mail.

"Twice, in the middle of the night, their campus home was vandalized with crude threats that were spray-painted on the garage door. The first incident happened shortly after the Sunday newspaper ran their famous exposé and first editorial. Filthy cuss words were painted on the garage door with a threatening statement to get out of town. That night, two bricks were thrown through their living room window, and the front yard was covered with huge mounds of stinky garbage.

"The campus facility crew diligently cleaned the yard, repainted the garage door, and replaced the broken picture window on the front of the house. About four weeks later, the community's barbarians returned under the cover of darkness and again painted obscenities across the garage door with another statement that threatened Woodrow's life if he did not leave. This second round of vandalism included a pile of horse shit dumped on the front porch and smeared all over the front door.

"There is a dark side of human nature where contagious impulses simmer. When they erupt, these timeless desires seek to conform to old byzantine tendencies like molten lava following established creeks and streambeds as it flows down the mountainside. Recall the crowds that assembled in the ancient Roman amphitheaters and their excitement when the scent of blood was in the air. Today, we still have Christian people in our communities who surrender to those same barbaric cravings, and they enjoy the thrill of 'mob violence,' when the crowd gives an old dog a bad name and then hangs him on main street. In less than sixty days, the community at large managed to violently destroy Woodrow's self-concept as they threatened his safety, crushed his dignity, and devastated his purpose in life.

"Like a rocket launched into space, this issue escalated from the foundation board's conference table to the university governing board's next meeting agenda. Mr. Allgood, the vice chair of the governing board, painted Woodrow in a very bad light to a number of community leaders whenever he had opportunities for private conversations. Trying to project his stalwart innocence, Mr. Allgood insisted that he was personally involved in this dirty business because he was trying to protect their treasured university. He used his leadership position on the board as a platform to advance brutal, unfounded slanderous accusations against Woodrow and his wife.

"As the pace of gossip and rumors accelerated, a kaleidoscope of prejudices swept through the community. Finally, after a special December 15th board meeting that was closed to the public, Woodrow was asked to leave the room before the board voted to terminate his contract for just cause. The vote was split, but there were enough board members swayed by Stevie and her brother-in-law to capture a majority ballot in support of immediate termination. The board used the "just cause" rationale to cancel Woodrow's contract without any buyout offer. And despite the approaching holiday season, the board issued a two-week eviction notice demanding that Woodrow and his wife move out of the presidential home before the first of January.

"JP, I arrived here a day early in order to set up our conference room and prepare my lecture notes. After I spent the morning sorting handouts and testing the audiovisual equipment in our meeting room, I decided to get outside for some fresh air and sunshine. It is just a short walk from our hotel over to the Alamo. As I toured the Alamo's grounds, I found myself thinking about my friend Woodrow. Like all those brave Texans who died for a noble cause defending the Alamo here in San Antonio, Woodrow's professional career died after he experienced an unbelievable modern-age version of public stoning. As practiced during ancient times, no single "stone" or word delivered the deathblow, but the cumulative effect of ongoing public slander, escalated by the practice of yellow journalism, slowly produced a complete and tragic character assassination that truly resembles the world's oldest form of execution—stoning.

"Needless to say, this professional betrayal was ruthless and barbarian. Woodrow stood as a lone voice against overwhelming odds, trying to do the right thing for the overall benefit of the institution. Unfortunately, two mean-spirited community leaders were able to torpedo a good man because he opposed their selfish investment plans. Trust me, JP, there was no critical thinking process used by the governing board. The charge was politically motivated, and the conviction was a foregone conclusion. The vote against Woodrow was fueled by emotional anger and guided by personal agendas. He became a victim of abusive power wielded by senior decision makers who believed the end justified their corrupt means. My friend never recovered from this premeditated political attack. Try to imagine the sense of shame he felt. Many of us will always remember this scandalous battle as Cartwright's Alamo. With the enduring stigma of board termination and the public humiliation that captured headline news, he was never able to find another university job. Woodrow's career was shattered like a beautiful oak tree destroyed by an unexpected bolt of lightning.

"Unfortunately, the story does not end with Woodrow's departure from Oklahoma. The second order implications of this termination were more tragic than you can imagine. Fate seemed to intervene with a cruel sense of humor. Woodrow was an active leader within two major national educational associations. Hoping to maintain his ability to network with professional colleagues as he looked for a new job, he appealed to the president of the American Council on Education for the chance to continue serving on two of their national committees. Without any explanation, he was removed from these assignments and disinvited to attend their next regular committee meeting. He simultaneously appealed to the president of the American Association of State Colleges and Universities for a senior fellowship assignment. He was told that their established board policy would not permit him to have the honor of a fellowship. It was AASCU's long-standing tradition to avoid any professional association with a president that had been fired regardless of his possible innocence.

"Do you know that ancient quote in the book of Job about being abandoned by your friends? Job said his friends scorned him while he became the laughingstock to all who knew him. Well, that was certainly Woodrow's experience. Many treated him like a leper.

"It is not easy to be around someone who is suffering, especially if that hardship has created a social stigma. A medical illness can be a badge of honor, but public slander creates a badge of disgrace. The victim emerges as a kind of social outcast. Woodrow was ostracized and avoided by colleagues who had known him for years. Most of his friends and trusted professional references refused to take his phone calls or answer his letters.

"His beautiful wife, Ashley, experienced the same betrayal and abandonment. You cannot believe the cruel way her friends treated her. But she remained emotionally strong and tirelessly supported her husband throughout this ordeal. I think she should be remembered as a saint. I cannot imagine the immeasurable pain she silently suffered and endured during this difficult period.

"For about three years, Woodrow struggled to keep his hope alive while he tried to find a job. His applications yielded hundreds of rejection letters. These dismal employment prospects spread gloom deep into the fiber of his bones. As his dreams became dust in the wind, he began to battle a serious depression. These dark nights of the soul eventually drove him to seek solace in the bottom of a whiskey bottle. I believe he was well on his way to becoming a true alcoholic during his last year of life. One night, after drinking too much and closing the bar, he tried to drive home, but he never made it. His car veered off the exit ramp on Interstate 80 in Omaha, and he hit the cement base of an overpass pillar head on. Many believe it was an accident caused by the alcohol, but the coroner ruled his death as a probable suicide because the evidence at the scene clearly indicated Woodrow never hit the brakes, and in fact, it appeared that he continued to accelerate as he drove straight into the cement column."

John stops and looks for some kind of feedback or reaction from JP.

"You know, John, your story outlines a major tragedy in human affairs. Your friend was a good man, and he deserved better treatment. Here we are participating in this seminar and enjoying this hotel's fine ambiance and ACE's hospitality, but I must say that I am truly disappointed to hear about the harsh actions of our professional colleagues in DC. Needless to say, as educational leaders at the national level, I would have hoped they would practice reflective thinking skills and take the time for an open-minded analysis. Their hasty rush to judgment was unfair, and their rejection of Dr. Cartwright seems shortsighted and cruel to me."

JP looks directly at John with a quizzical stare and adds a closing thought, "Have you ever noticed how often someone is considered guilty until they prove themselves innocent?"

With a philosophical glance, John responds, "I once read that there are two kinds of evil in this world. The first is the unexpected evil that happens to you. Generally, you trip over this evil, or perhaps you stumble badly and fall. The second kind of evil is the type you actively pursue or help make happen to others. Without question, both are orchestrated by the devil."

"John, I am frequently overwhelmed by the power of evil people and absolutely amazed that so many times, the silent majority of good people are content to stand back and willingly empower a few mean-spirited folks to do malicious things."

"JP, it is late, and I still have a few things to prepare for tomorrow's seminar discussion. In some small way, I hope this true story about my friend gives you a new paradigm to consider. Unfortunately, we live in a world where bad things happen to good people."

"Good night, John! Thank you for sharing this insightful story about Dr. Cartwright. Yes, I agree there is much food for thought in your narrative. In many ways, this conversation supplements the case studies we are discussing during our seminar."

Two days later, JP is completing a long day of return travel. His departure from San Antonio to Chicago is delayed because of weather, but he arrives at O'Hare International with just enough time to catch his connecting flight to Burlington. As he sits on the plane for many hours, drinking coffee and reading, he feels unusually troubled and unable to concentrate on his new book. As he gazes out the plane's window, he finds himself wondering which of the two great ancient thinkers have the most accurate theory about human nature.

JP's Catholic upbringing gives him a natural affinity for St. Augustine's premise that every person is naturally good and guided by a conscience that seeks to do the right thing. But John's story about his friend Woodrow makes a significant impact on JP. For the first time in his life, JP wonders if his hard work, meritorious accomplishments, and dreams for future career advancement can be erased by unopposed evil in a manner similar to Woodrow Cartwright's experience.

Perhaps it is the teachable moment for JP's character development, or perhaps, it is John's thoughtful reflections in conjunction with the seminar's assigned reading. Nevertheless, JP is experiencing a significant disconnect between his long-established values and his growing knowledge regarding human behavior. Recognizing the role of evil within human affairs, JP struggles to understand the purpose, context, and destination of his life's journey.

To be sure, there is a pronounced accuracy within the Confucian thought that describes the selfish, evil nature of some human beings. From time to time, JP has encountered evil people, but he has always considered them an anomaly or exception to the general rule. Now, as he ponders these rival theories, JP has a dismal feeling of uneasiness and internal turmoil. Intellectually, he wants to retain his idealistic framework. JP is not ready to change his beliefs about God and human nature. Since his early childhood days, he has believed God is a shield and protector who saves the honest heart and vindicates those who suffer false accusations. But emotionally, JP cannot stop thinking about the realities of unabashed evil that have caused Cartwright's Alamo. For the first time in his life, JP feels compelled to analyze his deep-rooted Christian values. And for just a few minutes, on the Chicago to Burlington leg of the journey, he wonders if Dr. Schmidt has worked behind the scenes with John to prearrange their dinner conversation and ensure that JP has this eye-opening experience.

16

The Trojan Horse

War is the continuation of politics by other means.

—Carl von Clausewitz, 1780–1831

April 1989
Springview, Nebraska

"Buzz, I want you to give this idea some serious thought. You are a natural for this job. And I can promise you the full support from our party's leadership."

The senator is grilling some of his famous T-bone steaks and trying to convince Buzz to run for his senate seat. Three weeks earlier, Senator Abe Turner announced his candidacy for the US House of Representatives race. Consequently, his state senate seat is up for grabs, and he wants to control whoever takes his place in Lincoln.

Turning around and looking at Dean Warton, the senator says, "What does our old dean think about my proposal?"

"I think it is a great idea. You know, senator, I checked the personnel manual like you requested, and there is an old 1958 policy that permits full-time university employees to serve within the legislature without losing their job. We could check with your friend, the chairman of the board, but I think a liberal interpretation of this policy would permit Buzz to keep his university job while serving in the legislature."

The senator beams as he carefully turns the steaks. With a skillful twist of the brush, he delicately applies his homemade BBQ sauce on each steak.

"I'm telling you, Buzz, I believe you are perfect for this position. And after I take over our operation in DC, I want someone back here working the floor of the senate that I can trust. To borrow one of your old Sun Tzu sayings, I need you to be my trusted spy in the legislature. You will be my quarterback as we push the party's agenda through the legislative process."

Dean Warton senses the senator's tension. He wants to spark some levity, and so with cheerful bravado, he raises his glass and proposes a toast.

"I want us to drink to our Remarkable Trinity! We are an unbeatable team, and together we will seize every possibility as the new opportunities multiply and we celebrate the election of Senator Buzz Granger!"

These words please the old senator and spark Buzz's confidence and enthusiasm. After years of drinking together, all three men automatically chug their glass of whiskey and simultaneously slam them on the table's wooden surface. Without a moment of hesitation, the senator turns to examine the steaks and immediately says, "Gentlemen, dinner is served! Grab your plates and I will pull your steak off the grill!"

Buzz sails through the primary race completely unopposed. His wife, Maggie, steps forward to support his political campaign during the months of September and October. Together they literally attend almost one hundred dinners, socials and public gatherings. Buzz gains twelve pounds on the campaign trail. Coached by Senator Abe, Buzz memorizes a brief campaign speech that glosses over the major issues and gives most of the audience a glimmer of what they want to hear.

Riding on the coattails of Ronald Reagan, the Republican Party enjoys a landslide victory from coast to coast. On election night, at about nine thirty, newly elected Senator Buzz Granger stands with his wife at the podium in Springview's new Holiday Inn. They are standing next to Congressman-elect Abe Turner flanked by family members and campaign managers. Both men step to the microphone to claim victory and graciously thank their loyal supporters for their vote of confidence and their wonderful assistance. The crowd explodes with applause when Congressman Turner says, "Ladies and gentlemen, my dear friends and our special guests, the chronicles of Republican Party history will record this occasion as truly a state day, bonfire night, and very special celebration. God bless each one of you, and God bless this great country!"

As the victory celebration escalates, the chandelier in the grand ballroom starts to sway. Congressman Turner politely excuses himself at about eleven thirty and retires to his suite on the third floor of the Holiday Inn. After removing his shoes and tie, he immediately goes to the telephone and dials his best friend's number. Within seconds, a solid brass telephone rings in a secluded cabin twenty-five miles north of Grand Island. After the fourth ring, an elderly male voice abruptly answers, "This is Ace."

"Well, good evening, my friend! Are you drinking champagne or brandy tonight?

After more than forty years of friendship, Congressman Turner knows his friend's habits like the back of his right hand. Mr. Ace is like his mentor and godfather.

"Hell, Abe, you know that bubbly shit is for sissies and women. Give me a fine brandy anytime. I am sitting here in front of the fireplace watching the television, trying to keep track of the West Coast election returns. We knew Ronnie would be strong in the West, but it looks like even the experts underestimated his political appeal."

Mr. Ace pauses to sip his brandy. "Congratulations, Abe, I am proud of you tonight! You will do well in DC, and that college boy of yours can keep track of things in Lincoln while you are working the hallways on Capitol Hill."

David Andrew "Ace" McNair, Jr. is a Midwest tycoon, land baron, and banker who grows up on a farm south of Hastings, Nebraska. During the Depression, his father has access to money, and frequently takes advantage of the economic bargains that develop every time the local community bank forecloses on a nearby farm. Incrementally, over a period of ten years, he purchases thirty-six farms for a nickel on the dollar. Andrew is raised on one of these farms, and as a young boy, he learns to work from sunrise until sunset.

In May of 1941, he graduates from Campbell High School with plans to be a farmer. However, after Pearl Harbor, Andrew joins the Marines and becomes a fighter pilot. He quickly achieves the rank of captain and flies many successful missions throughout the Pacific Theater. With seventeen confirmed "air-to-air" victories, he is awarded the Silver Star and goes into the record book as one of the great "flying aces" of World War II.

After the war is over, he returns home to the family farm and spends the next twenty years tripling the number of farms owned by their family corporation. His military nickname, Ace, becomes a household term among his family and friends.

During the early 1970s, Ace decides to diversify his wealth by carefully investing in bonds and the stock market. His Midas touch prevails, and he uses the soaring profits to purchase controlling interest in several major Nebraska banks.

Unbeknownst to the general public, Ace emerges as one of the top five wealthiest men in the Midwest. As he approaches his seventieth birthday, he divides his energy overseeing a complex web of financial investments and privately controlling the political landscape for Nebraska's Republican Party.

"You know, Ace, I ultimately want to live in the Governor's Mansion. I think of this assignment in DC as a furlough or a necessary detour that will eventually enhance my chances for the governor's job."

Ace chuckles. "Patience, my friend, patience! Your time will come. It is just a matter of time until you will be rambling around in that beautiful mansion with thirty-one rooms at 1425 H Street in downtown Lincoln."

The congressman counters, "We just have to be sure that shit-heel from Scottsbluff does not get the upper hand. I am sure he plans to push his agenda now that I will be out of his hair and two thousand miles down the road."

"Abe, remember our new secret weapon. Senator Buzz will work the senate chamber and pose as their friend, but in reality, he will be your spy. I don't think that old muckraker from Scottsbluff has a single clue that you just rolled a Trojan horse inside his castle walls. With the inside information from Buzz, you will always be one step ahead of your opposition."

"You are right! Shit, given our election results, we should be dancing on the tables tonight rather than worrying about those western Nebraska liberals who want to destroy the things we have worked so hard to build. Damn, Ace, do you ever get tired of the constant worry?"

A roar of laughter comes from Ace. "Hell no! When I climbed out of my uniform, I knew there was only one other civilized opportunity where you can get the same adrenaline rush that you experience in combat. That arena, my friend, is party politics. Next to the thrills of actual combat, the realm of politics represents the ultimate game of chess. Enjoy the ride, Abe. Take it from an old war horse who loves the scent of battle: it does not get any better than this. Good night, my friend."

Abe walks away from the telephone. The silence in his motel room pierces his heart. With a sense of pride and accomplishment, he marvels at the wisdom of his best friend. After pouring a glass of his favorite brandy, he smiles to himself as he ponders the strategic coup that his new Trojan horse represents. Amused and lighthearted, he mutters aloud one of his favorite mantras: "The prince who governs a state must do unto others as they would do unto him."

17

The Pilgrim's Mountain

The Hill called Difficulty
This Hill, though high, I covet to ascend,
The Difficulty will not me offend.
For I perceive the Way to Life lies here:
Come pluck up Heart, let's neither faint nor fear;
Better, though difficult, the Right Way to go,
Than Wrong, though easy, where the End is Woe.
…Difficulty is behind, Fear is before,
Though he's got on the Hill, the Lions Roar.

—*The Pilgrim's Progress* by John Bunyan, 1678

April 1990
Central State University

"Jenn, sorry to bother you at work, but I just got an exciting phone call from General Norman. The command selection board completed their quarterly meeting earlier today, and guess what?"

JP is ecstatic, but he has to subdue his voice because his university office provides minimal privacy. Two secretaries and a student worker sit behind desks that are less than fifteen feet from JP's two office doors.

"Oh, sweetheart, I hope they selected you for your next command! What did the general say?"

Jenn knows this is an important benchmark in JP's military career. She expects good news, because JP never calls to deliver bad news or sad information. For the past eighteen years, she has watched and supported her husband's many personal sacrifices as he juggles the demands of a dual career. Countless times, JP has gone the extra mile to achieve excellence while performing all his military assignments.

After completing his initial enlistment contract, JP talks to an Army National Guard recruiter about a year after marrying Jenn. He does the research, analyzes the facts, and becomes convinced that he wants to continue his military service. Driven by a sense of patriotism and a desire to establish a retirement pension, JP enlists in the Nebraska Army National Guard, completes the infantry officer's candidate school, and accepts an appointment as a rifle platoon leader within a mechanized infantry company. Jenn has lost track of the number of birthdays, anniversaries, and special family occasions he has missed because his military duties require his attendance at a meeting.

"Wow, Jenn! They are going to give me an infantry command sometime next fall. He said that I should be prepared to accept a new assignment shortly after the Thanksgiving holiday. Can you believe it? Holy cow! Let's celebrate tonight and go out for a nice dinner! How about it?"

"Absolutely, I am so happy for you! Congratulations, sweetheart!"

Actually, Jenn has mixed emotions, but she tries to curtail her worries and share her husband's moment of joy. She understands the importance of this command selection. With less than two years since his last promotion, JP is a fairly new lieutenant colonel in the Army National Guard. Presently, he has an excellent staff position working to support the state's chief of staff, but, JP has dreams to pursue and mountains to climb. He frequently explains in vivid detail that it is necessary to have a successful tour as a battalion commander in order to be nominated for the next promotion to full colonel.

"Hey, Jenn, I have to let you go. I have a two o'clock meeting that will start in a few minutes. I think Dean Messick is already waiting for me in the outer office area. I love you, baby! Can't wait to celebrate with you tonight."

JP finishes his telephone conversation and immediately steps out his office door to greet Dean Messick. Once she is seated in JP's small office area, she whispers and gestures with her hands that it would be better if both doors are closed.

During the next forty minutes, Dean Messick carefully outlines a complicated procedure that one of her department secretaries has used to steal money from the university. For many years, the department has maintained a cash box within their office in order to make change and sell the university's helpful guide sheets to individuals from the community who walk in as customers. The department chair has implicitly trusted his secretary to balance a weekly summary statement, and he lets her leave early on Friday afternoons in order to make deposits at the bank whenever the petty cash balance exceeds fifty dollars.

At first, the secretary takes a small amount with honest intentions of repaying the loan. She borrows twenty dollars to purchase some badly needed groceries. For a few months, she borrows and returns small amounts of cash whenever she needs extra grocery money. However, she eventually starts borrowing more than she can pay back. It does not take long for the problem to grow. Soon, she falls behind and no longer tries to pay anything back. Her flawless method enhances her bold sense of confidence. She is convinced no one is checking the weekly summaries, so she continues to use the cash box as a source of supplemental spending money.

Since this petty cash fund functions as an auxiliary and incidental account, the revenue and expenses never appear within the department's base operating budget. Consequently, no one detects any discrepancies or theft when the annual audits are completed by the university's business office.

Dean Messick has trusted the chair to provide oversight for this subsidiary account. She has never given this public service effort a serious thought. It has functioned below her radar. The occasional sale of guide sheets has been designed to be a simple, customer-friendly convenience for walk-in visitors. At the same time, the chair has trusted the secretary, and he has never checked the account until recently when the carry forward balance is too small to pay the upcoming printing costs for the new supply of guide sheets.

As Dean Messick concludes her review of the problem, she says, "This is certainly a sensitive problem that will hurt the university's reputation if it becomes public. I recommend that we let bygones be bygones and move forward with the chair's promise that he will watch this account like a hawk."

"Joan, I can't believe you want me to sweep this problem under the rug?" JP is simultaneously irritated and frustrated.

"Please, Dr. O'Bryan, for the sake of the university's reputation, don't try to press charges on this one. We have to find a way to resolve this problem and keep this trouble out of the news."

Dean Joan Messick is adamant. With twenty-eight years of dedicated service at the university, she is fiercely loyal and protective toward the university and its reputation. JP also senses that she wants to protect her department chair and the reputation of her school.

"Look, this is blatant embezzlement, Joan! I can't believe it! How much are we talking about here?"

Dean Messick tries to stall and evade JP's direct question. "Well, I don't know if we can ever determine the exact amount!"

With a firm voice, JP looks directly into her eyes speaking slowly while trying to control his Irish temper. "Look Joan, how big is this loaf of bread? How big is this problem? How much money has been stolen?"

"Well, we are not sure, at least several thousand dollars. We think about a hundred dollars per month for the last eight or nine years."

Dean Messick cringes and closes her eyes. She expects JP to explode with complete outrage. The room becomes stone silent. Dean Messick opens her eyes and looks at JP with her stoic face that conveys an unusual blend of remorse and well-practiced assertiveness.

Calmly, JP diplomatically tries to share his thoughts and appeal to her good judgment. "Joan, I don't want to sound too philosophical here, but I do believe we are like fellow travelers. Our current job assignments make us colleagues and kindred spirits on this complex journey called life. We need to work together to solve this problem. There is an old sixteenth century book that suggests the journey of life frequently delivers unexpected challenges. These problems can be difficult to solve. Often, one feels like they are trying to climb a steep hill—one step forward, two steps backward. But the secret to success and the way to solve these problems is by working together and pulling together in the same direction. Today, we are at a crossroads as we face this newly discovered theft, and together, we must choose the right way to go."

JP pauses, looking for some nonverbal signal of agreement; he hopes for some indication that they are on the same wavelength. But this brief pause becomes an opportunity for Dean Messick to interrupt and take control of the conversation. She does not like either the tone or direction of JP's comments.

"Look, JP, we are not standing on some pilgrim's mountain overlooking a spacious valley and debating the merits of Zen philosophy! I am telling you right now. Don't count on me for any support if you decide to ride your high horse and try to make a big deal out of this petty cash issue. By the way, you should know, the department chair has already contacted his faculty union lawyer, and they are preparing for battle. And his secretary refuses to talk with anyone unless her clerical union attorney is in the room. Once these two union attorneys start working together, you can expect an avalanche of grievances to fall on your head, and I don't plan to be standing next to you when they hit you!"

That same day, 1,600 miles west of Vermont, the sun shines across the rolling plains of Nebraska. Frantically, Buzz calls for an emergency meeting with his friend, the congressman. Precisely at 1:00 p.m., the proud members of the Remarkable Trinity assemble at the congressman's favorite table in the back corner of the dining room. Today they are a dynamite duo rather than a threesome. Tragically, one of the three great amigos has been found dead this morning in downtown Sioux City, Iowa. When Buzz hears the news, he hits the panic button. So, for the first time, there is a noticeably empty chair when the two men take their seats at the old wooden table with its matching, well-worn, padded oak chairs.

Congress has adjourned for a two-week Easter recess, and the wise old state senator, Abe Turner, is home for a few days of rest and relaxation. The timing for this luncheon is not good for Congressman Abe, but he senses the turmoil in Buzz's voice and decides he better try to calm his nerves and prevent him from doing something stupid.

As the Congressman takes his usual seat at the table, Buzz dispenses with the pleasantries of greeting his old mentor and blurts out with a high pitched voice filled with stress, "Did you hear how Big Dee died?"

Ever since their 1985 Montana elk hunting trip, Buzz has affectionately called his old friend, Dean Frank Warton, the "Big Dee." The "Dee" is an informal nickname for his academic title, the Dean. On that memorable trip to Big Sky country, Dean Warton had remarkable luck their first day out, shooting a trophy elk that claimed first place in Montana's hunting contest for the largest elk killed that year. Buzz has repeatedly said no other academic dean in the history of the university could claim the fame of being such a successful trophy hunter of four-legged game! When they drink together, Buzz always emphasizes the "four-legged" phrase to qualify and limit the dean's range of hunting skills. It is Buzz's way of highlighting his boastful, chauvinistic, manly claim that he is one of the most successful hunters of "two-legged game." That is, the "game" who wears short skirts, silk panties, and a size C bra.

"Yes, I heard all the gory details about his death!" The congressman is filled with grief and really does not want to discuss the specifics while they are seated for lunch.

Buzz presses onward, ignoring his friend's nonverbal clues and bubbling with an unhealthy attraction for the macabre.

"Well, I always heard it takes about four minutes to bleed to death when your cock is cut off. But since they also removed his balls, he might have died quicker since there would have been more profuse bleeding. Man, can you believe they tied his hands behind his back, put his cock in his mouth, and his balls in his shirt pocket?"

Buzz pauses long enough to gulp down his glass of ice water that is on the table. "Holy shit, what a way to die!"

The congressman cringes and turns white. He shakes his head in disbelief! At this point in time, inside this public restaurant, it is his opinion that Buzz is providing TMI—too much information. He raises his hand to signal that Buzz should stop talking.

"Please, Buzz, spare me all the details! I thought you wanted to eat a good lunch and talk about our buddy's upcoming funeral. We need to do something nice to help his family, and we need something more than flowers to recognize and remember our old hunting amigo in a special way."

As their luncheon progresses, Buzz becomes calmer, and gives the congressman the time and space to talk about the funeral. In some ways, Buzz is surprised by the congressman's empathetic decorum. This is a side of his personality that Buzz has never witnessed. He seems to be sincerely touched by Dean Warton's unexpected murder, and Buzz has never seen anyone display such grief at the loss of a friend. Buzz thinks that he perhaps has underestimated their bond of friendship.

After finishing their roast beef specials, both men order a piece of coconut cream pie. This mouthwatering, savory dessert is a house specialty at Mildred's Family Restaurant. With a homemade, flaky crust that is absolutely to die for, many people drive a lot of miles to enjoy Mildred's legendary trademark: her homemade, melt-in-your-mouth pie with hot coffee. Every time the congressman is home from DC, he makes it a point to rendezvous with Mildred's fresh gourmet pie. And he always says, "Her fresh coffee is surely the aroma of heaven."

While they wait for their pie, Buzz takes the opportunity to revisit Dean Warton's execution. It is common knowledge around town that his body was found behind a trash dumpster on old Fourth Street. This is a tough part of town near the stockyards and about one block from the abandoned train depot. Nothing good ever happens on lower Fourth Street. Once a thriving business district, the Fourth Street clientele has evolved from retail to crime. Over a period of twenty years, the street has become the police department's worst nightmare. Once the primary access route for the city's beautiful, bustling train depot, the badly worn red brick street has become the home for hookers, drug dealers, and ruthless bookies.

"Do you think Big Dee got in trouble with someone at the dog track?"

"Yes, I am pretty sure that he was in deep financial trouble. You know, the last few years he accumulated some exorbitant gambling debts. Did you know that a few months ago, I signed a special loan authorization for him at the bank? As chairman of the board, I guaranteed the loan with my signature. Our old hunting buddy was behind with his house payments, and he did not want his wife to know about his debts at the dog track."

Buzz is surprised. He has missed all the clues. After Dean Warton retires from the university, he drives to the dog tracks virtually every day the dogs run. Back on campus, Buzz is moving in his own ivory tower world. He quickly loses touch with the man he once considered both his best friend and main partner in crime. Their Sunday-morning conversations diminish to a few casual pleasantries after church while standing in the courtyard between the church and the parking lot.

Buzz lacks empathy for others, but he senses the need to sound respectful; so he tries to be philosophical as he says, "Well, all I can say is today is a sad day for our Remarkable Trinity! Life seems so unfair. It is like we are always climbing a steep hill while we are surrounded by problems. You know that old saying about taking the time to drain the swamp while you are hip-deep in alligators."

"Yes, Buzz, that is true. It is a very sad day. But more importantly, it is a tragic day for Frank's wife and their beautiful kids. And unfortunately, sometime after the funeral, I will have to tell her that my bank now owns their home. She does not have a clue about their debt. How I dread the day when I have to break that news to her."

The congressman finishes his coffee and excuses himself. He promises Buzz that they will talk more after Frank's funeral.

That evening, JP and Jenn go out for dinner. They elect to eat at the downtown Red Lobster because it is Jenn's favorite restaurant. She always orders their fresh salmon whenever they go there, and their homemade cheddar bay biscuits are always a special treat. This dinner should be a time to celebrate, but their conversation is very subdued because neither JP nor Jenn feel very lighthearted.

As they await the arrival of dessert, JP becomes very serious. "Jenn, do you believe we live in a society where the merits of a person's work primarily shape the progress of his career?"

"JP, you know we have talked about this topic before. Yes, I believe the quality of one's work is ultimately reflected in the performance evaluation and promotion process. But we both know that politics also influence the evaluation and promotion process. Are you thinking about military stuff or your work at the university?"

"Well, I know we are here to celebrate the news about my military career, but tonight, I guess I was thinking more about the university than the military. I had a very difficult conversation with Dean Messick earlier today, and she is deliberately avoiding the right thing to do because she wants to play politics. I am amazed by the absence of her moral compass and her desire to foster a conspiracy of silence around this embezzlement issue."

"Do you think she understands the serious nature of these facts and the subsequent ramifications that might emerge because of this issue? Maybe she does not value the same things you treasure. Perhaps all these years of work have calloused her sense of right and wrong."

JP takes a minute to savor his cappuccino. "For some reason, she wants to be silent about this embezzlement. She wants to ignore the problem and pretend like it does not exist. As an established campus leader, I am surprised by her willingness to sweep this under the rug and move on like it never happened."

Jenn responds quickly because they are retracing an old conversation. "You know, just because she is a dean, it does not mean she will act responsibly, JP! Let's go back to your original question. You always say that merit determines more than 50 percent of the promotion process, and politics plays only a minor role. What if it is the other way around? What if politics influence more than 50 percent of the promotion decision? Maybe even 75 percent! Are you prepared to play by those rules? Are you ready to surrender your moral compass to the political agendas of the day?"

Once again, JP asserts, "Hell no! Jenn, you know how I feel about this. I am not going to take the path of least resistance just because it is the politically desirable thing to do."

Jenn smiles and says, "Well, there you have it!"

They both laugh.

After finishing their meal, JP and Jenn return home. It is late, and Jenn is exhausted after a challenging day of work at school with her first graders. As the grandfather clock strikes one o'clock, Jenn is sleeping soundly and JP is pacing the living room floor in the dark. Their black-and-white Lhasa Apso, Colby, is taking advantage of JP's absence and sleeping on his pillow next to Jenn.

November 23, 1990, a Thursday, is a day JP will never forget. He and Jenn travel home to Missouri to celebrate the Thanksgiving holiday with their family. On this day, for the first time, the family assembles for their traditional holiday meal, and JP's dad is not seated at the head of the table. Mr. O'Bryan has died three weeks earlier after battling multiple myeloma cancer for more than four years. And to accent the day's sense of sadness, the traditional Thanksgiving Day football game between the Huskers and the Oklahoma Sooners is played in Norman and the Huskers lose 45 to 10. It seems like doom and gloom is hanging over the entire day.

Now with the holidays behind them, JP and Jenn have returned home and resumed their work. They have tabled most of their plans for Christmas because neither of them are in the mood to think about another quickly approaching holiday without Mr. O'Bryan.

On the evening of November 29, JP goes to bed early with a good book to read. At about nine thirty, the telephone rings and Jenn answers. After a few brief words, Jenn says, "JP, the phone is for you. It is Colonel Smith."

Quickly, JP grabs the phone next to the bed and says, "Good evening, Colonel. How are you doing? Hope you and your family had a great Thanksgiving holiday."

Colonel Greg Smith is long on business and short on pleasantries. He rarely talks about anything unless it is related to work. Tonight, he is calling to discuss a very confidential topic. "JP, as you know this Saturday, December first, you are scheduled to begin your new command assignment. Are you ready for it?"

JP is surprised. This seems like a strange question to ask at such a late hour of the day. He thinks to himself, *Hell yes, I have been ready and waiting for more than seven months!* Trying to be diplomatic and optimistic, JP responds, "Absolutely, sir! I am ready. I have been looking forward to this new assignment. It is an honor to be given this leadership opportunity."

Gruffly, Colonel Smith snaps, "JP, how are things with your family? How are things going at the university?"

Again, very surprised, JP is puzzled. How do you answer such a complex question within the boundaries of a brief phone conversation? Trying to be honest, JP says, "Sir, thanks for asking. You know it was really hard to bury my dad a few weeks ago. In many ways, he was more than my dad; he was also a best friend. But last week we traveled to Missouri, and we were together with everyone for a nice, traditional Thanksgiving visit. Now, as the eldest son in the family, I am trying to assume more responsibility and help everyone the way my dad used to do. As far as work is concerned at the university, right now I am super busy with budget reports, and we are in the middle of several difficult issues with the unions. But you know the old saying that you eat an elephant one bite at a time. So each day, I try to move forward in a positive manner."

The phone becomes silent. JP hears the muffled sounds of the colonel clearing his throat. "JP, this is not business as usual. You are not walking into a new command this Saturday in the routine way. You need to know that your unit just moved to "red" status on the defense department's mobilization chart. That means your unit is "hot" and could be activated to support the war during the next forty-eight hours."

JP is speechless. He is totally blindsided. He has been so engrossed with grief after his dad's death that he has never once thought his new command would be selected to serve in support of the Gulf War. But with a firm resolve, JP says, "Sir, I am ready for this responsibility. Tell me what you want me to do."

"Look JP, I am calling you because we are friends, and I want you to think carefully about taking this command. Are you ready? Are you ready to give your heart and soul to this assignment? If not, speak up now, and I will make arrangements to delay your command assignment and leave the current commander in his position. After all, he knows everyone in the unit, he knows the unit's strengths and weaknesses, and he can quickly take them through the mobilization process. I need to know if you are prepared to walk away from your family and your university job and throw yourself into this command as you run into the buzz saw of mobilization and deployment."

Without any hesitation, JP responds with a positive, can-do attitude. "Sir, I am ready to do this. I am ready to accept this responsibility. I will do my very best."

With noticeable emotion, Colonel Smith realizes he is sending a good friend into battle, and the odds indicate he probably will not return. Sternly, the Colonel says, "In that case, JP, tomorrow you need to go to work, and without telling anyone about this conversation, you need to prepare like it will be your last day at work. You can tell your supervisor, but that is it. No one else can know. If your unit is mobilized this Saturday during your weekend drill, you will never make it back to the campus. You will be swept into the fast currents of mobilization work as you prepare your new command for deployment. I think your unit could be certified for overseas deployment and on its way in about seven days. It will all depend upon the availability of airlift once you become deployable."

18

Dark Shadows Harbor
the Wiles of Evil

An old cowboy went riding out one dark and windy day,
upon a ridge he rested as he went along his way.
… As some riders loped on by him,
he heard one call his name.
If you want to save your soul from Hell a-riding on our range,
then cowboy change your ways today, or with us you will ride,
trying to catch the Devil's herd, across these endless skies.

—Johnny Cash, "Ghost Riders in the Sky," 1999

November 1990
Springview, Nebraska

Listening to music, laughing aloud, leaping from the chair, and looking out the window at the falling snow, Larry Gene Allen feels compelled to make another phone call. It is almost 2:00 p.m., Nebraska time, making it three o'clock in Washington DC.

As the recently elected chair of the university's board of governors, Mr. Allen finds it very ironic that he is now sleeping with the beautiful lady who was sleeping with the old fart, Buzz Granger. Last evening, over a glass of wine that followed a wild tumble of adulterous sex on crimson red silk sheets, Diana confides to her new lover that she is secretly leading an underground movement to conduct a "no-confidence vote" against Buzz's leadership as the department chairman.

Larry waits as the telephone rings four times. Expecting to roll into the message system, he is surprised to hear the familiar deep-pitched voice of his boss answer, "Yes, this is Congressman Turner. With whom am I speaking?"

"Hey, Senator Abe, this is Larry Allen calling. How in the world are you?"

"Fine, fine, what's up? Is everything okay at the bank?"

"Oh sure, we are doing fine at the bank. The market has been good to us, and we seem to be going through a nice growth spurt. Our last advertising campaign that highlighted free checking accounts really worked. I think it brought us about two hundred new customers. Things are good. Don't worry. I will have a complete report ready for you when we meet with the bank board in about two weeks."

"Great! Look, I only have about five minutes here to talk, and then I have to shag my butt down to the House Chamber in order to cast my vote on the President's new tax proposal. Damn, I am telling you, this is a wild and crazy time here on Capitol Hill. And now this mad man, Saddam Hussein, has really riled everyone up here in DC. Why the hell did he decide to invade Kuwait? Who knows? Well, enough of my problems. You did not call to hear me bitch. Larry, what can I do for you?"

"Well, Senator, I know Buzz Granger is one of your good friends. Ever since he took your place in the legislature, there have been a few people in town who question his right to double-dip with a salary from the university and a salary from the legislature.

As you know, he misses a lot of days on campus when he is in Lincoln working the legislature. His repeated absence is wearing thin on some of those old campus nerds. Anyway, I am starting to hear some rumbles that the faculty in his department might vote no-confidence against his leadership as the department chair."

"Well, shit! Damn it all to hell! Just when you think things are going well at that university, some fool throws a monkey wrench into the gears!"

Pressed for time, the congressman grows impatient. After a few seconds of silence, he says, "Look Larry. I pay you good money to run my bank. And I am proud you are serving as the university's board chair. Take my advice. You better get on top of this shit-storm and make it go away! I am counting on you to solve this mess. Goddamn it, I am almost two thousand miles away, and I sure as hell ain't going to be around town trying to smooth ruffled feathers and protect old Buzz's ass! I got my hands full trying to help the president with his tax plan, plus now we have this new hailstorm over Kuwait!"

That same afternoon, while Mr. Allen is talking to the congressman, another phone call is underway between two very good friends in Springview.

"Hey, sweet thing, how is my beautiful Jolee today? Can you talk now, or should I call you later?"

Jolee McBride is the assistant editor of the *Springview Press*. Since the summer of 1986, she has worn several hats at the newspaper office, but her primary duty requires her to oversee and edit all the local news. Every day, she supervises two young reporters who cover the local beat across town and prepare the first draft copy for each story.

With a hushed voice, Jolee acts casual giving everyone in the office the impression that she is receiving some church news updates for next Sunday's paper,

"Yes, Mitch, this is a good time to visit. How are things today with the Lutheran Church?"

For many years, Mitch Rahab and Jolee have been using the "Lutheran Church" code word to disguise their clandestine conversations about the university. Since Mitch is officially a part-time deacon with the Lutheran Church, it makes their conversations sound plausible to anyone at the newspaper office who might overhear Jolee's side of the discussion.

"Well, beautiful! I have a hot scoop for you! The grapevines on campus are really buzzing, and guess who the spotlight is shining on today?

Mitch pauses to give Jolee a few seconds to savor his breaking news. As she prepares to take some copious notes, he continues. "I am telling you, this is hot shit! I think this rumor could become your headline story on the top fold of next Sunday's paper. It seems our fair-haired senator, Buzz Granger, has his fat tit in a ringer. There is a significant movement underway right now to launch a vote of no-confidence against his leadership as the department chair."

Jolee smiles to herself as she fills her tablet with shorthand symbols and notations. For more than fifteen years, Mitch has worked as the vice president for student affairs at the university. Prior to that assignment, he was the director of student housing for almost seven years. Jolee is convinced that Mitch functions as the perfect mole because he is super connected on campus and a member of the president's cabinet. And he absolutely loves to share gossip that causes trouble.

It is so easy to keep this pipeline open with Mitch. To stay in his good graces, all she has to do is occasionally stroke his fragile ego with a few compliments and casually flirt with him on Wednesday evenings after their Bible study class at church. In many ways, Jolee thinks of it as a game. She is willing to do whatever it takes to keep in touch with all the campus rumors. Ever since her boss, Mr. Kronberg, gave her an end-of-the-year cash bonus for her work to trash Vice President Kelley, Jolee has been looking for another chance to pursue a sensational story that might yield another bonus. Besides, everyone knows her flirting with Mitch is meaningless. All the ladies at church know he is harmless. The standing joke is that it's the men, not the women, who should always give him a wide berth. Mitch is married for eighteen years before his wife files for a divorce. The father of three sons, Mitch tries to keep his homosexual desires in the closet, but his wife starts talking after their divorce. As an elementary school teacher, she explains to several colleagues at school that their "irreconcilable differences" happen every night in the bedroom.

After the Thanksgiving break, the academic pace on campus quickens as the faculty hasten to cover all the remaining content for each course. Simultaneously, the students rush to complete their assignments and prepare for final exams. Once these exams are finished, the fall semester adjourns and everyone has the chance to relax during the Christmas holiday. However, there is a three-week period just before Christmas when everybody is on the run, trying to keep up with a treadmill of events that are moving in high gear.

During the first week in December, Diana Dawson chooses to forego several culminating semester events and elects to work late in her office every night. Her friends assume she is dedicated to her classes and getting ready for final exams while preparing for the upcoming deadline when faculty must submit their semester grades. Several colleagues are surprised when she does not attend the Tuesday evening theater production of *The Grinch who Stole Christmas*. This annual extravaganza attracts children from area elementary schools and showcases faculty and students working together on stage. The proceeds from this production are donated to the community's "Toys for Tots Program." Diana also declines a gracious offer from her landlord, the head football coach, for a free reserved seat at one of the best basketball games of the season. This Thursday evening game against their archrivals, the Wildcats, will determine if the Panthers take over first place in the conference and enter the post-holiday tournament as the number one seed. Moreover, she disappoints several of her students by not attending the music department's Friday evening Christmas concert featuring the annual joint production between the talented chorale singers and the university's legendary hundred-piece orchestra.

Every night for more than a week, Diana has been in her office with the door closed and the telephone humming. She uses this time to personally call each faculty member within her department. Tonight, as she dials the home number for Professor George Swanson, she consciously focuses upon the tone of her voice. With a premeditated decorum, she sweetly says, "Hi George, how are you tonight? This is Diana Dawson. I hope this is a good time to visit. Have you finished supper?"

"Oh yes, supper is finished, and the dishes are washed. This is a good time to talk, Diana."

Diana knows that George is a key swing vote. This is a critical conversation. Dr. Swanson is one of the senior full professors in the department, and he most likely can sway at least three other votes with his opinion.

"George, you know we briefly talked in the hallway two days ago about this issue. I want to confidentially talk with you about the merits of trying to get us a new department chair. I think we currently suffer from absentee leadership. Buzz Granger is gone more than he is here, and I will never understand why we have to be the only department on campus with a chair that does not have his doctorate degree. I mean really, this whole situation is embarrassing and absurd."

Diana pauses, taking the opportunity to flatter George. She searches for a carrot that might tempt his ego and sway his vote. "You know, George, someone like you would make a great department chair. Would you consider the assignment if it becomes available?"

George chuckles aloud signaling his lack of interest. "No, no, I am not the least interested. I would be miserable trying to do that kind of work. I love teaching, and I feel like I have just entered my prime teaching years. There is so much I want to share with my students, and I relish those moments when I see the lights come on in their brains. I am not willing to dedicate half my time toward budgets and administrative duties."

Seeking to regain the initiative, Diana proceeds with her list of talking points. "George, have you ever thought about all the vice president's monthly academic affairs council meetings that take place with no one from our department seated at the table? Our collective voice is never part of those conversations, and Buzz thinks he is doing us a favor when he shares copies of the minutes from these meetings. Now really, those old minutes really offend me. Sometimes they are two months old before we get them. I think reading about those meetings after the fact is a cheap, secondhand way to pretend like he is working to keep us informed and represent our concerns."

"I have noticed the tardy nature of those published minutes, but frankly, I don't give them much attention. Over the years, I have learned to tolerate the administrative stuff by keeping it on the fringes of my work and out of my daily thoughts. I figure the dean gets paid to watch over our department's interests whenever Buzz is absent because he is working in Lincoln with the legislature."

"Well, that brings me to my next point, George. Do you think it is fair for Buzz to draw 75 percent of his university pay and keep all his staff benefits with the university while he also draws a full salary as a member of the legislature? As a taxpayer, I am offended every time I think about all the money he is getting each month!"

George senses Diana's outrage, and for a few brief seconds, she sounds jealous. The sweet tone in her voice is long gone. While he is sympathetic to some of her concerns, he is also reluctant to make waves across the campus and place his beloved department in the headlines of the *Springview Press*, or worse! He privately cringes at the thought of this topic becoming a public mockery on Craig Jacobson's radio talk show.

"Diana, I understand your concerns, but I am not sure we should make such a public issue out of all these matters. After all, Christmas is just around the corner, and it is supposed to be the time of the year for peace and joy and kindness toward others!"

Pressing hard, Diana counters like the old Grinch who wants to steal everyone's Christmas spirit. "George, I did an analysis of all faculty vacancies in every department since Buzz has been serving in the legislature. Do you know that the vacancies in our department take three months longer to fill than the vacancies in the other departments? Hell, Buzz is never around to do the interviews, and we end up suffering as a department because he is slow to recruit and fill our vacancies. How many times have you been asked to teach an overload class because a vacancy has not been filled and the class had to be taught?"

Growing weary and becoming defensive, George says, "Look Diana, if you did the analysis, I am guessing you already know the answer to that question. True, I have taught several overload classes during the last few years. But it did not seem that bad at the time. I try to be supportive of our team. Besides, I feel like my willingness to go the extra mile has been sincerely appreciated by the administration. Did you know that the dean has gone out of his way to thank me? And the VPAA nominated me for teacher of the year last spring, and someone in the president's cabinet convinced the university foundation that I should be recognized during our last homecoming celebration as a distinguished professor, and that five-thousand-dollar bonus check from the foundation really came in handy here at my house."

Diana persists. "George, confidentially, I will tell you that I already have enough signatures on a petition to place the confidence vote on a ballot for our next department meeting. The bylaws stipulate that the dean must schedule a department meeting within two weeks from receiving the petition, and he must be at the meeting to preside over the vote. I am hoping we can get a two-thirds majority to vote "no-confidence," but that remains to be seen. I hope you will give this discussion some serious thought and join me and many others who plan to vote against Buzz."

"Diana, you need to know that the cat is out of the bag, and many people around campus realize you are the ringleader for the no-confidence ballot. I have to ask: what in the world do you hope to gain from this mean-spirited effort? Aren't you trying to hurt the very man who just a few years ago supported your premature request for a full pay sabbatical while you went to graduate school to complete your EdD?"

With subdued anger and extreme sarcasm, Diana responds, "Look, George! That was then and this is now! I am trying to point out his shortcomings as a department leader. Ever since he became a famous state senator, he has shirked his responsibilities as our chair!"

Always the consummate gentleman, George remains polite and does not reciprocate Diana's aggressive assertion. "Good night, Diana. I think I understand your position. I will give our conversation serious thought, and I will be ready to cast my vote during our next department meeting."

Diana says good-bye and hangs up the phone just a few seconds before screaming to herself in rage. "Well, shit, that went just *swell*! I would like to make old George bend over so I could jam this phone up his ass and stick it in a place where the sun never shines!"

As George concludes the telephone conversation, his wife asks, "My gosh George, what was that all about?"

"Mary Ann, you would never believe it. Here we are getting ready for Christmas and the wiles of evil are casting their dark shadows across our campus. I have to tell you. The last few years, there have been times when the joy of teaching has been lost because I am surrounded with colleagues who spend most of their days trying to catch the elusive euphoria of power."

Diana is furious. She looks at the clock. It is 7:45 p.m., and there is just enough time to make one more telephone call. After hitting her speed dial, the phone rings twice.

"Hello, this is Larry. Can I help you?"

Trying to flirt with a sexy voice, Diana says, "Well yes, Larry, you can help me tonight. How much time do you have for me? It seems you are working late at the bank. Are you still trying to get ready for your board meeting?"

"Hey, Diana, my gorgeous gal, it is wonderful to hear your voice. Yes, I am crashing on a last-minute report that has to go in tomorrow's mail. We try to send to each board member advance copies of all the major handouts so they will have a few days to review the numbers before we get together for our quarterly meeting."

"Larry, darling, I have been thinking a lot about our last time together. Do you remember the fun time we had?" Diana giggles like someone recalling a very private, sexually intimate moment.

"You have to be kidding! How could I forget! That was one of my all-time favorite fantasies that you performed! Hell yes, I remember every amazing detail!"

With a sly grin across her face that Larry cannot see, Diana places both feet on top of her desk and tilts back in her office chair. "Well, good, sweetheart! I am glad you remember me hiding under your office desk and playing with your big, hard cock while you tried to act composed as you dictated letters to your secretary. I seem to recall a couple of times when you lost your train of thought, and I bet old Virginia still wonders about some of those letters you made her type. She is so over the hill, she did not have a clue what we were doing!"

Larry laughs out loud. He still marvels at how he has managed to be lucky enough to take this hot chick to bed. Diana continues the conversation.

"Larry, you told me that you would forever be in my debt if I agreed to crawl under your desk and make your dreams come true. Do you remember your promise, sweetheart?"

"Sure, and I meant what I said. Say, did you get those anonymous roses that I sent? I trust you knew they were from me. After all, I can't sign my name on a card that is going to be circulated in front of God and everybody."

"Oh yes, the roses were beautiful. But I need your help with something else. You see, if I can get a majority vote of no confidence against Buzz, eventually the VPAA and president must decide if they are going to keep him as chair or replace him with someone else."

Larry interrupts her comments. "Let me guess. You are hoping I might persuade the president to consider you as the replacement for Buzz. Does that sound about right?"

"Oh, perfect, you must have read my mind! I would love to have your support for the chair's job. And since you currently serve as chair of the university's board, I know the president will take your suggestion seriously. And if all this can be arranged and be part of my next annual contract, I promise to make another one of your fantasies come true!"

Larry is not surprised. He has been around the barn a time or two. With more than twenty years of banking experience, he has peered into the eyes of greed and jealousy many times while working with customer's loan requests. Ever since sharing that glass of wine with Diana, he has anticipated this veiled attempt to blackmail his position of authority. Now he has the precarious challenge of balancing Diana's special request with the congressman's harsh directive.

"Hey, Diana, I promise to look into this situation if the confidence vote goes against Buzz. Hey, honey, I must let you go for now. I better get back to work and try to finish this report so good old Virginia can get it in the mail tomorrow. You take care, sweetheart!"

Before returning to his desk, Larry walks over to his large west window. His fourth floor level places him above the city's tree line and gives him a clear, direct view of the horizon. From this spot, he has witnessed many sensational, lingering sunsets that reach across the endless skies and serve as a signature hallmark of the Great Plains.

With a half moon overhead and the evening nautical twilight still in place, the western sky is filled with gathering dark storm clouds. The spectacular cumulus congestus clouds look like the silhouettes of distant mountains reaching across an endless horizon. There are a few flashes of lighting streaking through the roiled clouds. As he gazes at this stunning sight, he thinks to himself, *How strange! The center mass of those distant clouds looks like an ancient dragon looming in the middle of a mountain range. It makes me think about my soft red dragon and her crimson silk sheets. I can't wait to jump again into bed with her! As my old grandfather used to say, carpe diem!*

Throwing caution to the wind, Larry is not worried about saving his soul or his marriage. He would rather please his new flame than listen to his boss, Congressman Turner. After all, she makes him feel special!

Unbeknownst to Larry, he is not special to Diana. His feelings are not reciprocated by her. Larry is just another man recorded in Diana's little black journal—another conquest on a long list of victims who have succumbed to the wiles of the red dragon lady. That night, Diana writes, "I love to hunt married men. Once I take them to bed, their soul belongs to me."

19

The Night Falls Heavy
When the Day Is Done

In the end, we will be held accountable for not only
what we said, but also for what we failed to say.

—John Dewey

December 1990
Springview, Nebraska

As the furnace begins to run, the timeless howl of the bitter winter wind is overcome by the sound of the telephone. Samuel looks at the clock and immediately becomes irritated. He has old-fashioned manners, and he believes it is very impolite to call anyone after 10:00 p.m. He drops his pen, turns away from his diary, and reluctantly answers after the third ring.

"Hello, this is Samuel."

With no introduction, a very excited female voice blurts out, "Hey, did you hear the news? Do you think we are really going to war?"

Samuel immediately recognizes the voice of his good friend and teaching colleague, Ellen Marie Martinez. "You know, Emmy, I am not sure about all this war talk. I did not watch the evening news tonight, so I don't know the latest. What is going on?"

For the next fifteen minutes, with an incredibly fast pace, Emmy explains every detail regarding the current actions of the United Nations and the deployment of Iraq's army along the border between Kuwait and Saudi Arabia. She sounds like someone giving an official Pentagon briefing on CNN.

Samuel listens politely. He has learned to humor his friend when she is in the talking mood. Occasionally, he is given the chance to insert a brief word or verbal sound that signal his presence or agreement. After years of friendship, he has learned to be patient with Emmy's eccentric ways. When her voice becomes high-pitched and her speech quickens to an unbelievably fast pace, Samuel knows she is having trouble with her medication.

It has been about three years since Samuel discovered one of Emmy's dark secrets. He hosted a small Christmas social at his home one evening, and he accidentally hears Emmy in the bathroom vomiting. The next day, with sincere concern, he stops at her campus office to inquire about her health and well-being.

At first she hints that it is just a bug, maybe a twenty-four-hour stomach flu. But for some unknown reason, on that day, at that time, while Samuel has his arms wrapped around her slender shoulders, Emmy starts to cry and confesses that she is fighting bulimia. She was initially diagnosed at the age of seventeen. Her lifetime battle against this disease has been filled with many setbacks.

Suddenly, Emmy exclaims, "Oh my God, Samuel! Look how late it is! I am so sorry. I got carried away and lost track of the time. Forgive me for rambling about this war stuff. I really called to talk about a completely different topic."

Really irritated, but always the consummate gentleman, Samuel calmly says, "That's okay, Emmy. What did you want to talk about?"

There is a long pause of silence, and then Samuel hears Emmy's faint sobs. "Emmy, what is wrong? What the hell is troubling you?"

"Samuel, you know I belong to our local chapter of PEO?"

"Yes, yes, that famous sisterhood that keeps sacred secrets. Your famous social sorority that parties every month and tries to raise money for educational scholarships. What about it?"

There is a standing joke between them; Samuel wants to know what PEO stands for, and Emmy always says, "If I tell you, then I have to shoot you in order to protect our secret."

With regained composure, Emmy says, "Tonight we had our monthly PEO meeting. It was our traditional Christmas party, but no one was in the Christmas mood after our chapter president told us that she just received word from a Miami, Florida chapter that Dr. Mary Jane Kelley is dead. The official cause of death was ruled as a heart attack, but some of her PEO sisters speculate that the heart attack may have been caused by a mixture of sleeping pills and alcohol."

Samuel gasps. "You are kidding! How could this happen? She is too young to have a heart attack!"

"Well, we do not know many details, but Mary Jane never recovered from all the slander she endured. After our board fired her, she could not find another job. She was unemployed for a long time. Finally, she landed a clerk's job selling books at a Barnes and Noble bookstore. I believe she incrementally fell into a deep depression." Emmy stops. The lump in her throat prevents her from saying any more.

"You know, Emmy, I have frequently thought that some of us should have spoken on her behalf. Maybe we could have made a difference, maybe we should have tried to help," Samuel's voice trails off like someone who just became lost in a forest of regrets.

"Samuel, I will never forgive our infamous "Springview Dee-Press!" I hold them primarily responsible for Mary Jane's character assassination. Their yellow journalism is unforgivable!

Their stories ignored the facts and fanned the flames of mob hysteria with all that bullshit gossip."

In silence, Samuel smiles. Many people have nicknamed their local newspaper the "Dee-Press" because the front page is always focused on bad or sad stories. Consequently, the daily news leaves most readers feeling depressed.

After a brief pause between them, a frail voice says, "Good night, Samuel, take care of yourself. See you tomorrow on campus."

With a heavy heart and a mind full of regrets, Samuel pensively hangs up the phone and returns to his diary. For the next two hours, he writes with passion and clarity of thought, like a man making his last confession to a trusted priest.

He closes his entry with the following thought:

"I will always remember the role of evil on our campus. On this sad occasion, the night falls heavy when the day is done. With the advantage of hindsight, I believe our collective silence helped betray a noble lady. I am convinced the goodness of mankind is diminished whenever the silent majority remains silent, and by default yields to the evil minority. Our failure to speak up really empowered their mean-spirited agenda against Dr. Kelley."

PART IV

The Man in the Arena

March on and fear not the thorns or
the sharp stones on life's path.

—Khalil Gibran, 1883–1931

It is not the critic who counts; not the man who points out how
the strong man stumbles, or where the doer of deeds could have
done them better. The credit belongs to the man who is actually
in the arena, whose face is marred by dust and sweat and blood;
who strives valiantly; who errs, who comes short again and
again, because there is not effort without error and shortcoming;
but who does actually strive to do the deeds; who knows great
enthusiasms, the great devotions; who spends himself in a
worthy cause; who at the best knows in the end the triumph of
high achievement, and who at the worst, if he fails, at least fails
while daring greatly, so that his place shall never be with those
cold and timid souls who neither know victory nor defeat.

—President Theodore Roosevelt
Speech delivered in Paris, France; April 23, 1910

20

A Bold Expedition

The gentle breeze of Father Time touches our memory
and soothes our recollection of difficult days. But,
experience is an unforgiving teacher. And, the harsh
reality of life reminds us that we are seldom permitted
the freedom to completely forget the lessons that
we learn during the hard times of our journey.

December 1990
Fort Leonard Wood, Missouri

A black phone sits on the right corner of an old gray metal desk. Years of accumulated rust have rendered the desk drawers inoperable. The broken wooden chair squeaks as it rolls closer to the desk. All three pieces of army furniture have seen their better days. Many years ago, they were designated as government surplus and relegated to storage. Today, however, they are back in use as the entire resources of Fort Leonard Wood strains to push an unprecedented number of troops through a massive mobilization process in support of Operation Desert Shield.

On August 7, 1990, Operation Desert Shield starts in response to Iraq's August 2nd invasion of Kuwait. Following the presidential executive order that authorizes the mobilization of two hundred thousand reserve troops, the secretary of the army directs the call-up of twenty-five thousand Army National guardsmen in combat and combat service support units.

A determined hand quickly moves the rotary dial on the old telephone. Three digits spin to gain access to a long-distance line. After a few seconds of hesitation, the area code and seven digit number methodically turn as a driven, energetic lieutenant colonel carefully cranks the numbers to reach his National Guard commander.

Unexpectedly, the call goes through on the first attempt, and after three rapid rings, a young female receptionist answers, "This is Mid-City Bank, how may I direct your call?"

"Yes, may I speak with Colonel Greg Smith? This is Lieutenant Colonel JP O'Bryan."

About three minutes pass as JP is placed on hold and given a recording featuring a mix of Christmas music. Ironically, Bing Crosby's classic "I'll Be Home for Christmas" is playing. JP looks out the old barrack's window at a parking lot that is covered with seven inches of fresh snow. He does not expect to be home for Christmas, and he realizes this will be the first Christmas since their marriage that he and Jenn will be separated. As his mind races past his private feelings, he tries to refocus his thoughts on the task of juggling dozens of logistical details. A tidal wave of responsibilities has swept JP away from life as he knows it. Uprooted and displaced from both his professional duties and daily personal routines, he carries a burden on a journey that will change his soul forever.

As old Bing finishes his song, the music stops and the line clicks. "Hello, this is Colonel Smith. Is that you, JP?"

"Yes, sir, how in the world are you?"

"Oh, I am fine. I just finished a meeting with my loan manager. More importantly, how are you doing, and how are your troops performing at Fort Leonard Wood?"

"Sir, I am pleased to report that we have hit a home run with all the mobilization requirements. Our long days and short nights have produced outstanding results. We achieved a 90 percent or higher score in each mobilization category, and our unit has been given an overall C-1 status. It looks like all our vehicles and equipment will be loaded and secured on railcars by close of business tomorrow. Because of the army's urgent need for manpower in theater, the post commander decided to forego painting the desert camo on our vehicles. This Friday night, the train is scheduled to depart for the Gulf Coast. I anticipate we will be certified as ready for immediate airlift on the eighth day of our mobilization sequence."

"Man oh man, JP that is really impressive! You should be proud of your unit. Your success will bring great credit to the state, and I know the adjutant general gave the governor a glowing report on your leadership efforts. By the way, the governor was impressed with your remarks when you spoke during the send-off ceremony on the lawn at the state capitol."

With a sense of modesty, JP replies, "Well, to tell you the truth, that ceremony seems like an eternity ago. I just tried to speak from the heart. I really did not have any written notes or planned message. It just seemed like the right thing to say."

"Hey JP, when do you expect to deploy? What is the availability of airlift?"

"Once we go into the deployment cue, I expect we will be gone in about forty-eight hours. But I have been told that there is a chance that our limbo status in the transportation cue could extend for about a week. Transcom is super short on cargo planes right now. After they assign our aircraft, chartered commercial buses will take us to Scott Air Force Base. Then it will be a matter of loading our personal gear and weapons on the C-141s."

There is a moment of silence and Colonel Smith clears his voice. "JP, I am proud of you. Thanks for taking this command on the run and producing such outstanding results under the most dire of circumstances. I think it is amazing what you have accomplished. You are about to begin a bold expedition to the other side of the world. While you are gone, I really hope you will take the time to maintain some kind of logbook or record of your experiences. You represent part of America's best talent, and you will be making history every day. You know, I may not see you for a long time, so for Christ's sake, take care of yourself. Keep your head down, and Godspeed, my friend!"

JP starts to respond, but the telephone connection goes dead. For just a moment, toward the end of the colonel's comments, it sounded like he was fighting an emotional lump in his throat.

JP turns to his executive officer, Major Nicholas Greever, and says, "Well Nick, I am surprised. You are never going to believe it. The colonel must have a soft spot in his heart. He sounded emotional toward the end of our conversation. Let's plan to keep sending the old man situation reports as long as we have access to a fax machine."

Major Greever quickly responds, "Wilco, sir!"

On December 17, while most of the Christian world is preparing to celebrate Christmas, the US Army is in the process of moving a mountain of equipment to support the largest ground force ever sent to an overseas deployment since the troop commitments for World War II. On this day, as a small part of this immense war effort, two C-141s are parked on the tarmac at Scott Air Force Base with flight orders for Saudi Arabia.

The sky is hazy gray, the temperature hovers at around thirty degrees, and the wind is gusting about forty miles per hour. In less than two hours, Lieutenant Colonel O'Bryan's infantry unit loads their duffle bags and weapons, secures their seat belts within their canvass strap seats, and privately anticipates their journey into the unknown.

Just before boarding the plane, JP directs Major Greever to find a fax machine and send another sitrep. The handwritten message says,

> Our dental and medical exams went well. Last night, we finished all rail-load duties including tie-downs, tape on windows, and number markings. This past week, I designated seven staff officers who completed a top-secret workshop that covered a variety of intelligence reports regarding Iraq's disposition and capabilities. I had to designate three NCOs as supercargo personnel to accompany our vehicles to Galveston, Texas. They will stay with our vehicles and equipment during the overseas trip. Currently, we are loading duffle bags and weapons on the C-141s at Scott AF Base, and we anticipate departure within the next hour. V/R LTC O'Bryan

The fax is sent on 17 December 1990, 1730 hours.

JP remembers Colonel Smith's advice. Before he leaves Fort Leonard Wood, he goes to the PX and purchases three large journals. That afternoon, he starts recording notes in his commander's logbook.

> Some traits of soldiers are timeless. One such characteristic is their bottomless, unending appetite for food. The terminal's snack bar did an exceptional business while we waited for permission to load our gear. Three of the four major food groups, cheeseburgers, French fries and shakes, were the number one best sellers. Everyone seemed to sense that this would be their last opportunity for many months to enjoy American food. Candy bars, chips, and soft drinks followed as the second most popular item on the menu. After a three-hour delay, we were cleared to load and board the planes. At approximately 1815 hours, we had wheels-up, and the first leg of our journey was underway.

Three hours later, two C-141s land at McGuire Air Force Base adjacent to Fort Dix, New Jersey. It is 2200 hours, local time, and JP's soldiers have been up and on the move since 0500 hours this morning.

Standing in the dark shadows of a cold December night, JP watches his people deplane. Many look tired. He turns to his executive officer.

"Nick, the loadmaster says those old blue air force buses on the other side of the tarmac are waiting for us. They are going to transport us over to the terminal. We have to wait about two hours in the terminal complex while they refuel these planes. Let's get a head count after everyone is seated on the buses."

The two-hour delay becomes a four-hour wait. Some of the soldiers use the time to sleep on the terminal's cement floor. Others play cards or eat one of their Meal-Ready-to-Eat (MRE) packets.

Finally, shortly after midnight, the planes are fueled and ready. The soldiers are instructed to re-board.

During the next two days of grueling travel, JP records the following entry in his commander's log:

> The flight over the Atlantic Ocean took approximately seven hours. We landed at Hereford, England. Chartered in 1189, Hereford is a city of 59,000 people located in west central England, approximately 120 miles northwest of London. It was 1300 hours, local time, when we arrived.
>
> At this point, it had been more than thirty hours since our last encounter with a bed and shower. Everyone is weary from travel. Since there were no buses, we walked across the tarmac to an old Quonset building that was serving as a makeshift waiting area. There were no restrooms, only a couple of port-a-potties that badly needed cleaning. There were no chairs, only a set of wooden bleachers that had been moved inside the old facility to provide temporary seating. There was no snack bar or restaurant, only a simple

table with a tall, insulated drink dispenser that contained lukewarm coffee but no cups. And, most disappointing, there were no telephone booths, so no one could call home.

The facilities were an old World War II British air force base that had been "mothballed" after the war. Recently reopened, the dilapidated, time-forgotten complex was providing refueling services to military planes en route to Saudi Arabia.

While some soldiers tried to sleep and others played cards, I used the time to write a letter to my wife.

Our refueling time in England developed into a major layover. Eventually, the message came to reboard our planes. As we walked back, I remember the gray skies and could tell that the winter daylight was fast ending with the approaching sunset. There was a sharp, cold wind blowing, and the atmosphere seemed to match our mood and silence. It was 1715 hours when I felt the plane go airborne. My watch was still set on Fort Leonard Wood time, and I tried to imagine what my wife was doing back home on a routine Saturday morning in Montpelier, Vermont."

Seated toward the front of the plane, JP looks across the aisle and speaks to his XO.

"Nick, pass the word that this next leg of flight time will take at least eight hours. Tell everyone to try and get some sleep."

"Roger, sir! One thing for sure, these old canvas seats are hard on the back and butt. They don't offer much comfort. Hopefully, the troops will use this time for a catnap."

The drone of the plane's engines make it impossible to talk. Once the loadmaster lifts the seatbelt requirement, some of the men move around the cargo area and find a place to sit and play cards. The rear of the plane has no heat, so the men wear gloves while they play cards.

Hours later, the speaker system in the cargo bay squeaks, and blares the loadmaster's voice.

"Gentlemen, welcome to the king's airspace. We are flying over the land of oil fields, drifting sand, and roving herds of wild camels. Return to your seats and buckle up tight. We anticipate a bumpy descent. Currently, the local time is 0345 hours, and the ground temperature is a balmy twenty degrees. We should be on the runway in about thirty minutes, and you will be walking on the soil of your new home! As they say, it is always great to be a guest of the king!"

Nick rolls his eyes and smiles as he looks at JP. At the time, neither JP nor Nick understand the political implications behind the phrase "guest of the king."

JP's ears are relentlessly popping. The pilot is executing a glide path similar to a falling rock. Air traffic control has directed a rapid, steep plunge because of the airfield's vulnerability to scud missile attacks. Amazingly, just minutes away from the runway, the plane jerks, the engines roar, and the nose of the plane abruptly pulls up. The jolt really surprises everyone, and the rapid climb causes several men to vomit.

After a few minutes of silence and worry among the passengers, the loadmaster announces, "Folks, hold on for an extended ride. Our airfield is under another scud missile attack, so it is not safe to land. We will continue to circle at a safe altitude for at least thirty minutes or until we get the word that we are clear for landing. Don't worry; we packed extra fuel because this scud missile thing is starting to become a nightly event here in beautiful downtown Dhahran!"

After forty-five minutes of circling, the pilot receives permission to land. Once again, everyone's ears suffer as the plane's landing approach complies with the rapid descent SOP. As the C-141's wheels hit the runway with a severe jolt, JP looks at his watch. The local time is 0450 hours. The plane comes to a rapid halt, and everyone steps out into the cool breeze of the Saudi night air. For the next seven months, JP's daily life is touched by the timeless desert wind of northern Saudi Arabia and southern Iraq.

Turning to his XO, JP smiles and says, "Nick, I have to tell you, man, you look like ten miles of bad road!"

Major Greever chuckles. "Yes sir, as my daddy used to say, I feel like the old horse that was rode hard and put away wet. You know, I can't sleep in the sitting position, and by my calculation, it has been about forty-five hours since we crawled out of bed at Fort Leonard Wood. Besides, we must have crossed nine or ten time zones. Shit, fire, that's what I call real jet lag!"

JP is empathetic, but completely focused on the work to be accomplished.

"We just have to suck it up, Nick! You know the drill. Make sure our section leaders maintain personnel accountability. We have to get our duffle bags and section equipment off the planes and loaded on those flatbed trucks that are parked next to that old building. Remember, we have about 360 miles of cross-desert travel ahead of us before we arrive at our KKMC base camp. Let's make it happen, man."

Major Greever salutes, turns and begins to walk toward the first plane.

A few minutes later, just as the work teams begin to unpack the pallets inside the C-141s, a blaring siren signals the next scud missile attack. Members of the ground crew scream, "Gas! Gas! Run to the bunker!"

Automatically, everyone drops everything and quickly dons their gas masks. Instinctively, JP's soldiers realize they must run in the same direction as the ground crew. The tarmac goes dark as the airport personnel execute complete black-out conditions. JP finds himself sprinting about 120 yards toward the old, cement-block warehouse building. It is incredibly difficult to breathe while running with a gas mask on his face. In a matter of minutes, however, JP is standing inside a large storage room, surrounded by approximately two hundred men all staring into a black darkness that harbors their fear of the unknown. The sound of heavy breathing fills the room while the deafening siren continues to blare for about ten minutes. As JP's eyes adjust to the dark conditions, he sees Nick standing about five feet away. JP shuffles through the crowd and taps Nick on the shoulder. Nick is severely laboring to catch his breath. His long-term smoking habit has reduced his lung capacity and diminished his ability to recover from their mad dash.

Nick turns around and shakes hands with his CO. His voice is garbled by the mask, but JP clearly understands his words: "Sir, as they say, it is sure great to be a guest of the king!"

21

The Humble Hero

Character cannot be developed in ease and quiet.
Only through experience of trial and suffering can
the soul be strengthened, vision cleared, ambition
inspired and success achieved. Silver is purified in
fire and so are we. It is in the most trying times
that our real character is shaped and revealed.

—Helen Keller, 1880–1968

March 31, 1991
King Khalid Military City, Saudi Arabia

The northern desert of Saudi Arabia generally soars to about 140 degrees in July and August. This year, on Easter Sunday, the daily high hits 120 degrees. As the sun slowly bakes the heavy-duty tent canvas into a brittle, paper-thin fabric, JP stands in an army GP medium tent trying to listen carefully to the chaplain's sermon. As sweat pours down his chin, the chaplain delivers an intense message about the importance of hope. The entire sermon is based on Isaiah 40:31.

JP tries to focus on the sermon, but his thoughts race between personal worries and leadership responsibilities. The rising heat and daily blasting sandstorms are taking their toll on the health and morale of his troops. Everyone is hanging by a thread of hope. Physically, they are tired and ready to leave right now. The rumor mill suggests they should expect to redeploy home on or around May 15. However, JP's desert commander, Colonel Joe Mercurio, has just given JP a confidential warning order that might alter and delay their redeployment timeline.

Colonel Mercurio indicated JP's unit is doing such a great job that ARCENT HQ in Dhahran wants to keep them in the country longer in order to sustain continued security across the northern boundary of Tapline road. The old highway, built in the early 1950s by Standard Oil, runs parallel to the Iraq border. Stretching across the east to west length of Saudi Arabia, it is located about twenty-five miles south of Iraq's border. Originally part of the Trans-Arabian Pipeline development, this two-lane highway is considered part of the army's key terrain and serves as one of the primary MSRs throughout Operation Desert Storm. It has to be secured while the entire army concentrates on a rapid withdrawal from Saudi Arabia.

Like most of the soldiers at KKMC, JP has not received any mail in more than a month. He is worried about Jenn and wondering how she is doing. The truck that delivers the army's mail to KKMC has been experiencing unusual problems. The last two semis have mysteriously caught fire while traveling across the desert between Dhahran and KKMC. The mail on both flatbed trailers is completely lost in the fires.

The chaplain finishes his message and closes the service with an upbeat song. Everyone is invited to sing "To God Be the Glory." About sixty men try their best while standing in the smothering heat of the weather-beaten tent. Their voices are off tune and their rhythm is offbeat, but they are enthusiastic participants.

As the soldiers start to leave, Nick stops JP after they have stepped out of the tent and into the scorching sun.

"Sir, this morning we have two more soldiers confined to their quarters. Sick bay is overflowing with patients, so now the doc is sending everyone back to their own cot. These guys are battling extreme nausea and they are plagued with horrible trots. It seems like we just keep passing this flu bug from man to man and tent to tent. I don't know about you, but I am counting the days until we get out of this hellhole. Only forty-five wake-ups, and we are on the big bird with a one-way ticket home! Shit, fire, Dairy Queen, here I come!"

JP smiles and suggests they walk over to the motor pool. He wants some privacy. As they walk through the concertina wire gate, the guard on duty salutes both officers. JP greets the young NCO and wishes him a happy Easter. Once inside the parking area, JP knows they are alone.

Without hesitation, while walking past a row of five-ton trucks, he starts talking. There is an intensity in his voice. "Nick, I know you understand that I do not control our assignment here. Unfortunately, there is a shit-house rumor going around our base camp that I love it here and want to stay."

Nick interrupts.

"Yeah, you can thank Major Doug Winters for that rumor. He is really working against you right now."

JP counters. "I know that, Nick. But when you look at his track record, you understand that he has never been willing to join my team or support our goals. He is a man driven by selfish motives. Anyway, it is ridiculous to think I am trying to keep us here. My God, nothing could be further from the truth! I want to get home as much as any man here. But for as long as we remain on duty, I will not permit us to lose focus and start doing our work with a half-ass attitude. While we are here, I want us to sustain our commitment to excellence regardless of these harsh weather conditions."

JP pauses, and Nick again jumps into the conversation.

"I understand, sir. I get it. It could be worse. At least we are not dodging scud missiles anymore. Hell, all we have to do is hang on for another six weeks. Then we will withdraw back to the lights of Dhahran with real beds, decent showers, and hot chow. Our only worry will be getting our vehicles clean and ready to load on those big ships. Hell, sir, compared to what we have been through the last five months, that redeployment task list will be a simple cakewalk."

JP knows there is no easy way to say what needs to be said, so he assertively recounts the basic facts. "Damn it, Nick! We may not leave in six weeks. Yesterday, Colonel Mercurio gave me a confidential warning order. We should be prepared to hold this position until the end of August or perhaps early September. Additionally, we should expect to inherit the responsibility for a larger area of operation as other units redeploy and we take over their mission."

Instantly, Nick becomes pissed. "Well, shit fire, and Happy Easter, Colonel Mercurio!"

Both men walk in silence until they come to the concertina wire on the back side of the motor pool.

JP speaks next. "Nick, I am confiding in you because you have a level head with great common sense. No one needs to worry about this turmoil right now except you and me. Give it some thought. If this extended stay comes our way, we need to have our heads in the game, and we need to provide the leadership that will help everyone suck it up and move forward. Every day, we get blasted by another sandstorm, and we seem to have a few more men on the sick-call list. We have already sent 11 percent of our personnel home on various kinds of emergency leave, and you know the army will not ship them back here now. So the bottom line looks like this: we have fewer people to do the work, and the list of things to do is probably going to increase rather than decrease."

That evening, JP sits in his GP Small tent. A single, forty-watt bulb hangs over a three-foot-wide army-green field table. The base camp's sixty-kilowatt, trailer-mounted generator is parked about ten feet from JP's tent, so he lives with the constant drone of the roaring diesel engine. A metal folding chair and a badly worn, shaky army cot represent the total contents of JP's living space. The desert wind accelerates, and everyone in the base camp braces for yet another harsh sandblast. JP tries to write a brief note before he has to place a wet washcloth over his face.

Commander's Log: Easter, 31 March 1991

Today has been a time of worry and turmoil. More than ever, I realize my troops want to get out of here and return home. This redeployment frenzy has touched everyone, and our base camp is rapidly dividing into two groups: the "haves" and the "have-nots." Those who have redeployment orders are filled with the joy and hope that the chaplain talked about this morning. But those of us who do not have redeployment orders are battling anger, frustration, and a rapidly deteriorating morale that is maddened by this ungodly desert wind. I often wonder how the Bedouins stand it day after day, year after year. To be sure, they are a resilient people that the modern world ignores.

By now, the desert wind is raging outside. The dust inside JP's tent is so thick it is like a dense fog. He struggles to breathe. The fog-like dust hovers around the center pole obscuring the light. It is time to get a wet cloth over his face. Reaching for the light switch, JP pulls the chain and the tent goes dark.

Out of habit, he automatically takes water from his canteen and soaks an old brown washcloth. During the next several hours, this cloth helps to filter the air he breathes while he sleeps. The desert night air has rapidly dropped from 120 degrees to about 80 degrees. JP feels cold when he crawls into his sleeping bag. As he silently says a prayer to Saint Jude, he hears the haunting howl of the same desert wind that has repositioned sand dunes since the beginning of time. This ageless moan, for more than three thousand years, has whispered in the ears of the spiritual leaders of three world religions.

During the next six weeks, the daily temperature rises as the soldiers' daily morale falls. For JP's unit, the volume of work increases while the number of troops, in-country decreases. The chasm between the "haves" and the "have-nots" widens while the thread of hope tapers.

Commander's Log: May 14, 1991

Today I traveled about thirty miles through the desert to the telephone communication center. The long-distance calls are super expensive, so I have limited my visits with Jenn to one call each month. Since today is her birthday, I wanted my call to be special, but it was a disaster. I traveled by myself because my driver was on guard duty at the motor pool. We are so shorthanded; I did not want to disrupt the duty roster and pull him away from his assignment. Mother Nature gave us another sandstorm this afternoon, and it was virtually impossible to see the road while I traveled. It reminded me of driving in the blinding snow during a horrible winter blizzard.

When I arrived at the communication center, there were no lines. In the past, I have stood in the sun for as much as an hour awaiting my turn. I entered the tent and immediately gained access to a phone. Because many soldiers have abused their telephone privileges, we currently have to limit our telephone conversations to ten minutes. After I wished Jenn a happy birthday, I had to tell her that our redeployment date has been officially delayed until early September. Jenn immediately cried, and that made me cry. I was trying to find words of comfort and encouragement when the NCO in charge of phone usage came by my table and depressed the receiver. He forced me to hang up because I had exceeded my time limit. I did not get to say good-bye to my wife. The tears were streaming down my face. Feeling angry and embarrassed, I quickly left the tent and returned to my old Blazer. It was a long, difficult drive back to our base camp.

—◦◦◦—

As the intensity and frequency of the summer sandstorms escalates, JP's unit witnesses a rare phenomenon one afternoon in early June. Looking across the southern landscape of red sand dunes, everyone is stunned to see a tsunami-like brown wall of sand crashing toward them. It moves like an incoming tidal wave as its height begins to block the midday sun. Within minutes, this extreme force hits the base camp like a devastating avalanche of red and brown sand. The storm's gale-force winds pop the support ropes on many tents like they are mere pieces of string.

Commander's Log: June 10, 1991

The month of June is a challenging time here in the desert. The daily temperatures have already reached 130 degrees in our northern location, and I expect we will peak at 140 degrees in less than thirty days. As I observe my soldiers working in this intense heat, my admiration for their perseverance grows. I believe that God is answering our prayers, because the secretary of defense, Mr. Cheney, made a public proclamation that seems to be influencing our redeployment status. We do not have access to any direct news, but I have been told that he appeared on television and pledged to have most of the American troops home by the Fourth of July. I hope that is true.

On June 21, 1991, JP is seated outside his tent watching an incredible desert sunset. The sky is aglow with brilliant shades of red, the air is clear, the wind is still, and the hundred-degree evening temperature seems pleasant after the 136-degree high.

Major Greever approaches the commander's tent and says, "Sir, this sealed message just arrived. It was delivered by a young lieutenant from ARCENT-Forward. I signed for it and promised to personally bring it to you."

JP opens the brown envelope and deliberately reads aloud, "You are hereby directed to prepare for redeployment to Fort Leonard Wood, Missouri. Your KKMC security mission will cease on the 28th of June, and your Riyadh operation must close on 29 June. Consolidate your personnel, equipment, and vehicles in Dhahran no later than 30 June and prepare for immediate departure. Authorized by the ARCENT G-3."

Nick screams with joy, "Jesus Christ on a bicycle, finally we are going home!"

JP examines the sunset. There is just enough daylight remaining to order an immediate formation.

"Nick, assemble all the troops. I want a formation in front of our flagpole as soon as possible. Every available man must attend. I will make this announcement, and I want everyone to be able to hear what I say, so kill that damn generator for the next thirty minutes."

Nick runs to the officer's tent to circulate the formation order.

The early morning hours of 2 July 1991 are a dream come true. The long-awaited day has finally arrived. Everyone eagerly climbs out of bed and hastily packs their personal gear within two duffle bags. JP schedules a staff meeting right after breakfast.

The tension in the conference room is thick enough to cut with a knife. You can almost taste the excitement that is mixed with anxiety, fear, joy, and worry. JP scans each face in the room and makes a mental inventory. Two officers are returning home to deal with divorce papers. One captain is returning to his wife and kids, but they have lost their home because of a bank foreclosure. The command sergeant major is returning to a twelve-year-old daughter who has been recently diagnosed with cancer. Three of his primary staff are absent because they have been sent home on emergency leave. Every man in the room privately worries if they will be able to fit back into their family units and their civilian jobs. JP knows this is the last time he will stand in front of his staff while they are in Saudi Arabia.

"Gentlemen, today we turn the corner and begin the final stretch of this journey together. I want to thank each of you for your support and hard work. We have accomplished all our assigned missions and sustained our commitment to excellence regardless of the circumstances. It is my hope that each of you find a sense of purpose behind our work here. It was not always easy, and deployment has taken a personal toll on each of us. As you search for the meaning behind this time in your life, I hope you feel a sense of pride and accomplishment. Collectively, we represent some of the best attributes of our great country. It was my pleasure to serve with you. Fortunately, we are taking everyone back with us, so I ask each of you to maintain personal accountability and attention to detail as we move to the airport and board the plane. Safety remains our top priority. Twenty-four hours from now, we will be standing in the USA!"

The men automatically clap and cheer. Their long-awaited redeployment journey is about to launch.

Commander's Log: 2 July 1991

We arrived at the airport facility late morning. Once we cleared customs, we moved into a restricted waiting area. Eventually, this seating area filled with troops from other units. We are scheduled to depart on a commercial aircraft, and I anticipate that every seat will be filled as part of the effort to comply with Mr. Cheney's guidance. While we were waiting, the chief of staff from Transcom headquarters arrived to bid us farewell and thank us for our hard work and valuable contributions to Operation Desert Storm. During his remarks, he commented that we were part of the last 5 percent of American troops to be redeployed. He was pleased to announce that more than

95 percent of all the soldiers who had been in-country had already returned home. I remember thinking that this was one particular mark of distinction that we would have preferred to not achieve.

Our aircraft was a chartered American Trans Air L-1011 with a seating capacity of four hundred. At 1900 hours, we were permitted to board the plane. Every seat was filled. At 2000 hours, the pilot announced that the attendants should prepare the cabin for takeoff. The plane started to taxi toward the runway at 2017 hours. I looked through the window and watched my last glowing red desert sunset. When the plane became airborne, I recorded the time as 2034 hours.

Nick is seated across the aisle from JP. He asks about the travel route.

JP responds, "I talked to the pilot, and he told me it will take about four hours to reach the Sigonella Air Base in Sicily northwest of here. After we refuel, the plane will fly due north for another three hours before we land in Frankfurt Germany. Then we will head northwest over England and continue on to Shannon Ireland. There, we will deplane for a few hours before we take off for Philadelphia. Once we land at Philadelphia, we will pass through US customs. So, Nick, my friend, now is the time for us to sit back, relax, and leave the driving to the man up front!"

During the early morning hours of 3 July, as the sun climbs over the horizon and the birds greet a new summer day, the wheels of a chartered Lockheed L-1011 TriStar hit the Philadelphia runway. Instantly, four hundred soldiers cheer and whistle with joy.

Before returning to Fort Leonard Wood, the army gives each soldier a four-day pass so they can enjoy the Fourth of July weekend with their families and friends.

JP receives a message that directs him to report to the adjutant general's office. As he walks into the building's main entrance, his friend and mentor, Colonel Smith, is waiting for him with a smile that glows from ear to ear.

The two men exchange salutes, and then the old Colonel gives JP a bear hug.

"Welcome home, young man! We are damn glad to have you back and proud of all the things you accomplished."

JP responds with a sense of modesty, "Thank you, sir. It is great to be back on American soil."

After thirty minutes of friendly conversation in the general's conference room, Colonel Smith asks, "JP, what do you consider your most significant accomplishment during this deployment?"

"Sir, before we left Fort Leonard Wood, I established two personal leadership goals. The first was to take care of my soldiers and bring each one back home safely. The second goal was to perform every assigned mission with a sense of urgency and commitment to excellence. I believe we accomplished both goals, and my men deserve the credit for the work we completed."

General Norman enters the room to join the conversation. "JP, we just received a fax from ARCENT HQ. The department of the army announced today that your unit earned the Meritorious Unit Commendation Award for outstanding service during Operation Desert Shield and Desert Storm! Congratulations, JP. Your unit is one of the very few National Guard units that was deployed for more than six months in the combat zone. This unit award is both unique and a historic recognition. We have not had a National Guard unit receiving this award since World War II. Moreover, I am pleased to confirm that your leadership has been recognized, and the army is awarding you the Bronze Star for your outstanding service."

JP is surprised, privately elated, but professionally unassuming. Colonel Smith jumps out of his chair to shake his hand.

"My God, JP! This is incredible. By my count, you have received five personal decorations for your active duty service, and now you bring home the gold, man. Wow, the Meritorious Unit Commendation is rare and special. What a credit to your leadership. Holy shit, you are so damn humble you don't even realize that most people consider you a hero!"

Commander's Log: July 14, 1991

"This will be my final journal entry for this journey that started almost eight months ago. Today is our wedding anniversary and I am separated from Jenn while I complete my final day of demobilization at Fort Leonard Wood. Tomorrow morning, we will climb on a plane and return home. Each of us must conquer our next challenge individually. Each of us must find our way back into civilian life, back into our family relationships, and back into our previous work routines. The mobilization process tears the roots out of your established life, and now we must carefully try to reestablish those root systems and those personal relationships.

Yesterday, I had a follow-up appointment at the post hospital. The senior physician of pulmonary medicine gave me some bad news that I did not expect. Besides the worry about returning home, I must face an unexpected health challenge. When I lost forty pounds, I thought it was just the long hours in the heat. When I started coughing, I thought it was just the damn dust from the sandstorms. But, I have been told that I am part of the select 1 percent of the army that returned from the war with active TB. Fortunately, no one else in my unit has this health problem, and I have not told any of my men about my circumstances. The doc says I am one millimeter away from the contagious stage. If I escalate to that danger point, I must voluntarily surrender to quarantine. Yesterday, I took my first dose of medicine, and I must continue this INH pill every day for the next six months. This medication hopefully will arrest the TB, but simultaneously, it will deteriorate my liver. So it will be a race to see which outcome arrives first. I hope my liver does not fail, and I hope I do not lose my job at the university because I must be quarantined.

Without question, this desert journey has changed my life and taught me many things about the malicious nature of some people. More importantly, it has cleared my vision, left an indelible mark on my soul, and purified the values that guide my character.

Hindsight tells me this cross of responsibility was part of my destiny. It took me a while to hear the message that the desert wind constantly whispered: the affairs and fleeting securities of this world are illusions that shift like the shape of sand dunes. Like Viktor Frankl said, the only thing we can control each day is the attitude we convey as we do our work.

More than ever, I believe God is governing the circumstances of my life. Each day, we live in the hands of divine providence.

22

The Lost Letter

I had a dream my life would be
So different from this hell I'm living,
So different now from what it seemed,
Now life has killed the dream I dreamed.

—*Les Miserables*

June 1995
Springview, Nebraska

Today is June 21, 1995, a Saturday. It is Dr. Boswell's thirty-seventh birthday. As the first day of summer and the established time for the vernal equinox, today will showcase the longest hours of daylight for this calendar year. It is a beautiful morning filled with abundant sunshine and an orchestra of singing birds. Robins, wrens, cardinals, and blue jays herald the beginning of a day that promises to be perfect for Samuel's rest and relaxation.

The month of June brings several late-evening rains that seem to stimulate the grass, trees, and flowers. From his back deck, Samuel admires Mother Nature's best showcase with multiple shades of green and arrays of several bright colors including red, yellow, and blue. His lilac bushes are in full bloom, and the lilac scent, while delightful for some, unfortunately ignite Samuel's spring allergies.

Samuel places his coffee on the patio table. A gentle breeze sways the treetops while occasional guests create a rustle and whistle through the spruce trees. Today, his major goal consists of reading a good book and never getting out of his slippers. But first, he has to sort and trash his weekly mail.

Every Saturday, Samuel makes a quick-paced walk to the downtown post office where he rents a mailbox. He considers this weekly two-mile trek a sufficient demonstration of his exercise program. After collecting his mail, he attends early mass at St. Mary's Catholic Church and then returns to enjoy what he considers to be one of the best times of the week.

His hands move quickly through routine pieces of junk mail. After living in Springview for twelve years, he has managed to get his name on just about every promotional list that exists. Brochures, fliers, and catalogs are tossed into his recycle bin. First-class letters and credit card statements are placed in a folder that generally resides on the corner of his dining room table. In his haste, Samuel tosses a badly frayed letter into the recycle bin because it carries the logo and return address for the Golden Palace Casino in Las Vegas. At first glance, it looks like a promotional letter, but Samuel's mailing address is written with a penmanship that looks vaguely familiar. So he reaches down into the plastic bin for a second look at the tattered envelope.

Puzzled, he examines both sides of the letter. There are four discernible postmarks stacked almost on top of each other: Las Vegas, Los Angeles, San Francisco, and Miami. There is another blurred stamp to the extreme left that looks like an old, faded Denver postmark.

Samuel's hands begin to quiver. He mutters to himself, "Can it be? After all these years? I say, dear chap, surely not!"

His eyes widen and his chin drops as he opens the letter and begins to read a hastily scrawled message.

Sunday, November 22, 1987, early am

Samuel,

I am in big trouble, and you may hear about my death before you get this letter. I may not make it home. It is 2:00 a.m., and I just had my worst-ever night at the casino. Lady Luck was against me, and I lost everything. I am in big-time debt here; my credit line is gone, and before I leave for the airport in a few hours, I have to meet with Big John.

Needless to say, I am scared shitless. I can't sleep. This could be the end for me. Big John is the casino's muscleman, and he does the dirty work for the mob's owner. In private circles, around town, people whisper his nickname: the "Merchant of Death." He gets paid to solve bad debt problems, and legend says his solutions are usually a painful death sentence for the debtor.

If I am going to die later today, there is something I must confess. I have to get this off my chest. My conscience has been killing me for years. Please try to understand my regret. I have made so many mistakes. If I could do it over, I would do it differently.

For several years, I have been selling drugs to the girls on my basketball team. This side business has given me the extra money to gamble. Buzz Granger found out because one of my girls was drunk while she was having sex with him. She told him the whole routine with all our code words. So, he used these facts as leverage against me and forced me to "pimp" for him whenever he wanted quick sex with one of my girls. That routine went on for almost two years. One night, Buzz was drunk and screwed one of my seniors and her sixteen-year-old sister. They promised to make him an Oreo cookie if he would process a change of grade form for our starting center, Samantha.

When Marsha Ann Montgomery was reviewed for tenure, the committee voted in favor of her packet. She is a really good person, very talented; she deserved to be tenured! But for some reason, Diana Dawson hates Marsha. Since Diana was president of faculty senate that year, she gave Buzz an ultimatum that we had to kill Marsha's tenure request. I think Diana has something over Buzz because he seems like such a wimp whenever she demands something. Actually, I think he is pussy-whipped by her.

Anyway, Buzz blackmailed me; if I did not cooperate, he was going to report my drug sales to the NAIA headquarters. I had no choice. He forced me to change the tally for the official tenure vote. Since I was the senate's recording secretary, I collected the ballots, which are cast in secret. The bylaws require three people must count, verify the votes, and record the outcome. Diana was there because she was senate president, Buzz helped because he was chair of the tenure committee, and then me. So only the three of us know about this illegal, unethical maneuver. And, now, my friend, you make number four.

If we have a chance to talk, and if I get back, I hope you will help me make some of this mess right. What we did was wrong. Diana is like a deadly black widow; her vengeance is lethal! But I am ready to stand-up against her and Buzz.

Got to go and find a stamp.

As always,
Mark

Samuel feels the simultaneous impact of fear and dismay. With a trembling hand, he reaches for his cup of coffee and misses the handle. *Crash!* His favorite orange Tennessee Vols cup falls onto the wooden deck and breaks into several pieces.

Like a thief troubled about his getaway, Samuel scans the backyard and worries that one of his nosy neighbors has seen him reading this blast from the past. He wonders, "How in the world could this lost letter arrive almost eight years late? All these years after Mark's death? Why me? Why did Mark write to me? Should I get in my car and drive over to the sheriff's office?"

Hours pass. Samuel's coffee pot grows cold. He has lost his desire to read and moves inside to his favorite La-Z-Boy recliner. Once inside, he does not leave the house for three days.

That night, Samuel's diary fills with a cascade of thoughts. He wants to do the right thing. He wants to stand up against these people like Mark has suggested. But he lacks the courage. Like the old Lion in the *Wizard of Oz*, he cannot find the courage to face his private fears. His mind repeatedly goes back to Mark's comment that only three people know the truth. Samuel recalls Ben Franklin's keen observation about human nature: three people can always keep a secret as long as two of them are dead!

Finally, after three grueling, sleepless nights, an exhausted Samuel is the first customer on Tuesday morning when the Farmer's State Bank opens its doors. Once he gains access to his safety deposit box, he tries to act casual as he places three large brown sealed envelopes inside the box. The first envelope contains Mark's lost letter. The second contains all of Mark's IOUs. In the months before he dies, the coach has been a financially desperate man, and he has borrowed more than $9,000 from Samuel. The third envelope contains a private, confidential letter from Samuel addressed to his SIU-Carbondale college mentor, Dr. Wesley Moreland.

Samuel is facing a moral crisis. He feels compelled to take action, but he cannot find the courage to take the first step. His mind is lost in a great fog of confusion. He is frozen with fear, like a man facing a great demon. The knot in his stomach never goes away. He cannot eat or sleep. The three days of isolation have given him the chance to bare his soul and write a twelve-page letter to his trusted mentor and sole confidante. But, to his frustration and dismay, Samuel lacks the courage to mail his private thoughts to Dr. Moreland. Once the envelope is locked inside his security box, Dr. Moreland's letter does not see the light of day for another twenty-three years.

The next day, Samuel sets his alarm clock for zero-dark thirty. He packs his suitcase and carefully prepares a one-week supply of food and water for his old cat, Maxie. Samuel leaves town in his car while it is still dark. As the early morning nautical twilight transitions into a brilliant sunrise, he is driving east and fighting the glare glancing off the newly resurfaced highway. Lost in thought and exceeding the speed limit, Samuel does not have a planned destination. He feels like he is on the road to nowhere. Samuel just wants to get away and avoid people. He hopes to find a sense of security by being anonymous.

After the first week on the road, he picks up the hotel telephone at about seven thirty one evening and calls his friend, Emmy. She answers after the second ring.

"Hello, this is Emmy speaking."

"Hey, girl! This is Samuel, and I just called to say hello. How are you doing, my good friend?"

"Samuel, where the hell are you? Are you okay? What are you doing? Did you secretly run off for some kind of interview? I have been so worried! Man, if you were standing here right now, I could just hit you so hard!"

"Now, now, Emmy. Calm down. I am just fine. I just decided to take a little vacation. You know, I just wanted to get away from the house for a few days. It was very spontaneous. Sorry about your worry. I should have called you sooner! Hope you will forgive me, dear friend!"

Emmy is so relieved to hear his voice. She quickly mellows. Once she realizes he is on vacation, she asks if he is doing anything super fun. He has a difficult time recalling the different cities and hotels so he glosses over most of the details saying his trip has been filled with lots of good food and plenty of rest.

"Emmy, I am planning another two weeks of travel, and I am wondering if you would be willing to look after old Maxie. He will need fresh water and more food and his litter box will need some care."

"Of course, I would be delighted. You know I love that old guy, and it will be fun to look in on him. Consider it done!"

Like a dog with a bone, Emmy is persistent and continues to question Samuel about his whereabouts. Under pressure, Samuel reluctantly confesses that he is in the downtown Marriott in Minneapolis. Finally, toward the end of their conversation, Samuel feels compelled to lie and says that part of each day has been devoted to writing a new journal article that he hopes to submit for publication by their September deadline.

During the next three weeks, Samuel drives 2,680 miles, sleeping in fancy hotels located within five different Midwestern cities. Every day, he uses room service to order great food, fine wine, and sinfully delicious desserts. But he always feels like hell, and nothing tastes good. He feels dirty, like he needs another shower. His conscience churns, and he feels embarrassed because he lacks the courage that Mark displayed in his letter. Every night he prays and wonders if he should go to confession.

For some reason, he cannot stop thinking about Mark's lost letter and the evil undercurrents that seem to dominate the culture of his beloved campus. He is glad to have this summer break. His academic life is so different from the youthful dreams he had during his graduate school years.

After hundreds of hours of private reflection, Samuel sits alone in the Sioux City Riverfront Hilton with a decanter of very nice house Merlot wine. The hotel room has recently been remodeled with a king-sized bed, an elegant wooden desk, and a comfortable reading chair; it also offers a scenic view of the mighty Missouri River. The carpet still smells new, and the walk-in shower features three overhead shower nozzles and a stereo music system. It is late when he starts writing in his diary.

When I was young, my love for books compelled me to attend college. The first time I walked onto the campus, the beautiful and peaceful environment plus the intellectual stimulation of my classes converged and made me feel like I was fulfilling my destiny. I had found my purpose in life. Then something inside of me, like a clarion call to arms, drove me to complete graduate school and start a career as a university professor. I was inspired by the memory of my father's dedication to teaching.

But I never realized until today that the people at a university represent a cross section of our total society. Consequently, we seem to have all kinds—some good, some bad, and some ugly—they all flourish on every campus just like we have a cruel mix within any other organizational sector of society. All these years I have been blind. Guided by hope and propelled by dreams and my educational aspirations, I looked at our organizational culture with rose-colored lenses. I failed to see the big picture. I consciously overlooked the reality of evil. I could only recognize the inherent goodness of a university. Somehow, I managed to turn a blind eye toward all the evil deeds and agendas of my colleagues. But today, I have gained clarity of thought. Today, I have come to terms with the reality of our campus life. Today, I see the private face of our public university with all its warts and blemishes. And I realize more than ever that when the silent majority remains silent, an evil minority can proceed without encountering resistance against their foul plans.

My life is so different, so turbulent from my original dream! This hell I'm living today has killed my dream—just like the Vegas mob killed my friend Mark, and my evil colleagues caused Dr. Kelley's untimely death a few years ago. For some reason, tonight, I feel like I share part of the guilt for those culprits who caused Dr. Kelley's career to be ruined. Oh, how I wish I could return to the sandy beaches, crashing waves, clear skies, and simple life on my beloved Tortola!"

23

Thou Shalt Not Whine

Don't let the incidents which take place in life bring you low.
And certainly don't whine. You can be brought low, that's
OK, but don't be reduced by them. Just say, "That's life."

—Maya Angelou, 1928–2014

March 17, 2013
Floyd University, Springview, Nebraska

"Happy Saint Patrick's Day, Lynda! Thanks for returning my call."

JP O'Bryan has been waiting for almost a week to have this conversation. While he does not understand nor appreciate Lynda's cold-shoulder treatment, he has come to accept her rudeness as the norm.

"Hello, Mr. President, what can I do for you?"

Lynda's tone is aloof and condescending. The power of her position has gone to her head. As a hometown girl with a high school diploma and two years of college, her only claim to fame still echoes in her ears. Whenever possible, she relishes the opportunity to talk about the night she skillfully dribbled down the floor and shot the winning basket as the buzzer sounded. Her midcourt basket glanced off the backboard and careened through the hoop to give the girls basketball team the one and only state championship ever garnered by any Springview high school team.

Lynda Stevenson marries her high school sweetheart about two years after graduation. Most of the time, she lives an unhappy life filled with acrimony until she files for a divorce and wins a bitterly fought settlement. While her daddy is serving as the city mayor, he manages to coerce a few of his pinochle buddies to advocate that his little daughter be hired as the new director of Floyd University's Alumni and Foundation Association.

"Lynda, have you had the chance to review that humanities grant that I sent to you last week?"

"Yes, I skimmed the executive summary and briefly looked at the proposed budget."

JP is disappointed, but patient.

"I hope you share my enthusiasm for this grant proposal. If we are approved by the National Endowment for the Humanities, we will have the chance of a lifetime to create a digital library in honor of John G. Neihardt. Just think! This electronic collection could become a national treasure. Nebraska's Poet Laureate will be available to anyone around the world who has access to the Internet. Just imagine someone in Paris, France sitting in a coffee shop visiting our website and reading Neihardt's poetry!"

JP's enthusiasm bubbles over the telephone. This grant would match every dollar raised through local donations with four dollars from the National Endowment for the Humanities budget. Each year, for the next four years, as the university raised $250,000 toward this project, the federal grant would award $1 million in matching funds. At the end of four years, a $5 million budget would be available to support the creation of this unique, state-of-the-art, digital library collection.

Lynda replies with skepticism, "I don't think my board will want to tackle this project. We already have established our five-year financial goals, and they are designed to double the net worth of our investments. There is really no room for any funds to be diverted toward this new idea."

Frustrated beyond words, JP tries to appeal to Lynda's common sense. "This proposal will give us a mark of academic distinction that will put Floyd University on the national map. The strategic partnership with the National Endowment for the Humanities will garner national publicity, and I believe this project will permit us to forge an extended partnership that will include the Library of Congress. Honestly, this is so huge that we cannot afford to miss this opportunity."

JP stops and waits for some feedback.

"I am telling you, Mr. President, our foundation board is very focused on our strategic plan. This poetry collection is kind of an unexpected, harebrained idea that does not fit into our established plans. Besides, just where do you think we are going to raise an extra quarter of a million dollars every year for the next four consecutive years?"

Totally exasperated, JP controls his Irish temper and calmly says, "Lynda, this grant application has a very tight timeline. If we hope to submit this proposal before the deadline, I will need a letter of support from your foundation board president by the end of the month. Would you at least give me the chance to schedule a telephone conference next week with your board's executive committee?"

"Well, if you insist, go ahead. Maybe your secretary can set it up. I am busy the next few days, so if you want to organize a phone conference, that is up to you. Just let me know the date and time, and I will call in to be part of the discussion. Needless to say, I do not plan to support any new ideas that will divert us from our strategic goals!"

That evening, JP talks with his wife during supper.

"Honestly, Jenn, I do not understand people sometimes. This federal grant could be an incredible opportunity for us. If it is approved, I know we can find the donors to support this new effort."

"JP, you know Lynda has opposed you ever since you came here for your first interview. You are never going to change her, and you will never convert her to believe in any kind of new religion, so you better make plans to tolerate her and work around her."

"I know you are right! But it just blows my mind when narrow-minded people stand in the way of progressive ideas. This campus is plagued with unit leaders like her who have never been to the other side of the mountain. They have no idea what is possible, and they have no motivation to pursue anything that requires change or fosters excellence. It is like a form of intellectual incest."

Jenn offers a gentle reminder. "You know Lynda is part of that hometown girlfriend club! They like to drink, party, and bash all the males in their lives. Trust me, honey, you have been bashed more than once since you became president!"

"Wow, this whole foundation mess reminds me of John's story about Cartwright's Alamo!" JP stops talking and goes into the kitchen to refill his coffee cup.

Jenn tries to be lighthearted as he returns to the table. "Honey, just remember your family slogan that proudly hangs in your mom's living room!"

JP smiles and they both simultaneously say in unison, "Thou shalt not whine!"

After a good laugh, Jenn says, "JP, let's go out for dinner this weekend. We should celebrate your second anniversary as a university president."

"Okay, where do you want to go?"

Jenn smiles. Intuitively, she knows this is a rhetorical question, and JP already knows the answer.

Again, in perfect unison, they say, "Let's go to Red Lobster in Sioux City!"

24

The Servant Leader

While servant leadership is a timeless concept, the term was coined in an essay published in 1970. A practical philosophy that replaces traditional autocratic leadership with a holistic, ethical approach. Servant leadership begins with the natural feeling that one wants to serve others and help them succeed. The servant leader is sharply different from one who is leader-first, perhaps because of the need to assuage an unusual power drive or to acquire material possessions. The following ten characteristics are central to a servant leader's style: listening, empathy, healing, awareness, persuasion, conceptualization, foresight, stewardship, commitment to the development of people, and building community.

—*Servant Leadership*, Robert K. Greenleaf, 1970

March 1, 2016
Floyd University, Springview, Nebraska

Approximately two weeks ago, President O'Bryan submitted his required annual self-evaluation. This base document provides the chancellor and the governing board with a summary of major accomplishments during each president's past year of effort. The maximum number of pages permitted within this brief document is five, and the narrative must address the following functional areas of responsibility: personnel, programs, budget, facilities, and community relationships. Each section must include a description of completed actions and an explanation regarding how these accomplishments support the board's statewide strategic plan.

JP has been looking forward to his appointment with Coach Singleton. Ever since Jess retired, he has emerged as a pillar within the community and the president of the Alumni and Foundation Association. This past year, he completed eight years of elected service on the city council, and he maintains a strong friendship with the current city mayor. As a member of St. Patrick's Catholic Church Board, Jess sustains an active schedule of community responsibilities while he and his wife dedicate as much time as possible toward spoiling their three grandchildren. As he enters the president's office, JP says, "Jess, it is really great to see you today. Thanks for taking the time to visit. Can I offer you a cup of coffee or a cold drink? Perhaps a Pepsi, Coke, or a bottle of water?"

"Thank you, Dr. O'Bryan. Yes, a black coffee sounds great."

The conversation begins in a friendly and casual manner. JP slowly turns the discussion toward a few key topics that he wanted to review.

"Jess, I am looking forward to the next quarterly board meeting with the Alumni and Foundation Association. Do you have any special topics you want me to address when I provide my regular progress report?"

"Well, yes, I do have a couple of suggestions. I think the board would enjoy hearing about your recent alumni meeting in Denver. It is always rewarding to hear about our active alumni chapters and keep up with the thoughts from our membership."

Jess pauses to drink some coffee. "Also, I know our board enjoys hearing about the plans for this spring's graduation ceremony. Oh, and be sure to tell us a little background information on the commencement speaker."

JP responds, "Absolutely, I will be delighted to include remarks on those topics. Anything else come to mind?"

"Well, I know we have been talking a lot about the new rec center, but now that it is officially dedicated and open for business, I think we all would like to hear about the daily usage and how the students feel about having some of their classes moved into that building."

"Great idea, Jess."

Both men pause to sip their coffee. JP continues with a reflective tone, "You know, Jess, almost a year ago we talked about my desire to have several spotters—people on campus and in the community who will provide me with honest feedback. I consider you one of my trusted spotters, and I need to know how things are going from the perspective of people in the community. What are you hearing? Are there any problems or concerns?"

Jess chuckles and waves his right hand as an assertive gesture. "I hear nothing but good things about you and your leadership. The community is very impressed with your work and your ability to move this campus forward in a positive direction. I know several alums who have commented positively about your monthly column in the newspaper and your quarterly report in the campus magazine. And now that the rec center is finished, people sing your praises because you were able to build it under budget and finish the construction on time despite the horrible winter we had here. Man, you really hit a home run!"

"Thanks for your kind words, Jess. You know how I feel about this community. It is a great town, and I very much appreciate the cooperation and support from community leaders such as yourself, the mayor, and all the members of the city council."

"Well, take it from me, you are without question the most popular and successful president this university has had in many, many years. Trust me, I know, because I worked for all the men who sat in your chair for the past forty years. All I can say is, keep up the good work."

JP's secretary knocks gently, opens the door, and politely says, "Dr. O'Bryan, your next appointment is here waiting to see you."

That evening, after supper, JP talks with Jenn while she quilts a new Americana wall hanging. JP shares some of the highlights from the day.

"Jenn, I had the most wonderful visit with Jess today. What a great man!"

"Sweetheart, you really like him a lot, don't you? Tell me what he had to say."

"Well, I consider him one of my key spotters, and I really count on him to help me stay in touch with community leaders and alumni members. He said really nice things, and he complimented me for my leadership."

Jenn probes deeper. "How did you conclude your visit?"

"Well, after he said I was one of the best presidents this university has ever had, I felt myself blush, and I asked him to share those sentiments with the chancellor since it will soon be time for my annual evaluation. You know, Jess and the old chancellor go way back together. Anyway, he said he would make it a point to call the chancellor and put in a good word for me. Plus, he voluntarily said he plans to ask the mayor to speak on my behalf next week when they both attend the governor's annual community leaders' conference in Lincoln."

"Wow that sounds great! You have worked hard, JP, and I think you deserve the highest evaluation scores that the chancellor can give!"

With a hint of family humor, JP says, "Jenn, I suppose that is your unbiased opinion?"

They both laughed simultaneously.

"You know, Jenn, it is really nice to sit in the presence of Jess. You can feel the goodness in him. He has a solid character, and I really admire all the amazing things he has accomplished. And sometimes, when I least expect it, he displays a mannerism or gesture that reminds me of dad."

JP pauses to overcome a lump in his throat. He looks down at the floor and speaks with a hushed tone.

"Jenn, I still miss dad after all these years. I still wonder if he was disappointed in me when I left the farm. I wonder if I should have stayed to help him, especially during those final years when he was fighting cancer, planting corn, and milking cows."

"JP, you can't go back and redo the past. You have to move forward and stay positive. I think your dad is looking down from heaven right now, and he is very proud of you and the work you do. Your destiny did not include farming!"

Jenn becomes verbally and nonverbally assertive.

"You have a gift, JP. You care about people, and you help them succeed. You are a great listener and a persuasive leader, and you bring out the best in people. You have dedicated your life's work to public education and service to others. You quietly help people make their dreams come true. Oh my Lord! Just look at our new rec center! It has been a dream in this community for more than twenty years. And you came along, you talked to people, listened to their ideas, created a comprehensive plan, and then provided the stewardship that made it become a wonderful reality."

JP smiles at his wife. Jenn takes his hand, kisses him on the forehead, and kindly says, "I am proud of you, baby-doll. And I know your dad is also very proud!"

25

Preparing the Poisoned Chalice

During antiquity, the Ides of March was considered a day to celebrate with picnics, drinking and revelry. Many primitive myths and rituals surround this legendary date reaching back to ancient Greek festivals marking the beginning of the New Year. In more modern times, the Ides of March is best known as the date on which Julius Caesar was assassinated in 44 BC. On March 15th, while going to the Theatre of Pompey, Caesar was stabbed to death at a meeting of the senate. It is estimated that as many as 60 conspirators were involved in this brutal murder. Caesar's death was a major event in the crisis of the Roman Republic, and triggered the civil war that would result in the rise to power of his adopted heir Octavian who later became known as Augustus.

—Internet Research and Wikipedia

March 10, 2016
Springview, Nebraska

Diana Dawson reaches across her desk and rapidly dials a long-distance number for the state capitol building in Lincoln, Nebraska. As she waits for the telephone to ring, she gazes out her office window at an old-fashioned raging blizzard.

This is one of those traditional winter storms that have been sweeping across the Great Plains for centuries. The howl and sharp bite of the wind reminds Diana of the classic blizzards that became legendary when Mari Sandoz vividly described in her masterpiece, *Old Jules*, the harsh physical realities and the struggle to survive on the wind-blasted Nebraska prairie. With heavy snow falling and winds exceeding forty mph, the visibility on campus is less than a city block. The weather forecast is projecting at least fourteen inches of snow by midnight. Everyone is hoping the president will announce an early dismissal and declare tomorrow a snow holiday.

After three rings, a mild, polite female voice answers with a timid decorum, "Good afternoon, this is Chancellor Granger's office. How can I help you today?"

Boldly, Diana said with a loud voice, "Yes, this is Diana Dawson. I'm calling to speak with the chancellor. Is he available?"

The secretary asks Diana to "please hold for just a few minutes" as she steps around the corner and down the hall to ensure the chancellor is in his office. After getting his approval, she returns to Diana and says, "Yes, Chancellor Granger is available. I will put your call through to his desk."

After one short ring, Diana hears Buzz try to speak, but his voice cracks and sounds garbled as he begins to talk with a slight hoarseness in his voice. Rudely, without covering the mouthpiece, he starts a timeworn ritual to clear the frog from his throat. Whenever Buzz is nervous, mucus settles on his vocal cords. This trait has plagued him since he was required to deliver oral book reports in his high school English class. This crude habit of simultaneously coughing and choking is something Diana experienced countless times when they were lovers and friendly colleagues thirty years ago.

Ignoring the formalities and traditional courtesies normally extended to his position, Diana takes the initiative and abruptly says to her estranged lover, "Hey, Buzz this is Diana. I hope you can talk privately. Are you alone?"

Buzz is leery and cautious as he responds. He has not talked with this lady for years.

"Well, Diana, long time no see. Yes, this is a good time to talk. What do you have on your mind?" Switching to a sarcastic tone, he says, "I trust you are calling because you need something!"

"Buzz, I am pressed for time here and in a hurry to get to my next class so I will cut directly to the chase. I just had a run-in with President O'Bryan, and I am telling you this guy has to go. Nobody says no to me and lives to talk about it without deep regrets. I want him to suffer. I want you to fire his ass!"

With each word, Diana's voice escalates until she is near the pitch of a scream.

"I want you to cut off his balls and put them in his shirt pocket like they did old Frank Warton. Do you hear me, Buzz?"

Completely stunned by this blast from the past, Buzz really wants to tell his old flame to go to hell. Privately, he thinks she still sounds like a spoiled little diva who always wants her way. His initial thought is to tell her to take a flying leap. After all, this is the lady who forced a no-confidence vote against him many years ago. But he senses her rage, and he knows from experience that he must be careful.

"Diana, you sound very, very angry. This reminds me of the day back in 1985 when you were in my office and mad at Vice President Kelley. Do you remember?"

"Hell yes, I remember. And according to my notes, you got your rocks off that afternoon while I serviced your horny little brain and licked your miniature cock in the middle of your office!"

Seething with rage, Buzz hates to have his manhood criticized. But he manages to control his words and the tone of his voice. "Look Diana, I don't want to go back and relive all the sordid details from the past. Just tell me how you expect me to fire a university president who just completed a phenomenal year of work. He has several major accomplishments that have been realized this year, and the board president, Jack Blackmore, wants me to recommend a 7 percent merit salary increase to recognize his outstanding performance evaluation. Furthermore, on more than one occasion, O'Bryan's exemplary work and diplomacy has been mentioned with accolades by the governor during his monthly cabinet meetings here in the capitol. I am telling you, it would be impossible to fire this man right now. Everyone thinks he is doing a great job!"

Buzz stops short and does not share all that he knows. The last few years he has feared and envied JP's ability to get things done. Recently, an old drinking buddy from Buzz's legislature days told him that the board has been talking about the need for a new chancellor, and the chairman would like to see JP promoted to replace Buzz.

With an explosion of temper, Diana interrupts Buzz.

"Goddammit, Buzz Granger, let me put it to you in plain English! Either you fire President O'Bryan, or I will publicly disclose so much dirt on you that you can stand in the middle of a shower nonstop for the next two years and you won't be able to ever get clean. I guarantee you will lose your cushy political job and probably your wife. You might even discover a jail cell with your name on it!"

There is a long pause of silence. Buzz resents being on the receiving end of this kind of blackmail. He prefers to be the blackmailer rather than the one receiving the ultimatum. In less than thirty seconds, however, he realizes Diana has the clout, connections, and the ammunition to make her threats credible.

"Well shit! Let me look into this situation, and I will get back to you next week. Today is Thursday, and I have to testify in front of the legislature tomorrow morning. I will be presenting the board's proposed collective budget for our four state colleges. This is an important time in front of the appropriations committee."

With another volatile outburst of anger, Diana raises the volume of her voice to the point where Buzz has to move the earpiece away from his head. "Like hell, Buzz Granger! Don't you dare try to give me your famous stall tactics. I expect you to get on the phone and start turning the wheel of fortune. And by God, when that wheel stops moving, it better land on the peg that says 'Fired Immediately'!"

"Okay, Diana. I get it! I understand your message. Give me some time to make a few phone calls. Let's plan on meeting with a few trusted friends sometime next week so we can develop a strategy. This is going to be a difficult task, and I sure don't want it to backfire on us!"

Frustrated, angry, and wanting revenge so bad she can taste it, Diana screams into the phone as she kicks her office trash can. It flies across the room and hits the backside of her closed door. Reluctantly, she accepts Buzz's proposal for a meeting. As she prepares to end the conversation, she says, "Buzz, if you can remember my hatred toward that bitch, Vice President Kelley, then take that level of anger and multiply it by *ten*, and you will have some understanding of my feelings today. I will not compromise on this issue. I want him fired! The sooner, the better! I will start making a list of selected people that I want to attend next week's meeting! Good-bye!"

On Tuesday, March 15, a small group assembles for an evening dinner at Louigie's Italian Restaurant in Columbus, Nebraska. This restaurant is famous for its authentic lasagna, incredible Cabernet cranberry sauce, and homemade, thick-crust garlic bread. Buzz has reserved the small, private dining room on the east side of the restaurant and has requested a round table with seating for six. In the center of the table, three bottles of Cavallotto Piedmont Bricco wine proudly await the arrival of all the dinner guests.

Four of the guests drive about two hours from Springview to Columbus. They travel in three separate cars and arrive within a fifteen-minute time interval. The two ladies travel together, and the two gentlemen travel separately. The chancellor leaves the capitol building twenty minutes behind schedule. His legal counsel, Peter Sedworth, rides with him. The roads are clear and dry. With the chancellor's heavy foot, they soar from Lincoln to Columbus in ninety minutes. Everyone is seated at the dinner table by 7:00 p.m., and Buzz suggests they order from the menu so each person can enjoy their favorite individual entrée.

The first thirty minutes of dinner conversation are stilted and awkward. But Diana smothers everyone with charm and compliments while Buzz performs the role as gracious host. By the time dessert arrives, the wine bottles are empty, and the group seems to be more comfortable and willing to freely talk about current issues at Floyd University. Only one man, Larry Gene Allen, remains unusually quiet. Two years ago, his boss at the bank and the current state governor had reappointed him for a second term on the university's governing board. He had served eight years on the board back in the mid-1980s and early 1990s, but the board's bylaws permitted the governor to reappoint someone after a five-year break in service. Currently, he is in the role of vice chair of the board and is scheduled to become the chair on July 1st after Mr. Blackmore's appointment expires.

Clearing his voice with a loud cough, Buzz captures everyone's attention and opens the formal part of their evening discussion.

"Ladies and gentlemen, let me begin by again thanking each of you for your willingness to join me tonight. I realize we organized this meeting on short notice, and each of you had to adjust your personal plans in order to travel a couple of hours to get here. Thank goodness we have a break in this weather, and the roads are in good shape. Tonight I want us to have a very frank conversation that each of you must consider extremely confidential. This discussion simply cannot become public knowledge to anyone outside this room. We must pledge to each other that we will carefully guard our thoughts and our strategy. As old Sun Tzu would say, 'Proceed with caution and achieve success by using the element of surprise.' In my opinion, our only hope for success will be our ability to move with rapid speed that is completely stealth and organized as a total surprise."

Buzz pauses to again clear his throat and gather his thoughts while he sips on his glass of wine.

Diana glances across the table at her friend Carol. They both roll their eyes at the same time. Diana inadvertently smiles at her friend while thinking to herself, *Oh no, not more Sun Tzu shit!*

Buzz continues. He wants everyone to think that he is protecting the university's high ground. He wants to transform this cause into a crusade against a single opponent. He musters his best attempt to sound motivational, hoping to disguise his real intentions so no one suspects he is covering his own ass.

"I am convinced that we are together tonight with one thing in common. That is our love for Floyd University and the enhancement of its future. And that brings me to the central topic that I hope we can discuss openly and honestly. The leadership of President O'Bryan is not the type of leadership we need for our beloved university's future. I hope you will join me in the difficult task of removing the current president so we can replace him with someone more suitable, someone more fitting. Someone who is willing to take our ideas and convert them into action plans. We need a different leader who will take Floyd University to new heights—a leader who has the vision to prepare our university during the next ten years to celebrate its wonderful 125th anniversary!"

Buzz stopped and looked around the table. He is trying to sound inspirational. He is hoping for some signal from the group that they are motivated. He has to be sure they are ready, willing, and able to support his proposal to remove JP O'Bryan.

At the same time, Diana looks around the table at each guest and inwardly smiles. As she reflects upon Buzz's opening words, she remembers her little black book tucked in the nightstand next to her bed. She thinks, confidentially, that everyone at the table really has two things in common! First, and probably most importantly, each of them has been in her bed and experienced the salacious glow of her fine silk sheets and warm, soft body! And second, as Buzz suggests, they all share a love and loyalty for their hometown university.

The silence in the room lingers for several seconds. This brief period of time seems like an eternity to Buzz. During the past three days, he has several telephone conversations with Diana, and she has assured him that everyone is on board with their goal and ready to help. The fact that she has personally recruited each guest prompts Buzz to think that she is coercing each person to do her bidding. As he suspects, after completing extensive research in her little black book, Diana has issued individually tailored personal ultimatums to each guest in order to ensure their full cooperation.

Professor Carol Nodland finally breaks the silence. "Buzz, I have known you for better than forty years. We started teaching together back in 1974. If you think President O'Bryan has to go, I am with you all the way. The past few years, he has charmed the socks off our faculty senate, but there are still a few of us old salts on campus who are always skeptical of any administrator, and we think it is fun to hit 'em below the belt and poke them in the eye! Besides, I think some of us learned from past experience when the Four Horsemen prevailed that if we are well organized and assertive, the silent majority will cower like sheep and pretty much let us do whatever we want to do. You know that old-fashioned saying: kill the shepherd and his sheep will scatter!"

Diana wants to keep the momentum of this conversation going. With vivid memories of sexual conquest racing through her mind, the excitement from this clandestine power game has made her panties wet. She immediately concurs. "Carol, I could not agree more! I think we can make this happen, and as far as I am concerned, there is no time like the present!"

Coyly smiling, she reaches over to touch the right arm of the seventy-year-old man sitting to her left,

"Don't you agree, Jess?"

Feeling the peer pressure that permeated the room, the retired football coach, John Edward Singleton, nods his head like a puppet just prompted to move.

"Yes, I do agree. Well, speaking as a proud alum, a retired faculty member, and the current president of the Alumni and Foundation Association, I know many friends who want only the best for our university."

Looking directly at Buzz, Jess says, "Chancellor, we have known each other for many years; in fact, more years than I care to admit. In some ways, those early years seem like yesterday to me. I can remember you strolling across the campus as a young buck during your first year at the university. As I recall, you still had a full head of hair back in those days, and both of us were ten inches smaller around the waist."

A friendly chuckle emerges from around the table. Jess continues.

"We have shared many memories together, and your lovely wife is a dear friend. She has been a true blessing to my wife. We will never be able to thank her enough for the times she helped my Rosie while she was battling cancer. So if you say this president has to go, then I will do my best to help. You can count on me!"

Feeling uncomfortable with the direction of this conversation, Larry squirms in his chair while he assertively tries to wave a flag of caution. "Folks, not so fast here! I cannot speak for the board, but I can tell you what I do know about board politics. We will have to get a majority vote from the board in order to cancel O'Bryan's contract, and I don't think that decision will come easy! He has achieved so many good things!"

Turning his head and looking directly at Diana, he continues. "You may think there is no time like the present, and the sooner the better, but I know that as long as Mr. Blackmore is on the board, we will never be able to get rid of O'Bryan. My advice and words of caution suggest that we wait until after July 1st before we try anything. Once Mr. Blackmore's term expires, he will go off the board, and I am scheduled to become the next chair. At that time, we will have a better chance of influencing the membership of the board to go our way."

Buzz wants to be supportive of Mr. Allen. Using his most respectful and subservient voice, Buzz says, "Larry, you are exactly correct! Besides, I think it will be better if we remove O'Bryan during the summer months when the campus is quiet and empty. We should plan to make our move against O'Bryan when the faculty and students are gone for the summer break. I don't want those two campus senates becoming agitated and passing any resolutions that would support O'Bryan. Furthermore, I recommend we plan to have a new acting president on the campus by the time fall classes begin."

Diana turns and looks directly at Mr. Sedworth. She senses his nonverbal resistance to the cause, but she is convinced her threats have forced him to cooperate. She has him by the balls, and he knows it! With an insincere smile, she tilts her head in a flirty way and says, "Hey, Peter, you have been awfully quiet. What do you think? After all, you are the legal expert here tonight!"

Peter Sedworth has just completed forty years as a legal counsel within Nebraska's university environment. As a corrupt, polished bureaucrat, he has excelled since moving to Lincoln. His situational ethics are a perfect fit for someone working in this chancellor's office. Like a flag blowing in the wind, he can shift directions quickly whenever the political currents demand flexibility.

After the governor assertively removes Buzz from his chief of staff position and gives him the chancellor's assignment, Buzz recruits Peter from Floyd University. They have worked together for many years on the Springview campus, and their wives are close friends through their membership in the church choir. Buzz knows that Peter has witnessed the dark side of every scurrilous crevice behind the façade of public university business. His years of experience have made him a master of disguise and a connoisseur of slime and slander. Peter can besmirch or damage the enviable qualities of a saint, and Buzz admires the way he practiced the skillful art of character assassination.

"You know, I have been thinking about this issue ever since Diana called me two days ago. I have a Rotary friend who volunteers as a clown at children's hospitals. He travels the entire Midwest and entertains terminally ill children. He tells me the secret to success rests upon his ability to create illusions while doing his magic act. By diverting the kid's attention, he is able to make things appear to be real through staged deception. Sometimes the impossible seems real in the eyes of his audience because they have false impressions planted in their head. You know the deal, like the rabbit in the hat trick! The key is smoke and mirrors!"

Growing irritated with this rambling, Diana interrupts and says, "Peter, what is your point here?"

"Some of you may remember back in 1985 when we removed Sue Barton from her position as department chair."

The tone in Peter's voice transfers this rhetorical question into a declarative assertion. Buzz looks down at the table and pretends to write some important notes on his yellow tablet.

With a detectable tone of frustration in his voice, Peter continues. "My point, Diana, is this. We placed some old documents on the table in front of Sue Barton and suggested we had the evidence to fire her. It was an illusion! We bluffed her out of a tenured job. We created the false impression that those letters, receipts, and phone records were grounds for termination. Her mind was stunned and overcome with fear. Emotion clouded her thoughts and hindered her good judgment. On the spur of the moment, she panicked and signed a resignation statement that I had conveniently prepared before the meeting."

Buzz jumps into the conversation. "My God, Peter, Sun Tzu would be proud! You just described the perfect example of what can be achieved with the element of surprise. Let's hold on to that thought and try to use it as part of our strategy against O'Bryan."

Carol quickly jumps into the conversation. "Chancellor, do you think we could find some old emails and use them against O'Bryan?"

"No, I suspect he is a cautious man and very careful with his emails. Most presidents realize these days that any newspaper can file a simple 'freedom of information' request and get all the emails they want. My guess would be his email account will be a dead end for our purposes. We need something more creative. Perhaps a report or audit that will appear as an intimidating document, something we can slap on the table with complete surprise. I want to cloud his judgment with something that will put the fear of God in him. I really like Peter's idea of pushing him into a resignation."

Larry smiles. For the first time this evening, he is pleased with the direction of the discussion.

"From the board's perspective, a resignation is much easier to deal with than trying to get a majority vote to fire a president. You know, Chancellor, if you bring us a signed resignation, we will most likely publically express our dismay and regret, and then automatically go into closed session. Subsequently, I would call for a vote to accept the resignation and quickly move forward appointing a new person as interim president. After the meeting, our news release could be short, sweet, to the point, and very dispassionate in tone."

Buzz looks at the time and realizes the hour is late.

"Folks, it is already 9:30 p.m., and we all have to drive a couple of hours to get home. We better adjourn for now. Thank you for your willingness to help me formulate the initial phase of our plan. We made a lot of progress here tonight. During the next few months, I will continue to dig for some dirt that we can use against O'Bryan. I really like the idea of timing this termination during the summer months when the faculty and students are not on campus. Again, let me emphasize the critical importance of keeping this effort confidential."

The first person to leave the dining room is Larry Allen. In less than fifteen minutes, he is moving down the highway on his way home. As he leaves the city limits and turns onto Highway 81, he hits the speed dial on his cell phone and waits for a response. After four rings, his boss answers the phone.

"This is Governor Turner. Is this Larry?

"Good evening, Governor. Yes, this is Larry. Sorry for the late hour. Do you have a few minutes to talk?"

"Larry, I caught your number on my caller ID. Hell, yes! I have time to talk. I am sitting here in my favorite easy chair in my slippers enjoying a fine glass of JW Red Label Scotch. I hope you have some good news about our pending merger. I really want to secure the controlling interest in Creighton's state bank before the word leaks to my opponents. Tell me you have some good news!"

"Governor, I am in my car right now, just leaving Columbus. I really think the merger is on track and about to be approved. I should know for sure sometime during the next two days, but I am calling to give you an update on a different subject. We need to talk university business."

"Goddammit, Larry. I want that merger so bad I can taste it. I expect you to call me day or night whenever you get the word. Do you understand?"

"Absolutely, Governor! You will be the first to know once I receive their decision."

"Good, good. Now what the hell is going on with our universities?"

"Well, governor, our Universities are doing just fine. But I think our chancellor is out of control again! He just had five of us around the table for a confidential discussion regarding his plans to fire President O'Bryan. Has he briefed you on this topic?"

"Jesus H. Christ, Larry! What the hell is he doing? He casually stopped me in the hallway yesterday afternoon and said that we need to get rid of O'Bryan. I told him that was a very bad idea, and if he tried, it would blow up in his face like a huge shit-bomb! Why the hell can't he leave this alone?"

"Governor, I don't know if you have met Professor Diana Dawson, but she is the bitch who pushed the no-confidence vote against old Buzz about sixteen years ago. Do you remember? It was back in 1990 if I am correct; about the same time as the Gulf War."

"Hell yes, I remember. I was working in DC—in the middle of that congressional shit-storm, and you tried to protect Buzz, but she seemed to have the clout to go after him. So what is she doing now?"

"Well, I am not sure, but for some reason there seems to be an unholy alliance between Buzz and Diana. They have joined forces against a common enemy—President O'Bryan."

"Holy shit, Larry! I will tell you that there is a limit to my patience and willingness to protect old Buzz. Just because we have been friends for many years and we go deer hunting every fall, I am not giving him carte blanche protection. Do you understand my position? I cannot continue to underwrite his outrageous actions!"

"Governor, I am no psychology expert, but I have been around people for many years. I think old Buzz is jealous of O'Bryan. Maybe it is the PhD thing. You know how those academic folks are about their credentials. Old Buzz never had the intellectual clout to get that doctorate degree. Or maybe it is O'Bryan's incredible ability to get things done. He is an effective leader— well-liked and respected by most. You know that old saying about never outshining your boss."

"Goddammit Larry, this really pisses me off! Thanks for the heads-up. I'll tell you what I am going to do. I plan to call Buzz tomorrow so we can have a come-to-Jesus meeting. I want this O'Bryan thing to stop. The last thing I need right now in my cabinet is a big scandal that tarnishes the reputation of our public universities and makes me look bad! I will tell Buzz to put this crazy idea on ice! Goodnight, Larry! Be sure to call me when you have something on that merger!"

"Yes, sir, Governor! Thanks for your time tonight!"

The digital clock on the dashboard displays 10:45 p.m. Jess is about halfway home and lost in deep thought. For the past hour, he has been reliving his years at Floyd University. For the most part, they have been good years. But tonight, his guilty conscience overwhelms him as he struggles with this moral crisis.

In the fall of 1973, Jess walks onto the football field at Floyd University as the new assistant coach in charge of the offensive backfield. While working for the legendary head coach, Joe Harlow, Jess excels in a program that has a winning tradition and an explosive offense that routinely averages four hundred yards each game. After ten years, Coach Harlow decides to retire, and Jess is given the opportunity to become head coach. During the next thirty years, he maintains a relentless, demanding schedule of travel and recruiting. His hard work translates into rich dividends. Over the years, his teams win countless conference titles and compete several times in national tournaments where they always make it to the final four in the playoffs. Finally, with his wife's health failing, Jess completes his fortieth year at Floyd University and then he retires in 2013.

In 1996, he celebrates his fiftieth birthday and unfortunately experiences all the classic symptoms of male menopause. After he buys a red Corvette convertible, his wife stops speaking to him for more than two months. He stops going to church. The difficult weeks turn into months as he spends more time traveling, recruiting, and drinking and less time with his wife at home.

Jess cringes as he recalls his walk down the slippery slope of adultery. For about twenty years, he has maintained a small rental house just three blocks from the campus. He still remembers with great detail a young Diana Dawson renting this house in the fall of 1984. She is beautiful to behold and fun to be around. As her landlord, he finds himself increasingly stopping to check on the house and see if she needs anything. Finally, after years of enjoying her flirty ways, he jumps into bed with her one late night in 1996 after returning from an away game.

Their affair lasts the better part of an academic year. When he stops their sexual relationship, she becomes ugly, mean-spirited, and difficult as a renter. There is always something wrong in the house. At times, he suspects that she is consciously breaking things just to harass him. Finally, in the summer of 1998, he wants to avoid her completely so he convinces his wife that it is time to sell their rental property. They decide to invest the profit from this sale in a retirement condo near Boulder, Colorado.

The past three years, he has enjoyed his wife and time with their grandchildren. As a distinguished member of the community, he has many friends and serves on several boards. When Diana threatens him, he feels compelled to comply with her demands because he cannot bear to think about the debasing embarrassment that would unfold if his infidelity becomes public.

—*∿*—

Buzz drives in silence and basks in the joy that one feels after they have flawlessly completed an important project. It is 11:00 p.m., and Peter appears to be sleeping as they cruise down the highway. Buzz smiles surreptitiously as he reviews the sequence of events from their evening discussion. He muses with pride knowing that he has followed Sun Tzu's recommended guidelines.

Lost in his thoughts, Buzz accidentally mutters aloud, "Step one, unite your troops around a cause. Step two, fill their bellies. Step three, lead from the front!"

The third step is his favorite, and the very thought of his distinguished leadership role makes him chuckle with smugness.

Peter awakens from his light sleep. He places his hand against the kink in his neck and drowsily asks, "What did you say, Chancellor?"

"Hey, Peter, you are awake! I was just reviewing tonight's meeting and thinking about the next steps. I really like your suggestion to slap a report or some kind of document on the table and put the fear of God in O'Bryan. I need that resignation, and your experience with Sue Barton fits this situation perfectly."

Somewhat confused and still trying to clear his thoughts from a wine-induced sleep, Peter says, "I am not sure I follow your thinking. What are you suggesting?"

"Well, Peter, it is clear to me that you are the man! I need your legal expertise to write a report and create that illusion that you were describing."

Peter is momentarily stunned, but he is now wide awake and thinking about the magnitude of this assignment.

"But wait! I can't pull something out of thin air and make it seem real. You are asking for some kind of miracle!"

"No, Peter, this will not be a miracle. As you said tonight, it will be smoke and mirrors! Think of it as pulling that rabbit out of the hat!"

The chancellor laughs aloud. He is quoting Peter from the meeting and enjoying the opportunity to make him squirm. Now the old attorney has to practice what he preaches.

"Chancellor, if you want me to do this writing, you at least have to give me a topic. I need some kind of project where O'Bryan has been the key leader and therefore vulnerable and liable."

Once again, the chancellor laughs and hits his steering wheel with enthusiasm.

"Peter, Peter, oh ye of little faith!"

Surprised at the chancellor's lighthearted humor, Peter begins to wonder if the wine is still lingering in the chancellor's brain.

"Well, judging from your laughter, I take it you have already selected the topic for this report. What is it?"

"Peter, I recently received O'Bryan's self-evaluation. He believes his most significant accomplishment for this last year has been the construction of that twenty-four-million-dollar recreation center. He claims it was accomplished on time and under budget."

"Chancellor, you know I reviewed all those construction contracts, and I personally supervised the public bidding process. I cannot imagine how we will find anything wrong. From my perspective, this project was done by the books. And besides, we both attended the dedication ceremony and listened to the governor praise everyone for this effort. I don't think it would be wise to throw egg on the governor and his best friend, the Springview mayor, in order to paint O'Bryan as the bad guy."

"Peter, Peter, once again, I must remind you that all you need is faith the size of a mustard seed. Remember, this is an illusion. It does not have to be anything real. Make it up as you go! Make it happen!"

Peter remains skeptical and begins to counter argue. Before he can utter two words, the chancellor's mood swings from giddy to angry; he hits the front dashboard with his fist and interrupts Peter in midsentence.

"Let me put it to you in a different way, Peter! You are hereby ordered to write this report! Do you understand my plain English? Consider this a formal directive!"

———*◊◊◊*———

At this very moment, a red LSF Sport Lexus is cruising north on Highway 81. Diana is talking, laughing, and having such a fun time that she fails to monitor her speed. With her headlights on high beam, she catches a glimpse of two deer crossing near an approaching bridge. As she hits the brakes, she glances at the speedometer and realizes she is going seventy-eight mph in a sixty-five-mph zone.

"Shit, Carol! Did you see those two deer? I better slow down and pay attention to my speed."

"I can see it now, Diana. Your name printed in bold letters within the Courthouse News section of the paper—pleading guilty for excessive speeding and paying some huge fine as a penalty. Then you can go around campus and try to explain to everyone why you were out on the highway between Columbus and Springview at midnight!"

They both laugh at this thought.

"Well, old Buzz would crap his pants if he thought the element of surprise had been lost thanks to my heavy foot!"

"Do you think Buzz has the balls to fire O'Bryan?"

Diana responds with an immediate assertion. "Hell yes! He has no choice! He knows I will cut off his balls and serve them to him raw on a platter if he does not cooperate with this plan! Let me put it to you this way: I have his two tiny balls in my handheld nutcracker, and he is feeling the pressure right now as he drives into Lincoln. I'll bet his fat ass is pinching buttonholes in the seat covers!"

Diana gestures with her right hand to simulate squeezing the handles of a plier. "Carol, I can't wait for our next night out with the Sexy Six! I am dying to tell our girls about the plans. I intend to ask them to start digging up dirt that we can use eventually to fuel the rumor mill."

Carol looks out the car window on the passenger side and marvels at the snow-covered fields glowing with the light from the stars and moon.

"Diana, this is going to be more fun than watching two naked ladies fighting in one of those old mud pools. Do you remember when the sororities at college used to sponsor those mud fights and sell admission tickets to all those horny frat boys?"

Once again, both ladies laugh like silly school girls as Diana presses the accelerator and the speedometer hits eighty mph. Lost in their own world of conversation, Diana unknowingly passes Jess like he is standing still. About thirty miles outside of Springview, she passes Larry while he is talking on his cell phone to one of his vice presidents.

As the red Lexus soars around his car, Larry recognizes the driver and subconsciously says over the phone, "Well, there goes the red bitch from hell!"

26

Dirty Hands

Life is a game with many rules but no referee. One learns how to play it more by watching it than by consulting any book, including the holy book. Small wonder, then, that so many play dirty, that so few win, that so many lose.

—Joseph Brodsky, 1940–1996
US Poet Laureate in 1991

March 16, 2016
Lincoln, Nebraska

The morning sun radiates through the four large windows on the east side of the state capitol building. The governor's outer office is a massive two-thousand-square-foot space filled with historic pieces of furniture and scenic oil paintings that adorn the walls. The twelve-foot-tall grandfather centennial clock chimes ten o'clock as the receptionist signals to Buzz that the governor is off the phone and it is okay to enter his private suite.

As Buzz enters the governor's inner office, he immediately senses a cold reception from his old hunting buddy. The governor remains seated behind his massive, shiny walnut desk. Buzz leans forward and extends his hand across the width of the desk toward the governor. Their curt handshake feels strange to Buzz. For a few fleeting seconds, he recalls their last night in deer camp when the Remarkable Trinity emptied three bottles of Jack Daniels and shared the warmth of manly camaraderie.

The governor is anticipating a heated discussion and does not want anyone in the outer reception area to overhear their loud voices, so he suggests they step into his adjourning conference room. Foregoing the amenities of coffee and friendly conversation, the governor sits in his heavily padded, swivel-tilt leather chair at the head of the table, leans back, intensely glares at Buzz, and says, "Buzz, I happened to be on the phone last night with Larry Allen. He was giving me an update on the bank and mentioned that he had attended a meeting in Columbus hosted by you. What the hell is going on?"

Instantly, Buzz goes red-hot with anger. In less than twelve hours, the group's confidentiality agreement has been broken. Now he must defend his actions to his boss.

"Governor, you will recall a few days ago that I mentioned the need to dump O'Bryan. The meeting last night was designed to start a confidential conversation that will ultimately give us a workable strategy. I think—"

Thumping his hand on the table, the governor interrupts him. "Goddammit Buzz, don't try to bullshit an old bullshitter! I specifically told you not to touch O'Bryan! I sure as hell don't want you to start some kind of scandal that will haunt my reelection bid. What the hell are you thinking? My God, where are your scruples?"

Buzz glares directly into the governor's eyes. A switch flips in his brain. The filter between his thoughts and mouth instantly stops working. Like the dog compelled to bite the hand that feeds him, Buzz's bizarre temperament hampers his mental balance. In the presence of his mentor and godfather, he goes on the offensive with a blazing outburst of ranting anger.

"Hey, governor, don't talk to me about scruples. You would not know one if it walked into this room and sat in that chair next to you! I hope you haven't forgotten who taught me everything I know. Do you think I can remain Mr. Clean as I sit in the chancellor's godforsaken hot seat? You once told me leaders who avoid dirty hands are weak, and they invariably end up defeated."

Buzz aggressively leans toward the governor. "I have fostered deceit, betrayal, and killed many political actions because you sent me into battle with a clear directive to make it happen!"

Buzz stops. His face, crimson with anger, glows with a condescending smirk as he continues. "Have you forgotten who taught me the art of an unscrupulous ruler? For more than two decades, I did your dirty work. I have dirty hands because I have been loyal to you."

Extending both hands across the table, Buzz escalates the volume of his voice. "Look at these hands! They are dirty up past my elbows because you always needed me to get down in the mud to fight your shitty battles."

The governor tries to interrupt, but Buzz continues. "You know I have embraced every opportunity to support your career. No matter the cost, I was always there working to advance your agenda. Years ago, I stopped caring about what others think, and I stopped counting the number of political opponents we crushed. You taught me to be an apostle of Machiavelli. It never mattered who got hurt inside the circle of collateral damage. You taught me well because I firmly believe the end always justifies the means."

Blatantly lighting a Camel cigarette in the governor's no-smoking conference room, Buzz continues his tirade.

"Every time you needed a soldier to walk across the killing fields in that great legislative chamber we call the senate, I was your man. I was the gladiator you sent into the arena to bash heads and get things done."

Buzz pauses to flip ashes into an elegant brass coaster that was custom-made for the state's centennial celebration. "You owe me, governor. You owe me big-time!"

Waving his right hand toward the governor's face, Buzz, explains "You know, about two thousand years ago, my favorite Chinese philosopher said that whenever a wise leader masters power, he can have anything he desires. Well, governor, that's me. And I tell you now, O'Bryan is the prey, and I am the predator!"

Totally stunned by this display of arrogance and insubordination, the governor's first thought is guided by anger. But just before he is about to scream, "Get the hell out of my office," he remembers all the times his godfather, Mr. Ace, said, "Never let your opponent know your true feelings."

As the governor watches Buzz flip more ashes on his antique Brazilian mahogany conference table, he hesitates for about twenty seconds, regains his composure, and says, "Buzz, you know I have always valued your loyalty. I am going to ask you to go back to your office and reconsider this O'Bryan thing that you seem so hell-bent to accomplish. Why don't you and your lovely wife come over for dinner this Saturday evening? We will talk some more while we enjoy a good steak with some fine whiskey."

Buzz leaves the room by using the governor's private backdoor. As he rides the elevator to the tenth floor and returns to his office, he feels sharp pains across his chest, and he knows his blood pressure is probably going off the chart. Once he is seated at his desk, he automatically begins to open his email.

Slamming his fist on the desk, he is frustrated and ready to chew on a nail. Distracted, his thoughts are fogged by his self-pride and boiling anger. The first email he opens is the "Thought for the Day" message. It is from George Bernard Shaw, and it says, "I learned long ago, never to wrestle with a pig. You get dirty, and besides, the pig likes it."

Totally out of control, Buzz curses to himself. He hits the delete key so hard he breaks the keyboard as he tries to trash this simple email.

27

In the Eye of the Storm

Dreams of a lifetime,
Thrills from long ago,
These years of joy now have flown,
Silhouettes in a mirror...
Seasons are changing, winter of my life,
The memories still survive, and the dreams of my love,
Are coming down like rain...
She meant everything to me,
Scarlet woman with eyes of gold,
She's out on the edge of my dreams,
In the eye of the storm.

—Taylor Dayne, "Eye of the Storm," May 2010

March 18, 2016
Springview, Nebraska

During the last ten years, Diana Dawson has served as the catalyst
to assemble a group of ladies fondly known to each other as the
Sexy Six. Publicly, they call themselves the "Ladies in Red." This

girlfriend club routinely makes time every third Friday of each month to get together for a ladies' night out. Their purpose is simple. Have fun, drink, eat, and share some good old-fashioned gossip. Frequently, one of the ladies serves as the host for these gatherings, but four or five times each year, on birthdays or special occasions, they go out to eat and party at a restaurant or bar.

Tonight, Carol Nodland is hosting their ladies' night out. She has prepared a marvelous buffet layout of delicious finger foods on her dining room table. With two large Gott coolers filled with beer on ice, the stage is set with the ingredients for a lively evening of freewheeling conversation. The doorbell rings and Diana walks in with two chilled bottles of Canard-Duchene authentic brut rose champagne and a decorative serving tray filled with assorted crackers and caviar.

"Hey, girl, I hope you have six nice stemware glasses that we can use for this superb champagne!"

Carol is surprised and delighted.

"Oh my gosh, this is great! Are we celebrating a special occasion tonight?"

"You better believe it, girlfriend! I talked with the chancellor this afternoon, and he is moving forward with our plans to ambush the old president! I can't wait to make the announcement tonight and recruit everyone's help!"

Diana is acting giddy, like a young schoolgirl who just received her first kiss on the playground. Carol suspects Diana has started happy hour a little early today with her favorite drinking buddy, old Ray Wheelwright.

Just as Carol enters the kitchen to get some nice glassware, the doorbell rings again, and Jolee McBride walks into the room carrying a large grocery sack filled with assorted bags of chips. Dr. Ann Spencer enters right after Jolee. As a senior full professor of chemistry, Ann is Carol's best friend and office neighbor. About twenty years ago, Ann moved into a private office directly across the hall from Carol in the Thornburg Science Building.

As the new arrivals exchange greetings with their host, the doorbell signals another arrival. Lynda Stevenson enters with a silver tray filled with homemade fudge brownies. Lynda is a lifetime resident of Springview and always fun to be around, especially after her second drink. She thrives on community gossip and knows where all the skeletons are buried around town. After her divorce, she was unemployed, so her daddy pulled a few strings to get her a job. About six years ago, many in the community were shocked when she was appointed as the director of the university's Alumni and Foundation Association. Without question, her local political connections enhanced her application status. Feeling the local pressure, President Gill hired her just before he retired. Many of Lynda's friends were surprised when she got the job because the original announcement stipulated a bachelor's degree was required. Lynda only completed a two-year associate degree in accounting after she finished high school and then she married and raised three sons. Now she works as a member of President O'Bryan's cabinet.

Diana is anxious to pop the cork on the champagne and make her announcement, but she wants to wait until everyone has arrived.

Carol opens a bottle of beer for each guest. As she pours the beer into glasses, the front door opens briskly and Ellen Marie Martinez rushes into the house, rambling an apology for her late arrival.

Emmy traveled directly from campus to Carol's house. She had attended the Annual Awards Day ceremony in the auditorium because she was recognized by President O'Bryan for completing thirty years of service to Floyd University. As she gushes with apologies for her windblown hair and disheveled appearance, she proudly flashes her thirty-year service certificate in front of everyone.

Diana waits patiently for Emmy to regain control. Everyone has learned to be patient with Emmy's eccentric ways. She constantly struggles to manage moments of tension while she tries to please everyone. Usually, after about five minutes of rapid chatter, she becomes calm, almost introverted.

Finally, Carol gently taps the side of a champagne glass with a small butter knife. The unmistakable ring of elegant glassware brings everyone to complete silence as Carol loudly says, "Ladies, ladies, our dear friend Diana has a special announcement that she is dying to share."

Emmy squeals. Ann and Jolee clap their hands and Lynda says, "Hear, hear! You go, girl!"

Diana asks each lady to fill their champagne glass because she wants to make a special toast. Carol moves around the room, carefully filling each glass to the very brim.

Diana carefully raises her glass above her shoulder and boldly announces, "My dear sisters, we are assembled together this evening in warm friendship. Whenever we are together, we wear red clothes and share a timeless bond that is articulated in our ancient pledge to always protect each other. Once each month, we share with each other our personal hopes and joys. Well, tonight I joyfully want you to be the first to know that Floyd University will soon have a new president!"

A loud clamor of voices echoes around the room. Lynda, now into her third drink, shouts, "Go, girl. You go, girl!"

Diana continues. "This is very confidential, but I have received a personal promise from the chancellor that he will trash President O'Bryan sometime early this summer. The old army colonel is in the eye of a big storm, and he does not have a clue. So tonight we drink to the demise of JP O'Bryan and the dawn of a new era under a more reasonable leader. Drink up, girls, and let the games and gossip begin!"

In less than thirty seconds, all the champagne glasses are empty, and everyone becomes engrossed with speculation and excitement. After all, there is nothing like the thrill of giving an old dog a bad name.

The balance of the evening is devoted to the planning of countless opportunities to spread hot rumors and juicy gossip about a man who valiantly stands in the middle of the arena known as Floyd University. Fueled by beer with champagne chasers, six wicked souls prepare to launch the ancient sport of character assassination.

28

The Magnificent Deceit

Crush the enemy is a key strategic tenet of Sun Tzu, the author of *The Art of War*. Have no mercy. Crush your enemies as totally as possible. All great leaders since Moses have known that a feared enemy must be crushed completely. Crush your opponent, not only in body but in spirit.

—Robert Greene, *The 48 Laws of Power*, 1998

May 2016
Sioux City, Iowa

"Jesus Christ, Craig! Oh, I don't know how you do your magic. You seem to get better every time we are together! You remind me of a fine wine that improves with age! That was amazing, my dear!"

Diana always flatters her love-toys while they are in the afterglow of sex. During the past four years, she has made it a point to spend at least one weekend per month with her friend and lover in his renovated townhouse. In many respects, they are partners in crime—both specializing in the commodity of slander. They have a friendly mutual agreement that has been in place since their first night in bed together. He skillfully uses his tongue to take her into sexual fantasies that give her unprecedented climaxes. In return, she gives him all the inside rumors, gossip, dirt and hot-poop that she can recall from the university so he can use it during his radio talk show.

Built on a bluff, Craig Jacobson's living room has a large floor-to-ceiling window that faces south and overlooks the Highway 20 bridge that crosses the Missouri River. Day or night, Diana loves to stand naked in front of this window, watching the traffic on the bridge and the boats on the river while Craig kneels in front of her and performs his sexual wonders.

Craig fondly reminds Diana that his sexual prowess is not as good as it has been in the past, but certainly better than he ever was for a one-time encounter. Feeling invigorated, Craig says, "I hope you are in the mood to go out for dinner? We have a new steak house that opened just across the street from the River Boat Casino. How about it? Their steaks are supposed to be sensational. Are you game for a night out on the town and maybe a few slot machines after we eat?"

"You know, I don't feel like getting dressed. How about some Chinese and a nice white wine? Let's call for delivery, and I will take a shower while we wait for the food to get here."

"Super! I have some nice wine that is already chilled. You hit the shower, and I will call in our order. Do you want your traditional cashew chicken with fried rice and extra soy sauce?"

Diana lingers in front of the large window like a model pacing the runway at a fashion show. Somewhat distracted, she casually responds, "Sure, that will be great!"

Craig places the food order and fills two wine goblets. He is surprised to find Diana still gazing out the window and not in the shower. As he hands her the wine glass, she says, "Well, honey, what would you say if I told you Chancellor Granger is going to fire President O'Bryan?"

In the middle of drinking his wine, Craig is visibly surprised and almost spills some wine on the sofa. "You are kidding, right? Holy shit, my sources in Lincoln tell me the chancellor is on shaky ground, and he is the one that might get fired. Why would the chancellor go after O'Bryan?"

"Well, I am not sure, but some of us think Buzz is jealous of O'Bryan. I think he is intimidated by the president's poise and talent. I think the old chancellor fears O'Bryan might someday take his job. I was at a private meeting a few months ago, and Buzz seemed insecure. There is a rumor going around that the board chair already asked O'Bryan if he would think about a future assignment as the next chancellor."

"Well, hell yes, old Buzz should feel insecure, but not because of O'Bryan! I hear the governor forced him out of the chief of staff position and gave him the chancellor's job just because they are old hunting buddies, and Buzz needs a few more years to secure his second retirement plan. The word I hear is the governor is tired of cashing Buzz's checks! His mouth always overruns his feeble mind. Did you know when he was chief of staff, he told the Republican Party's majority leader to go to hell and suggested he take the attorney general with him? At the time, it was a huge uproar in the capitol building, and the governor had to step in and become personally involved as a mediator in order to mend the broken fences. It almost split the party."

Diana pretends to look surprised as she smiles and sips her wine. After years of seething hatred for her old lover, she enjoys hearing anything negative about Buzz. She knows firsthand that he is a blundering fool and totally incompetent.

Moving gracefully across the room, Diana turns her slim body directly toward Craig. Years of aerobics have kept her muscles agile like a ballerina dancer. As she showcases her new breast implants, she slowly bends over to touch her toes. With a sexually suggestive tone, she says,

"Well, sweetheart, you just stand by and watch the fireworks. I think Floyd University will have a new president before you know it. Why don't you kiss my little red dragon while we wait for our food to be delivered?"

On Monday morning, Craig arrives at work more than an hour early. He jumps on the telephone and begins trolling his network of moles. He is on the hunt for breaking news, searching for any details or hints signaling the immediate downfall of a university president.

PART V

Crucible of Humiliation

My Son, accept whatever happens to you;
In periods of humiliation be patient.
For in fire gold is tested,
And worthy men are tested in the crucible of humiliation.

—The Wisdom of Ben Sira
Circa 175 BC

29

Abuse of Power

A preferred approach in Unconventional (Dirty)
Warfare is to take the line of least expectation. The 36
Military Strategies from Ancient China suggest each
military maneuver has two aspects: the superficial move
and the underlying purpose. By concealing both, one can
take the enemy completely by surprise.

Generally, people expect your behavior to conform
to known patterns and conventions. Sometimes the
ordinary is extraordinary because it is unexpected.

—Robert Green, *The 33 Strategies of War*, 2006

June 2016
Lincoln, Nebraska

On June 6, JP leaves home at 5:30 a.m. and drives into Lincoln
to meet with the chancellor at 11:00 a.m. The purpose of their
meeting is to discuss JP's performance evaluation.

Their conversation moves quickly as the chancellor reviews all
the category ratings that are scored either *excellent* or *outstanding*.

After approximately forty-five minutes of discussion, the chancellor reaches across the conference table and taps JP on the shoulder. The last couple of years, the chancellor has frequently used this nonverbal gesture with JP and some of the other campus presidents to signal that he is standing next to them. He always reminds them that he supports their leadership decisions through thick and thin.

Finally, the chancellor says, "JP, I want you to think of me as your mentor, guide, coach, and friend. I will always stand shoulder to shoulder with you, and together we can work as a team to solve your problems. Count on me to be right there with you whenever you have a difficult situation or challenge to your leadership decisions. I am here for you!"

"Thanks, chancellor. I always appreciate your support and helpful guidance. In many ways, this has been one of my most challenging years as president, but given the things we have completed, I must say it has been one of the most successful years of my entire career in higher education."

The chancellor continues, "Well, I am pleased to sign this annual performance evaluation. As you can see, I have given you an overall rating of *outstanding*. I hope you realize that I generally do not give ratings this high, but you have earned it. Also, the board chair and I have agreed that you should be nominated for a merit pay increase. Right now, we are thinking that you will receive the standard 4 percent increase because of your successful evaluation plus another 3 percent increase for merit. If the rest of the board agrees, that will give you a 7 percent increase for this next year. And I will recommend to the board that we extend the length of your contract so you will have another two years added to your contract length. How does that sound?"

"Really? Great! Thank you, chancellor! I sincerely appreciate your thoughtful feedback and willingness to make these recommendations to the board."

"JP, as you know the board is scheduled to meet in ten days, on June 16. I will be presenting all the contract recommendations for each campus president. I do not anticipate any pushback. I have been keeping the chair informed as I have prepared each performance evaluation. This will be Mr. Blackmore's last meeting as a member of the board. The vice chair is scheduled to assume the chair's position, and the current secretary will move up and become our next vice chair. Your new contract will be effective on July 1 and synchronize with the next fiscal year. Once the board approves my recommendations on the sixteenth, I will prepare a new contract and send it to you. Please give it your immediate attention. Sign it and return one original to me for our permanent records. Our personnel policy requires me to have everything completed before the new fiscal year begins. Besides, I plan to take my wife to Florida for a long Fourth of July weekend, and I need to have these contracts in place before we leave."

JP senses the conversation is coming to a close. He responds, "Absolutely, chancellor. I will get the contract back in the mail to you the same day it arrives on my desk. I hope you have a wonderful trip to Florida with your wife. Are you flying?"

"No, we plan to drive and enjoy the scenery along the way. There is a chance we may loop into North Carolina on the return trip and visit my son and his new wife."

JP leaves the capitol building and walks across the south parking lot to his car. He should feel joy and personal satisfaction, but his intuition tells him to beware. Once inside his car, he hits the speed dial on his cell phone.

"Hey, Jenn, just want to call and give you an update. I think my evaluation went very well."

After briefly explaining the ratings and proposed salary increase, JP stops to let his wife talk.

"Honey, that is really terrific. Congratulations! I am proud of you. All your hard work and endless hours have paid off and given you the recognition that you have earned! All that worry you have been doing turned out to be false signals. Don't you feel like you are on cloud nine right now?"

There is a pause in the conversation, and JP hesitates. Finally, he says, "You know, Jenn, I am grateful for the high ratings, and we can sure use the salary increase. But there was something in the chancellor's demeanor that just did not ring true. I can't put my finger on it. Basically, he seemed insincere, like he was just going through the motions because it was expected behavior."

His wife laughs.

"JP, you are a true Virgo! You find things to worry about when you should be celebrating. Now you want to worry about something you vaguely feel simply because you don't have anything real or specific to worry about."

"Okay, okay, Jenn, you are right. Let's put my worries aside and go out for a nice dinner tonight. I should be home in about four hours and then we can make some plans for dinner. Love you!"

On June 15, JP drives to Lincoln and stays at the Best Western Motel. The next morning he is in the capitol building by 7:30 a.m. and seated in the board's conference room by 7:45 a.m. The meeting starts promptly at 8:30 a.m. Mr. Blackmore follows the agenda and projected timeline. After lunch, the chancellor presents his personnel recommendations for each president's salary and new contract. After the chair expresses his appreciation to each president for their hard work and successful year of accomplishments, the board votes unanimously to approve the chancellor's contract recommendations.

That evening, as JP drives home, the *Springview Press* calls. JP answers his cell phone, and Jolee McBride is on the other end. This seems unusual. Generally, JP interacts with one of the reporters who works for Jolee. She wants to ask JP about his renewed contract and his merit salary increase. The entire interview seems strange to JP. The questions are routine; it is a standard news interview. But Jolee acts clever, almost haughty—like she knows something JP does not.

At one point toward the end of the interview, Jolee asks, "Now that your contract has been extended, what do you hope to accomplish during the next year?"

JP responds in an articulate manner recounting the work remaining to be done to advance the goals within the university's strategic plan. As he finishes his comment, he says, "I look forward to the opportunity to work with our campus and the Springview community as we strive to achieve our vision of becoming one of the premier universities within the Midwest."

Unexpectedly, Jolee surprises JP and bluntly says, "Well, it remains to be seen if that work will happen."

That night JP talks to Jenn about this unusual interview and Jolee's strange editorial comment toward the end of the conversation. He wonders if her words refer to his personal involvement with this work, or if she is questioning the credibility of their vision to become a premier university.

"Jenn, I know you think Virgos like to worry, and we sometimes make a list of worries to worry about, but Jolee talked like she was very skeptical about my future career. She came across like the Cheshire Cat from Alice in Wonderland who knows some kind of secret."

Jenn usually gives JP a heavy dose of reality whenever he needed an attitude adjustment,

"JP, you are amazing. You should be savoring your victories rather than wearing a black band of crepe. Remember how your dad always told you to focus on the donut and not upon the hole? Well, you have many reasons to be optimistic and full of hope. So stop worrying and go read your new book about China."

JP moves into the living room and quickly settles into his favorite reading chair. Jenn is right. His dad's daily demonstration of positive thinking has become something of an aspirational North Star for JP's moral compass.

30

Dead Man Walking

Any man who tries to be good all the time is bound
to come to ruin among the great number who are
not good. Hence, a prince who wants to keep his
authority must learn how not to be good.

—Niccolo Machiavelli, 1469–1527

August 1, 2016
Floyd University

Seated in his office, JP answers his telephone after the second ring. A familiar voice says, "Hello, President O'Bryan. This is Maribeth, the chancellor's secretary. Are you available to speak with the chancellor?"

JP responds, "Hi, Maribeth. How are you today? Did you have a nice vacation at Silver Dollar City?"

Maribeth is markedly cold and aloof. "Yes, we had a good trip. Please hold for Chancellor Granger."

The telephone clicks, and a recording of routine "elevator" music plays. JP is on hold until the conclusion of the second song.

A gruff male voice abruptly breaks into the music.

"JP, thanks for taking my call on the spur of the moment. I want to talk with you, face to face, so I am going to ask you to drive into Lincoln first thing in the morning. Plan to be in my office at 1:30 p.m.!"

JP is surprised and wonders about this spontaneous, uncharacteristic demand. Trying to be cooperative, he answers, "Sure, I can do that." JP hesitates, carefully selecting his words.

"I have a couple of meetings here in my office that I will reschedule for a different day. By the way, how was your family vacation in Florida?"

"Our trip was fine! Look, JP, I have to run for my next meeting. Just be sure you are on time tomorrow because I have a tight schedule with back-to-back appointments."

The chancellor's tone of voice has become terse.

"Chancellor, is there anything specific I need to be prepared to discuss? Do you want me to bring anything for our meeting?"

The chancellor's voice quickly alters to a cordial tone.

"Oh no, no, nothing to prepare. I have a report here on my desk, and I want to go over it with you. We can discuss it when you get here!"

JP is very puzzled. So he probes with another question. "Chancellor, would it help if I read the report tonight and came ready to talk about it? You could send me an email copy, or you can fax it to me."

"That won't be necessary. There is no need for that. Just come ready to talk, and I will introduce the report to you when you arrive."

The next day, at 1:15 p.m., JP rides the elevator to the chancellor's wing on the south side of the building. As he enters the office suite, he is surprised to see that all four receptionists and secretaries are gone. No one is present within the entire entrance area. JP quietly takes a seat in one of the guest chairs.

About ten minutes later, Maribeth comes around the corner and coldly but politely says, "The Chancellor is ready for you. Please go on back."

JP thinks to himself, *Wow, after all these years, this is the first time I have been here for a meeting and Maribeth did not offer me a cup of coffee.*

JP proceeds down the long, narrow hallway past four other empty offices. Both vice chancellors are gone, and their offices are dark. Both financial analysts are away from their desks, but their office lights are on. Reaching the end of the hallway, JP knocks on the chancellor's door.

"Come in, JP. Take a chair at my conference table."

Another first is noted by JP. The chancellor did not greet him with a handshake.

JP takes his routine guest seat on the backside of the conference table. It is a standing joke among the other campus presidents that no one dare sit in the end chair that faces the window. That position is exclusively reserved for the chancellor because he likes to daydream out the south window whenever he becomes bored during a meeting.

As he walks across the room from his desk to the conference table, the chancellor throws a large report-like document across the table toward JP. It hits the table with a loud thud and slides like a hockey puck the full length of the table toward JP.

JP senses the nonverbal animosity and the chancellor's hostile decorum. The awkward silence is quickly broken by the chancellor.

"Do you see that report, JP?"

Without giving him time to respond, the chancellor continues. "Turn to page five and read the conclusions. I want you to read aloud so I can hear you verbalize these charges."

Shocked and dismayed by this crude proceeding, JP opens the document to page three and politely complies with the request.

> It is therefore concluded that President O'Bryan deliberately used state-appropriated funds to pay for construction costs that were legislatively mandated to be paid by donations. Furthermore, President O'Bryan coerced his business staff to alter the accounting ledger. It is clear

that his premeditated leadership efforts sought to hide this misappropriation of state funds. Moreover, during this past year, President O'Bryan issued two individual construction contracts that exceeded $25,000 without following the legislatively mandated state bid process. It is evident that these illegal actions were maliciously orchestrated by the president because he wanted to falsify the records and ensure the total construction cost for the new rec center would remain under the authorized budget as directed by the board and required by state law. Therefore, be it resolved that President O'Bryan has willfully attempted to deceive the chancellor and the board and in the process committed a felony by stealing more than $50,000 from state appropriations.

JP looks across the table at the chancellor. The bald old man is chewing gum and grinning from ear to ear. Leaning forward across the table, he assertively extends his right arm, forms a fist with his hand above his head, and hits the conference table so hard that JP's notebook bounces.

"Mr. President, I expect your resignation on my desk by three o'clock this afternoon. Do I make myself clear?"

JP remains calm. He immediately scans the report. There is no signature or signature block. The last ten or twelve pages seem to be attachments that are typed transcripts from interviews. All the names and dates are blacked out. Repulsed and defensive, he tries to object.

"Where did you get this report? Where in the world did you come up with these crazy ideas? They are false. My God, they are pure lies!"

The chancellor interrupts and reasserts control. "Never mind how I obtained this report. My attorney and staff have been working on this research for months. We have caught you red-handed!"

JP counters, "But these are false charges. I did not do these things. You want me to resign for something I did not do. And if I resign, by default, it will look like I am admitting guilt."

The chancellor's temper explodes as the volume of his voice escalates. "I said three o'clock and not a minute later. Take that damn tablet of yours and go write your resignation. All I need is a single sentence, handwritten! Do you understand?"

With his face beaming red and the veins on his forehead visibly throbbing, the chancellor looks like a man ready to stroke out.

"Chancellor, I will not write a resignation without talking with my wife. I am not guilty of these charges. I need time to drive home and talk with Jenn. I am willing to call you in the morning, but that is the best I can do."

"God damn you, JP. You are such an arrogant son of a b———. You can't even follow a simple directive! I want that resignation, and I want it today! If you don't cooperate, I will charge you with insubordination!"

Stunned and disheartened, JP struggles to think clearly while remaining respectful. "Sir, I understand your directive, but I cannot comply. I insist that you give me time to talk with my wife."

Pushing back from the conference table, the chancellor stands and leans across the table as part of his nonverbal bullying technique.

"God damn it, get the hell out of my office. I expect your resignation call first thing in the morning, promptly at eight o'clock, and if I do not hear from you by eight thirty, I plan to hold a press conference tomorrow and release this report to the media. The new board chairman, Larry Allen, fully supports my decision. Hell, you are nothing but a dead man walking. Trust me, your reputation will be totally destroyed if you don't play ball by my rules. You will never work again at any university after the newspapers, social media, and Internet get done with you. Shit, you won't be even able to get a janitor's job. Now get out of here right now. I don't ever want to see your insubordinate ass again!"

JP leaves the capitol building. For a few minutes on the elevator, he contemplates stopping at the governor's office to ask for help. Then he thinks about the lieutenant governor and the wonderful friendship they have developed since collaborating on the rural leadership grant.

After a rapid assessment of the situation, he concludes that it is, most likely, impossible to prevail over the chancellor's political clout and long-standing friendship with the governor. As he walks across the south parking lot to his car, his hands tremble as he hits the speed dial on his cell phone.

After five rings, the call rolls into voice messaging.

"Hey, Jenn, I just finished my meeting with the chancellor. It was really bad, just horrible beyond description. He is demanding my immediate resignation. I refused to resign, and I am in the car on the way home. Give me a call when you have the chance. Truly, today is a dark day. Love you!"

31

Crushed by the Perfect Storm

A leader should never start a war out of wrath.

—Sun Tzu, fourth century BC

August 1, 2016
Highway 81, south of Springview, Nebraska

It is a heartbreaking drive for JP. After his devastating meeting with the chancellor, he has immediately started his return trip because he wants to talk with his wife. Despite his mental anguish, he is thinking clearly and trying to find a solution to this terrible ordeal. About twenty miles out of Lincoln as he approaches Seward, JP calls one of his trusted friends, Coach Singleton.

"Hello, Jess, this is JP O'Bryan. Did I catch you at a bad time? Do you have a few minutes to visit?"

Coach Singleton is prepared to dodge this conversation. He elects to remain cool and aloof.

"Well, hello, Mr. President. How are you? Oh sure, I have a few minutes, but then I must run downtown. What is on your mind today?"

JP believes he is talking to a trusted friend and confidant. He also knows that Jess has deep roots in the community, strong connections with the chancellor, and indirect influence with the governor. In some ways, talking to Jess reminds JP of the way it used to be when he talked with his dad. JP is not ready to beg, but he is ready to ask for a helping hand.

"Hey coach, I am on the cell phone traveling between Lincoln and home. I just got hit by a bolt of lightning. I drove into Lincoln early this morning at the request of the chancellor. When I met with him, he accused me of many false charges regarding the construction of our new rec center. About an hour ago, he demanded my immediate resignation."

JP pauses. For the first time, he feels the despair of this situation, and the emotion creeps into his throat. Trying to say more, he finds himself unable to talk. After several long seconds of silence, JP struggles to continue.

"Jess, I consider you a true friend. I really need your help."

The old man's squeaky voice cracks as he begins to talk. He is extremely nervous and carefully selects his words like a man slowly walking across the circus high wire.

"Did you resign?"

"No, Jess, I did not! I will not admit guilt for something I did not do."

Sensing a major problem brewing, Jess coyly denies his knowledge of the situation.

"I don't know anything about this issue. But it sounds very political to me, and I am not willing to get involved. The way I see it, this is between you, the chancellor, and the board."

JP is stunned. Before calling, he was convinced Jess would intervene and try to help.

"Coach, you always said to let you know if I ever needed any help. Well, today, I am asking you to speak on my behalf. I sincerely need your help."

Once again, JP is forced to stop talking because the lump in his throat is now about the size of a football.

Jess searches for some weasel words.

"Look, JP, maybe it is time for you and Jenn to seriously think about moving on. Why don't you take this opportunity to go find another job at a different university?" Jess hesitates. "You know, I just looked at the clock, and it is getting late. JP, I have to run or I am going to miss my appointment. Maybe you should talk with the board chairman, Larry Allen, and see what he has to say."

JP is desperate. He is now ready to beg, but before he can say another word, the phone connection goes dead. He is not sure if Jess hung up or if he hit a dead zone on the highway causing his cell connection to be lost.

Ten miles down the highway, JP's cell rings, and the caller ID flashes his wife's name.

"Hey, baby, thanks so much for returning my call. Did you get my message? Are you okay?"

Jenn is crying. In-between sobs, she says, "Honey, I am so sorry. I knew something was wrong even before you called."

"My gosh, how did you know, Jenn? You must have ESP going."

"Well, my dear PEO sister, Emmy, called this afternoon and told me that Craig Jacobson's radio talk show highlighted rumors from Lincoln, Nebraska that indicate you are being fired. While they were live on the air, Craig called the board chair's office, but Larry Allen was traveling and unavailable for comment."

"Jenn, this is an unbelievable turn of events. It seems like a living nightmare. How can this be happening? Just forty-five days ago, I received a great performance evaluation and a contract extension. Now I feel like that ship caught by the perfect storm."

"I don't know, honey. Right now all I want is for you to get home safely. Concentrate on your driving and be safe. I just want to hold you in my arms when you get here."

"Jenn, I will be fine. Hey, you know how much I think of our friend, Jess?"

"Of course, in many ways he is a trusted sounding board, and he reminds you of your dad!"

"Yes, well, while I was waiting for your return call, I decided to talk with Jess and ask him to intercede. I would have bet the family farm on his willingness to pitch in and help, but instead, he gave me the brush-off and said he did not want to be involved with the politics."

"What is that clicking sound on the line?"

"Jenn, I have another call coming in. I will let it go into voice messaging, and I will catch up with it after we finish talking."

Between Seward and Columbus, JP talks nonstop as he explains the sordid details of his meeting with the chancellor. Jenn's tears slowly turn to anger, and she is ready for a fight. Finally, JP asks, "What do you think? Should I call in the morning and resign?"

"Hell no! You did not do anything wrong. JP O'Bryan, when you get here, we are going to jump on the telephone and find you a lawyer. This is not right! You have to fight this blackmail."

"Okay, Jenn, I know you are right. Needless to say, your Taurus temper is showing. I am just outside of Columbus so I plan to stop at McDonald's for the restroom and a cup of coffee. See you in a couple of hours, sweetheart!"

JP pulls into the parking lot. Before going inside, he hits the message icon on his cell to listen to his voice mail.

"Dr. O'Bryan, this is Jolee McBride from the *Springview Press*. I just finished reading an interesting report that accuses you of fraud and theft. It appears that you will be facing felony charges, and I want to ask you some questions. So, give me a call, and I look forward to our visit. If you want your point of view included in this story, I need to hear from you before six o'clock tonight. Trust me, we are going to press this evening, and you will be our headline story in tomorrow's paper. So give me a call."

While JP agonizes and makes the long drive home, Chancellor Granger and Peter Sedworth are having a drink at Lincoln's most popular after-hours bar, Patty's Shamrock. Seated in the last booth at the back of the pub, the two men are enjoying happy hour and their second round of drinks.

"Damn it, Peter! I wish you could have been there to enjoy the show. The old army colonel turned white as fresh snow while I was hollering in his face. Truth be known, I bet he shit his pants! Hell, he can take that Bronze Star of his and flush it down the toilet because his ass belongs to me!"

The chancellor grabs another handful of pretzels and chugs his beer.

"Maybe so, chancellor, but I have to tell you that I am worried. This did not go like we planned. The whole strategy was based upon the element of surprise and the assumption that you would scare him into an immediate resignation. What the hell are we going to do if he does not call in the morning?"

"Relax, Peter, my man! Don't get your panties in a wad! Everything is under control! Trust me, he's a wimp and he won't fight. Hey, let's order another round, how about it?"

One hundred miles west of Springview, Larry Allen is driving home after a bank meeting in Broken Bow. He initiates a call on his car phone.

"Hello, governor, this is Larry."

"Yes, Larry, what's up? You caught me at a bad time. I am trying to squeeze into this damn tuxedo, and the pants won't button. Hell, I think these trousers shrunk when I sent them to the cleaners."

"Sir, I am sorry to bother you, but we have a real problem on our hands. Can you give me five minutes to explain?"

"Well, hell, I am already going to be late for the fundraising dinner. Go ahead, what's another five minutes? But be brief man."

"Governor, the chancellor had a meeting with Dr. O'Bryan today and tried to shock him into an immediate resignation. Well, it did not work. Peter Sedworth had written a report that contained a bunch of trumped-up charges. I specifically stipulated that no signatures would be on the report, because if we got the resignation, I planned to have the report destroyed. Anyway, O'Bryan left without resigning. Now, the chancellor expects him to call in the morning with his resignation, but somehow there has been an unfortunate leak, and the *Springview Press* received a backdoor copy of our report. The news editor, Jolee McBride, is chasing me for a statement. She plans to make this report headline news in the morning. Once this story hits the AP news line, it will go viral."

The governor is enraged. "God damn it, Larry. We talked about this four or five months ago. Shit, I thought you put this crazy idea to bed. Are you guys all running around with shit for brains? Now we are going to look like fools!"

"I am sorry, sir. What do you want me to do?"

"Oh hell, yes. Now you want me to clean up your mess. Here I am trying to raise money for reelection, and I have two dumb turds running around playing personnel games and creating scandals within my administration."

The governor stops briefly and mutters some profanity as he inhales and buttons his trousers. He immediately continues.

"For Christ's sake, Larry, you better pray that O'Bryan calls in the morning with his resignation. If he doesn't, I can tell you that the old bald chancellor has his fat tit in a huge ringer."

JP is about thirty miles from home when his cell phone rings. He assumes it is Jenn trying to check on him. However, the caller ID displays a number from the university.

"Good evening, this is Dr. O'Bryan. Can I help you?"

"Mr. President, this is Bo Polinski. Can you spare a few minutes so I can share a concern?"

Woodrow "Bo" Polinski is a tenured, full professor with a PhD in agricultural economics. With more than twenty years of service at the university, he functions as an opinion leader both on and off campus. Bo also serves as the current president of the Springview Public School Board and is an elder in the Methodist Church. JP considers him a friend, trusted colleague, and one of his valued spotters.

"Of course, Bo. What is on your mind?"

"Well, this afternoon, our campus faculty started receiving an avalanche of emails that are filled with derogatory comments about you. Most of the messages seem to emanate from Professor Nodland and Lynda Stevenson. They are suggesting that you are a crook and a thief and that you were fired today."

JP sinks further into the depths of despair. "Bo, I hope you know that all these false charges are a figment of the chancellor's imagination. I have no idea how all this mess got started."

Dr. Polinski continues. "Have you ever met our new high school track coach? The young, good-looking guy who sometimes runs around with Diana Dawson? Anyway, many people believe he is the mystery man behind that nasty say-anything blog. Under the cover of anonymity, people are going crazy saying the most horrible things about you and your wife. I have been reading that crap all afternoon, and I am worried about your safety. This blog is like some strange form of mob violence that is transmitted effortlessly across a world made flat by the Internet. The crowd psychology on this blog seems to sweep through the masses and override a person's good manners. The frenzy causes blurred judgment and undiscriminating, cruel impulses. I am embarrassed to think these people live in my hometown!"

"Bo, I have used my cell to periodically check office email. In the past two hours, I have received more than a dozen emails demanding my immediate resignation. One alumni member sent an incredibly malicious message and said I need to get out of town if I know what is good for me."

"Well, there is more, sir, if you have a few additional minutes?"

"Yes, Bo, I am listening."

"This afternoon, Ann Spencer and Carol Nodland started an email petition among the faculty demanding an emergency, special meeting of the faculty senate. They are calling for a no-confidence vote against you. I don't think they will be able to get a 51 percent majority vote, but they are really stirring the pot, and I noticed that Jolee McBride is copied on all their messages so you can be sure the newspaper has all this information."

"Bo, this firestorm is moving like a raging, out-of-control, wind-driven prairie fire. I hope you and your colleagues will be willing to help me."

As the conversation closes, JP thanks Bo for his kind words and thoughtful update.

JP begins to ponder this crucible of humiliation. After several minutes of haunting silence, he decides to turn on the radio. By coincidence, "If You're Going through Hell," Rodney Atkins' great hit, is playing:

> Well you know those times when you feel like
> There's a sign there on your back that says
> I don't mind if you kick me, seems like everybody has,
> Things go from bad to worse
> You think it can't get worse than that
> And then they do.
> If you're goin' through hell keep on going
> Don't slow down if you're scared don't show it
> You might get out before the devil even knows you're there.

32

Guilty until Proven Innocent

> Many tragic events and disasters stand as a powerful
> reminder that it can be terribly dangerous, even
> perilous, to assume that because people hold positions
> of responsibility they are therefore acting responsibly.
>
> —David McCullough, *The Great Bridge*, 2012 Edition

October 14, 2016
Lincoln Nebraska

It is a beautiful Friday morning. The blue sky frames the sun
while colorful autumn leaves rustle in a gentle breeze. The entire
city of Lincoln braces for Saturday's home game and the influx of
eighty-five thousand wild-and-crazy Big Red football fans. Two
well-dressed men sit in the governor's conference room. They
are nervous. Both of them fear the wrath of God is about to
descend upon them. Larry Allen is so tense that he is pinching
buttonholes in the leather seat cover on his chair.

Trying to be lighthearted, the governor's chief of staff,
Washington "Chip" Peterson, attempts to crack a joke. His feeble

effort to be humorous completely bombs. Larry smiles but does not respond with any laughter.

Mr. Chip Peterson has worked for the governor for the past three years. He replaced Buzz Granger after the governor pushed Buzz out the door and up the elevator into the chancellor's job. Chip is a talker who thrives on the government's grapevine of gossip. He loves to eat and drink and tell off-color jokes whenever he feels safe to expose his racial and ethnic prejudices. More than one hundred pounds overweight, his knees can no longer support his weight so he walks with an exquisite, vintage walnut cane that showcases a genuine polished horn handle. With piercing blue eyes and a silver gray mustache, his intense gaze intimidates the bravest soul. Around the hallways of the capitol building, everyone refers to him as the governor's hatchet man.

About fifteen minutes past their scheduled appointment, the governor enters the room, takes a seat, and glares at his two subordinates. His facial clues signal a man too angry to speak. The silence continues for a couple of minutes. But to Larry and Chip, it seems like an eternity.

Diverting his gaze toward the south window, the governor barks, "Gentlemen, we have a king-size mess on our hands. I have a chancellor who seems to have lost his mind. First, he totally ignores my guidance and blatantly goes after O'Bryan just a few weeks after giving the man an excellent evaluation and contract extension. O'Bryan calls his bluff, hires an attorney, and challenges these damn trumped-up charges.

"Next, we dispatch a highway patrolman on a Sunday afternoon to drive two hundred miles one way in order to hand deliver a written directive that prevents O'Bryan from entering any building on campus including his office."

The governor's tone of voice becomes sarcastic.

"You can bet! That move really resonated with John Q. Public, the taxpayer who voted us into office! Then we confiscate his cell phone, computer, and all the files and papers in his office. After a team invests thousands of hours of reviewing this mountain of information, we can't find one shitty email or handwritten note that remotely looks like evidence of a smoking gun. No documentation whatsoever to substantiate this horrific cluster that was started by the chancellor! And then, like a man grasping for a straw, old Buzz goes public and calls an emergency meeting of the board's executive committee. Like a fool, he tries to convince you to fire O'Bryan for insubordination. Jesus Christ, what a damn farce! My God, we are talking about a decorated war veteran and retired army colonel who probably does not have an insubordinate bone in his body. What the hell were you thinking, Larry? God damn it, you should have refused to have that executive committee meeting. But, oh no, you all seem to have shit for brains and demonstrate a collective IQ of about 80. And to make matters worse, when the damn meeting is over, you let the chancellor go on the evening news to talk about it! Brilliant, just damn brilliant!"

Sensing the governor's escalating anger, the chief of staff tries to diplomatically enter the conversation.

"Shut up, Chip. You will speak when I ask you a question. Right now, you listen while I talk! Do you understand?"

Chip's embarrassment shows. "Yes Sir!"

"Now as I was saying, I have a chancellor who is abusing his power. He has gone past the point of no return with me. His behavior and comments are nothing but bizarre! He is acting like some wild, drunken cowboy trying to take the law into his own hands and make a public spectacle out of O'Bryan. Do you assholes ever read the paper? Do you guys watch television? Do either of you ever look at the Internet? Are you following Craig Jacobson's radio talk show? My God, we look like complete fools to the average citizen who might be following this hocus-pocus fiasco! I asked our public relations office to give me a news media summary. Since this all started seventy-five days ago, dumb-ass Granger has conducted fifty-seven press conferences, appeared on television news twenty-one times and on radio talk shows seventeen times, and has been quoted 105 times by four major newspapers in ninety-five different stories. Do you turds understand guilt by association? I am sad to say Buzz Granger is associated with me! We have been friends and hunting buddies for almost thirty years. You know I supported him when he ran for state senate. Hell, everybody knows he was my chief of staff, and most everybody with a brain knows I gave him that chancellor's job! So now, I am guilty for part of this mess because Granger is on my cabinet, and I have been associated with him for years."

With a heart full of remorse, Mr. Allen tries to apologize. "Governor, you are right, and I sincerely apologize for this terrible ordeal. I should have—"

"God damn it, Larry. I don't want to hear it! Don't sit here and whine! Don't even open your mouth unless you have a proposed solution for this nightmare!"

Both men remain silent and stare at the surface of the wooden conference table, wishing they could somehow disappear from the room like two schoolboys trying to avoid eye contact with the teacher during a math exam.

Leaving his chair, the governor walks over to the window and looks out across the south lawn of the capitol; he slowly turns and points at his chief of staff.

"Chip, next spring I want some new rose bushes planted near that outdoor bench and I want a circle of yellow mums planted around the fountain. This time next year, they should be in full bloom. Do you understand?"

"Yes, sir! We will get it done."

"Good, now Chip, I want to talk some more with Larry. Wait outside my office, and I will let you know when I am ready for you."

"You bet, Governor!"

The chief of staff is very glad to leave the room. Once the door is closed, the governor walks back to the table and sits in his favorite chair.

"Larry, you have really dropped the ball on this one. Now we have to work together and hope we can do some damage control. Since the chancellor reports to you, I am going to publicly wash my hands of all guilt and hang this mess on you. If you are half as smart as I think you are, you will let this shit roll downhill and hang as much as possible on Buzz."

Eagerly trying to cooperate, Larry replies, "Yes, sir!"

"So for now, I want you to get his attention and start controlling the chancellor's interaction with the news media. For God's sake, no more press conferences, and try to minimize the number of interviews he does with radio and television. Every time he opens his mouth, he sounds like a bumbling fool. He has become a spectacle and embarrassment to all of us in this capitol building. Any questions?"

"No sir, I completely understand, and I will do my very best."

"That's all for now, Larry. Send Chip back in as you leave."

The chief enters the room with a humble decorum.

"Sit down, Mr. Chief of Staff. You better get ready to take some notes because I am only going to say this once."

"Yes, sir. I am ready whenever you want to begin."

Pacing like a caged lion, the governor begins to slowly walk around the conference table. He likes to think and walk at the same time.

"Chief, between you and me, from this day forward, O'Bryan is guilty until he proves himself innocent. Am I clear?

"Yes, sir, crystal clear."

"When you leave here, I want you to walk directly to the attorney general's office and privately talk with Parker. There will be no emails and no written correspondence regarding my directive. You will do this with limited access to others and only share this information by word of mouth! Work with Parker. I know he hates Buzz, but this time we have to save the old fart in order to protect my reputation. Got it?"

"Yes sir, crystal!"

"Tell the attorney general that he must handpick the administrative judge from his staff who will preside over the O'Bryan hearing. It has to be someone he explicitly trusts. Tell him regardless of the evidence; there is only one verdict that I will accept!"

The governor stops pacing. With fire in his eyes, he looks directly into Chip's blue eyes and says, "O'Bryan must be found guilty. The chancellor must win this hearing!"

"That's easy, sir. I am sure we have many loyal, dedicated lawyers on the AG staff who will be pleased to rule in favor of our great state. I did a quick check, and nationally about 90 percent of these personnel hearings go in favor of the state."

"Remember this kangaroo court is going to be open to the news media, so our handpicked judge must play the role and pretend to be impartial."

"Yes, sir, we can make this happen. Anything else?"

"Yes, one more thought. Talk with Parker and see if he can put the pinch on this lawyer who is defending O'Bryan. He is from Grand Island, and I don't know anything about him. Try to find a way to encourage him to play ball with us, if you know what I mean."

"Absolutely, sir!"

"That's all for now, Chip. But, I am placing a marker on the table that I want you to remember."

"Yes, what is it?"

"When this malicious drama is over, you and I are going to clean house upstairs in the chancellor's office. I want the scalp of every staff member who was involved with the creation of this ridiculous, fraudulent report. And I personally want to fire the asshole who leaked the report to that goddamn *Springview Press*."

The governor returns to his private office. With the door closed, he hits the speed dial for his best friend and mentor. After the phone rings six times, a frail, ninety-two-year-old male voice answers. "Well, hello, Governor. I have been expecting your call.

How the hell are you doing in the midst of this circus of news stories? By the way, you need to tell the chancellor that his bald head creates quite a glare on my big screen television!"

Both men chuckle.

"Ace, I need some advice. I am really torn. Old Buzz and I go way back. My God, I could not count the number of bottles of whiskey we have drunk together. And yet, I am so damn mad at him, I could kick his ass down O Street in front of a hometown football crowd lining both sides of the sidewalk and cheering me on!"

"Yes, I know what you mean. He has been a good soldier for you and a loyal voice for our party, but in the game of chess, every good king knows that knights are expendable."

"I know you are right, Ace, but damn, he is a good friend!"

"Look, governor, I once had a golden retriever who was the love of my life. We hunted together all the time. She was a great field dog and loyal companion. Every night she sat next to my chair, wagged her tail, and guarded this house with her life. Unfortunately, one day she came back from her morning run and started to act sick. It did not take me long to realize that she had rabies. Her temperament completely changed, and I had to put her down."

"I know where you are going with this story, Ace."

"Governor, you have a chancellor who needs to be put down. He has become totally bizarre. If you don't get rid of him, he might bite you when you least expect it!"

"Ace, I know you are right! Thanks for taking the time to listen to me blow steam. It is always good to hear your voice. Take care, my friend."

That evening, the governor watches the evening news. To his chagrin, the chancellor is the lead story. He announces that the state auditor is working directly with his staff and they have launched a review of all O'Bryan's travel expenses."

The governor mutters to himself, "Well, shit, we have started another witch hunt!"

The next day is Saturday. Before departing for the football game, the governor calls his chief of staff.

"Chip, did you see last night's news?"

"Yes, I did. This situation just seems to go from bad to worse. Old Buzz is acting like a possessed man. The more he rants, the wackier he looks."

"Yes, Chip, I agree completely. Here is the deal. When we get this mess resolved, you are going to be my hatchet man! I want the chancellor to immediately announce his plans to retire. I want you and Larry to divert the public's attention toward some big-ass national search for a new chancellor, and I want the new chancellor in office by next June. Do you have any questions?"

"No, this makes perfect sense."

"One more thing. Between now and Buzz's departure, I do not want to see him in my office. You handle all his questions and keep him out of my hair. Got it?"

"Crystal clear, sir!"

PART VI

Shattered Dreams

So much for your promises,
they died the day you let me go.
Caught up in a web of lies,
but it was just too late to know.
I thought it was you,
who would stand by my side.
And now you've given me, given me,
nothing but shattered dreams, shattered dreams;
Feel like I could run away, run away
from this empty heart.

—Songwriter: Clark Datchler
Sung by Johnny Hates Jazz, Worldwide Hit in 1988

33

The Legend of White Fang

But the tigers come at night
With their voices soft as thunder.
As they tear your hope apart,
As they turn your dream to shame.

—Les Miserables

November 25, 2016
Baton Rouge, Louisiana

It is the day after Thanksgiving. On this special day, Samuel basks in the warm friendship of his old mentor and college advisor. Dr. Will Moreland is celebrating his ninetieth birthday, and Samuel has just completed a two-day trip by car in order to be part of this memorable party.

After a busy afternoon filled with cake, balloons, kisses, and hugs, Dr. Moreland invites Samuel to his modest, one-bedroom apartment for a quiet evening, dinner, and a glass of brandy. Like stepping back in time, Samuel immediately renews an enduring link of friendship with his dear friend. Their bond is anchored by a deep sense of trust. After an hour of conversation, it feels like time has stood still. Tonight, for a few fleeting hours, Samuel feels like a young college student whose advisor is carefully listening to all his problems and private worries. Whenever they are together, Dr. Moreland's calm decorum is always a touchstone that emanates security.

While they enjoy two pieces of leftover birthday cake, Samuel asks Dr. Moreland to read Coach Moore's lost letter. After Dr. Moreland finished reading, Samuel immediately gives him the confidential letter he wrote almost twenty-one years ago. The sealed envelope still has Dr. Moreland's university office address on it. Both men sit quietly. The silence lingers for several minutes, broken only by the elegant ticktock rhythm of Dr. Moreland's seven-foot-tall antique grandfather clock. Samuel makes no attempt to explain why he kept Dr. Moreland's letter sealed in the safety deposit box for almost three decades. Really, no explanation is needed. The old man's intuition already knows the reason.

Like a worried man meandering in the confessional, Samuel starts talking in a nervous, high-pitched voice. He attempts to minimize or whitewash more than a quarter century of moral failings. Most of his mistakes were caused by fear, insecurity, and the human frailty that encourages one to walk the path of least resistance. His conversation jumps from topic to topic while he rationalizes his actions, defends his decisions, and avoids eye contact with his best friend.

Dr. Moreland listens carefully without making any judgmental comments. Slowly, incrementally, Samuel reveals a litany of facts, events, and personal regrets that had been held in the deep recesses of his long-term memory. By 8:00 p.m., Samuel is baring his soul and openly explaining his deepest laments. For the first time, he admits his lack of courage during the unfair character assassination of President JP O'Bryan.

Once he breaks through this self-imposed wall of silence that has limited his ability to talk about the malicious ways of his campus, he races through an exposé of evil deeds that recounted how a handful of mean-spirited faculty, guided by low instincts, unfairly ruined countless careers. Samuel briefly talks about Dr. Sue Barton, Vice President Kelley, and the reign of terror fostered by the notorious Four Horsemen. He also recounts some of the second order implications from these malicious deeds. At least one innocent person was pushed, unfortunately, into the depths of despair that culminated with suicide.

Dr. Moreland reflectively listens without any editorial criticisms or interruptions. He waited, as they say back in Carbondale, for Samuel to clear his conscience and "dump the whole load of hay."

As an old bachelor, Dr. Moreland treats Samuel like the son he never had. Always a consummate teacher and talented storyteller, he wants to help Samuel sort his thoughts and discover a sense of meaning from the turmoil and chaos that he has experienced. After hearing the gory details regarding President O'Bryan's public stoning, Dr. Moreland decides to give Samuel a very special gift—a story that his mother's family has shared with each other for many generations.

Dr. Moreland refills their brandy goblets. His decorum quickly becomes intense, like a man preparing to pray Psalm 51, the Miserere. The old man begins.

"Samuel, please listen carefully as I tell you a tale that I learned from my grandmother. It is the story of a great dog with a beautiful spirit and brave heart. For many generations, my family has shared the legend of White Fang with the hope that it will help the listener synchronize their moral compass. Please consider this story a sacred gift. You are the first person that I have ever told. I believe my ancestors will be pleased!"

Getting comfortable, Dr. Moreland places his two feet on the footstool in front of his easy chair. As he adjusts his position, both brown slippers fall to the floor. After clearing his throat, he begins the century-old tale.

"There was a time in the late 1890s when my great-grandfather, Black Hawk, tried to eke a living as a resident within the small town of Sundance, Wyoming. He was a popular medicine man in his Lakota tribe, but he separated from his people when they moved onto the reservation. At first, he lived as a hermit in the Black Hills. Eventually, his aging bones forced him to move into town where he lived in a makeshift lean-to behind the blacksmith's stable. He survived by making and selling small cloth rugs and sleeping mats. Elderly, with more than sixty winters behind him, he carried two battle scars on his face. As a young man in his prime of life, he had fought against General Custer in the summer of 1876 during the Battle of the Greasy Grass, now known in history as the Battle of the Little Big Horn.

"One day, a thin but beautiful, all-white stray dog appeared in Sundance. For several weeks, he was chased, cussed, and threatened. The kids threw rocks at him, and the men tried to kick him whenever they could get close enough to make contact. Virtually skin and bone from starvation, this dog eventually sought safety by sleeping behind the woodpile near Black Hawk's shack. Soon, the dog befriended Black Hawk, and they became inseparable companions. Black Hawk named him White Fang because he often displayed his pearly teeth as he growled at passing strangers.

"Like most dogs, White Fang could sense a person's character. Every day, numerous people walked past White Fang as Black Hawk sat on a wooden bench across the street from the new post office. White Fang would wag his tail if he liked the person, or he would utter a low-pitched, deep-throated growl if he questioned the person's intent. A few of the ladies in town would sometimes bring White Fang table scraps, and whenever the opportunity developed, he would truly enjoy chewing on an old steak bone. Occasionally, if someone tried to give Black Hawk trouble, White Fang would defend his master with fierce barks, growls, and a show of his massive white teeth.

"One day, a young cowboy named Buck rode into town. They called him "Snake" because of his love for gambling with dice. I guess he had unusually bad luck and rolled many snake eyes with the dice. It was the month of October, the moon of changing seasons. His pockets were full of money because he had been punching cows and branding calves for six months in the North Dakota Badlands.

"It did not take long for a pattern to develop. After a few days, old Snake became a regular fixture in the saloon. Each afternoon, when he was full of whiskey, he bragged about his manly prowess and his hate for Indians. Frequently, he stood in the middle of the street and mocked Black Hawk while he sat on his work bench making rugs. Late one windy afternoon, Snake's hollering echoed so loudly that White Fang responded with defensive growls and barks. Drunk and having difficulty maintaining his balance, the cowboy violently screamed and cursed the dog. The situation could have easily escalated, but old Snake had enough sense to back down and walk away. However, from that point on, Cowboy Buck truly hated that dog, and I think the feeling was mutual from White Fang's perspective.

"It was early November, the moon of falling leaves, when a fancy lady with a big hat and a pretty dress arrived on the train. She was pushy and demanding and gave the depot agent a difficult time. She became furious when the agent told her she would have to walk to the hotel. She did not want to get mud or dirt on her pretty shoes.

"As she passed Black Hawk's bench, she made several ugly racial remarks about Indian scum running loose in the streets. White Fang sensed her personality and growled. She tried to kick him, and he started to bark. Once he showed his white teeth, the lady screamed and became outraged. She told everyone that this trashy dog had tried to bite her, and since he was such a mangy critter, he probably had rabies.

"In the middle of the lady's hysteria, Mr. Snake exploded like a burning short fuse hitting a stick of dynamite. Cowboy Buck had been looking for a good reason to get rid of this dog. He told everyone this dirty mongrel had to go because he was dangerous and bad for the town. Most likely, he would start biting the town's children any day. Fueled by an afternoon of beer spiked with whiskey, old Snake managed to rant, carry on, and quickly assemble a crowd of curious onlookers. His boasting, bravado, and false accusations against White Fang escalated into a frenzied pitch. Soon, Main Street was lined with community members who wondered about this unusual ruckus.

"Now in a rage with anger and booze, Cowboy Buck mounted his horse, rode down the street, and stopped in front of Black Hawk's work bench. With a masterful toss of his rope, he lassoed the old white dog while White Fang stood guard trying to protect Black Hawk.

"Once the rope passed around the dog's neck, Snake turned his horse and galloped up and down the street carefully aiming for every mud hole he could find. The crowd roared and cheered as the helpless dog passed in front of them. Not one person tried to intervene. No one cared as old Black Hawk frantically begged to save his dog.

"After several trips through the street, Cowboy Buck stopped at the old cottonwood tree in front of the bank. He threw his rope over the first limb and pulled the dog into the air. Death came quickly for White Fang. He already was badly mangled after being dragged for so long. Once the dog stopped moving, old Snake secured the rope to the base of the tree and proudly left White Fang hanging about five feet off the ground like a trophy kill on display.

"That evening, the mayor called a special meeting of the town council. Countless false rumors were circulating about that mangy old dog. Truly, Mr. Snake had done a good thing, and he deserved some kind of special recognition. So, in order to show their appreciation, the council voted unanimously to give Cowboy Buck a twenty-five-dollar cash reward because of his meritorious service and his initiative of ridding the town of that nasty stray dog that probably had rabies.

"The next day, the morning sun found White Fang still hanging on the cottonwood tree. Snake felt rich, and he used his cash to buy more beer and whiskey while he gambled. Then at about 3:00 p.m., feeling like the town hero, Cowboy Buck started another ruckus and discharged his pistol in the air. And as the crowd lined Main Street, he took his rope from the tree, mounted his horse, tied the rope to his saddle, and dragged the dead dog up and down the muddy street. Everyone cheered and enjoyed this commemorative event. They wanted to humor their new hero, so the roar of the crowd was louder than the previous day.

"The rain from the previous night had left the street very muddy. After several trips past the post office, it was impossible to see the dog's original white hair. White Fang quickly became a clump of mud-covered flesh.

"Now, human nature is sometimes hard to understand. Every day, at about 3:00 p.m., for the next two weeks, Cowboy Buck drank his whiskey and rode his horse through the streets dragging the remains of White Fang through the mud and dirt.

"Each day, the assembled crowd became smaller and smaller; Snake was becoming an embarrassment, but no one had the courage to speak up. Finally, only a few drinking buddies cheered Snake as he performed this morbid ritual.

"Behind closed doors, people talked about the cowboy's very bizarre behavior. But publicly, no one would say a word against the town's hero. After all, he had been commended by the mayor and city fathers.

"One night, Black Hawk could no longer bear the sight of his beloved dog hanging in the cottonwood tree. The flies and crows had destroyed most of the body pieces that still remained. Black Hawk wanted to bury his old friend. So, at about midnight, he quietly approached the tree and prepared to cut the rope. Someone across the street at the saloon alerted Cowboy Buck. He burst outside, shouted several cuss words, and told Black Hawk to leave that mangy mutt alone. Old Snake told Black Hawk that he was nothing but the scum of the earth. He boldly ordered Black Hawk to low-crawl back to his hut. Deeply angered, Black Hawk jumped toward the tree and quickly cut the rope that held White Fang in the air.

"A shot rang out, and Black Hawk fell to the ground. Cowboy Buck's bullet hit his left leg, just below the knee. From that day forward, Black Hawk never regained the full strength or movement of that leg. He walked with a distinct limp until he died.

"The next day, Cowboy Buck was on his horse dragging poor old White Fang through the streets. A well-dressed stranger had just arrived on the afternoon train. He stood and watched this strange scene. The mayor happened to walk past the stranger, and the visitor asked, 'Why is that crazy cowboy dragging an old muddy gunny sack through the street?' At that moment, through the fresh eyes of a stranger, the mayor realized that the remains of White Fang could no longer be recognized as a dog. The mud had completely covered the dog's body, and the fragmented remains looked more like a gunny sack than a dog.

"That night, the mayor had another special, closed-door meeting with the city council. They all agreed that Cowboy Buck had to go, but they were unsure how to proceed since they had previously declared him a great hero. Finally, each member of the council personally donated five dollars in cash and immediately created an incentive fund.

"The sheriff was given the task to deliver the money and the message. Late that same night, two men were seen riding through the shadows of main street, headed south toward Newcastle. The sheriff was physically escorting old Snake out of town. Early the next morning, the sheriff returned by himself.

"Legend has it Cowboy Buck continued his wild and bizarre actions. Eventually he made his way into Colorado where he managed to kill a man during a barroom fight. Ironically, they sentenced him to death and hung him in an old cottonwood tree."

Dr. Moreland pauses. He becomes completely silent. With his head reverently bowed, he mutters a brief prayer in memory of his grandmother.

Samuel sits in his chair with a huge lump in his throat. The story touches his heart and rekindles some long-forgotten memories dating back to his childhood days on a boat dock in Tortola.

After a few minutes of comfortable silence, Dr. Moreland said, "Samuel, this is a true story passed to me by my mother's ancestors. I ask you to ponder the meaning within this story. This tale harbors some important secrets about life, especially for someone trying to do the right thing when they are surrounded by varying degrees of social injustice. There are three levels of human nature that you should consider.

"First, think about the actions of Cowboy Buck and the townsfolk who stood by and watched. Most of the community cheered his bizarre behavior. There is much to learn about human interaction and individual conduct in the midst of a frenzied crowd. Every time a large group assembles, you can be sure the good, the bad, and the ugly are present. I still marvel how some people who call themselves devout Christians continue to enjoy an old-fashioned, public bloodletting. Our society still nurtures cruel byzantine desires, like the Roman crowds cheering when the lions devoured those innocent souls in the great amphitheaters.

"Second, think about centuries of time filled with people like Mr. Snake and the challenge many good people like you face when it is time to step up to the plate and do the right thing. I am amazed how a few people can motivate a crowd to batter an innocent person of prominence with an avalanche of conniving false accusations. They act like a frenzied mob pounding a tottering fence until it falls to the ground and lies in total destruction. When we know someone like White Fang is falsely accused or wrongfully slandered, we have three options: say nothing as we safely watch, join the contagious fun, or stand up and set the record straight. It takes courage to intervene; it takes moral conviction to step in front of actions that are prompted by the devil. Like that old song says, the tigers always come out at night. It is risky to oppose any kind of evil. You must be willing to leave the comfortable ranks of the silent majority when you face the wrath of an angry tiger or a fierce dragon.

"Finally, think about the spiritual meaning behind this story. Each person walks a path that requires them to interact with mean-spirited, unscrupulous people. Don't let the tigers tear your hope apart. During our precious life, we have a purpose or mission that must be performed, and somehow, we are invited each day to advance God's plan. You, my friend, are on this journey, and I trust you will find the solution to your present worries within the context of this old story."

Samuel feels overcome with emotion. His mind is clouded, and he feels like the ship watchman standing on the bow of a fogbound steamer, striving to reach a safe harbor and carefully listening for sounds while straining to see oncoming ships that are hidden and wrapped within the dense mist. Raising his glass, he swallows the last of his brandy with a single gulp and says, "What do you think I should do?"

Dr. Moreland shakes his head and shrugs his shoulders in a noncommittal manner. "Ultimately, you must select the path to walk. It would not be proper for me to make that decision for you."

Throwing his hands in the air like the situation is hopeless, Samuel says, "But, after all these years of silent surrender, I doubt that anything can be done to make our campus a better place. These evil people have been in control for so long!"

Samuel pauses, and then continues. "This river of dark energy runs deep. I am not sure my actions would make a difference."

Looking at the ceiling and feeling helpless, Samuel rhetorically mutters, "Where to start?"

The old man smiles at his young friend.

"You may be right, Samuel, but they say God draws with crooked lines! Our life's journey is in his hands. Many times the improbable can produce a good outcome. Sometimes, God confers benefits through tribulation and adversity. Permit me to share two quick thoughts. First, remember Thomas Jefferson's observation: one man with courage is a majority! Second, I can tell you that after ninety years of experience, I remain convinced that there is no statute of limitations on telling the truth."

Dr. Moreland's words hit Samuel like a thunderous bolt of lightning! Once again, his old mentor helps him gain clarity of thought. Decades of study, journal writing, and praying coalesces for Samuel as he starts to integrate Dr. Moreland's guidance. He quickly begins thinking about his next steps.

"Samuel, you know my life draws to a close. Like Emerson said, this is my time to be old, to take in my sail; I must trim myself to the storm of time. For me, the winds die. Soon my ship will sail toward Saint Brendan's island of light and hope. But you, my dear friend, have miles to go and important work to accomplish. Hoist your sail, face the wind no matter how harsh it might be, and find out where your story will go."

After all the years of turmoil and confusion, finally Samuel starts to discern what he needs to do when he returns to Springview. Courage boils in his veins. It is a new sensation for Samuel.

The hour is late. Both men know it is time to gracefully say good night. In Samuel's heart, this good-bye means, "Hey, see you next time." But for Dr. Moreland, the handshake and hug are his final parting. He tightly clasps Samuel's hand and nonverbally signals his desire to linger for a moment.

With an unusually deep, calm tone in his voice, he says, "Samuel, trust in the slow work of God. You are impatient to reach your goals without delay. Remember, our tears are stored in God's flask, and the law of progress requires that you experience some instability and difficulty. Keep your hope and dreams alive. I believe God's spirit is gradually forming you and leading you toward what Father Time will make of you tomorrow."

Samuel feels energized. A cascade of wonderful memories rushes through his mind as he briskly walks to his new Buick. As he approaches the car, the headlights turn on and the engine starts. Samuel reaches for the touch pad, and his fingerprints unlock the door. Before taking his seat, Samuel feels compelled to glance back toward the apartment complex. There, he sees his best friend standing in the front window. His frail physique silhouetted against the living room's mellow light. Dr. Moreland waves farewell.

Four months pass. Then the unexpected happens. Once again, the angel of death surprises Samuel! Just two days before Easter, he receives a heartbreaking phone call from an old college acquaintance.

"Hey, Samuel, this is Harold Bruner. Do you remember me? We briefly talked at Dr. Moreland's birthday party."

"Yes, Harold. I certainly remember you old chap! How are you? It is nice to hear your voice."

"Well, Samuel, I am fine, but I am calling under difficult circumstances with some very sad news. I must report that Dr. Moreland just lost his battle with bone cancer. He died peacefully in his sleep earlier this morning. Fortunately, during the past several days, the doctors did everything possible to keep him comfortable. He was living under the muddle that is induced by heavy-duty painkillers."

Harold continues to explain that while the morphine drip eased the escalating pain, it seemed to give Dr. Moreland strange delusions.

"You know, Samuel, those drugs really clouded his brain. He did not recognize anyone, not even his favorite pinochle partner,

Father Patrick, when he arrived to administer the last rites. I talked with a couple of people who looked in on him, and no one really understood what he was trying to say during those last days. He continually rambled and muttered about an old muddy dog named White Fang. His words made no sense. To the best of our knowledge, Dr. Moreland never owned a dog."

Tears cover Samuel's face. Unable to continue the conversation, he abruptly says good night to Harold.

Within the privacy of his living room, Samuel is overcome with an outburst of grief. He automatically begins to chant John Donne's 1624 Meditation XVII, like a man compelled to recite his favorite prayer during a time of urgent need.

"No man is an island, entire of itself. Every man is a piece of the continent, a part of the main. If a clod be washed away by the sea, Europe is the less."

Samuel pauses. Tears stream down his face and drip from his chin. His words are interrupted as old Maxie unexpectedly jumps into his lap. With a sad smile, Samuel gazes into Maxie's wise eyes as he finishes the ancient verse that years ago inspired him to write the last chapter within his PhD dissertation:

> Any man's death diminishes me, because I am involved in mankind, and therefore never send to know for whom the bell tolls; it tolls for thee.

34

One Hundred Days
The Rush to Injustice

Injustice never rules forever.

—Seneca 4 BC–65 AD

November 29, 2016
Sioux City, Iowa

"Goooooooood morning, Sioux City Land! You are listening to the powerful KSUX and the Craig Jacobson Hour! Each day, Monday through Friday, we roar down the mighty MO River as we come into your life and spend some quality time examining current events and topics that interest you. Today is terrific Tuesday, and I want to welcome you our listeners, to the Midwest's most provocative, no-holds-barred talk show. This is *the* show where your views can be heard and your opinion counts! Right after this brief commercial break, we will go live with today's special guest, Nebraska's Chancellor Buzz Granger!"

The technician hits the play button for the first sixty-second commercial featuring River Side Ford's holiday specials on new 2016 Trucks. As the music fades, Mr. Jacobson announces, "All right, folks, we are back, and joining us live from the great city of Lincoln, Nebraska, we have Chancellor Buzz Granger. Welcome, Mr. Chancellor! Thanks for taking time to be on the air with us today."

Buzz tries to respond, but his first words are garbled by the frog in his throat. Awkwardly, he tries to quickly clear his voice. Mr. Jacobson attempts to overcome this rough start by continuing the conversation,

"Now as I understand it, a decision has just been released this morning by the attorney general's office. The administrative judge found President JP O'Bryan guilty of misconduct and misuse of state funds while overseeing the construction of Springview's new rec center! Is this correct, Chancellor?"

"Yes, Craig, that is correct! And let me say thanks for inviting me to be with you today."

"Certainly, Chancellor. It is always our pleasure to have you on the show. Now let me ask you this question. In your opinion, what evidence sealed this guilty verdict?"

"Well, I am really not sure. Actually, you never know how the judge considers the arguments and counterarguments, but I would like to think my testimony carried a significant weight in the eyes of the judge. I mean, after all, I do supervise every president in the state, and JP O'Bryan reports to me, at least until the board takes action to get rid of him."

"Ah, yes, you mention the board's next step, and I would like to come back to that point in just a minute. But first, let's go back to my initial question with a quick follow-up. Many people followed the three days of this hearing, and some of my brave listeners have taken the time to read the hearing's entire transcript, all 1,267 typed pages. They maintain that your side never presented one shred of evidence that proved these charges. You seemed to wander from topic to topic and just throw everything but the kitchen sink at O'Bryan. I think one call-in listener said it was like watching someone throw spaghetti on the wall with the hope that a few pieces would stick. What is your response to that observation?"

"Well, Craig, I would say they missed the main points of our argument. Actually, there is no way these construction funds could have been transferred from state budget lines to donor budget lines without a conspiracy directed by the president."

"Let's hold it right there for just a moment. It is my understanding from O'Bryan's testimony that your office attorney, Peter Sedworth, personally authorized those construction contracts. So if that is true, how did your office approve those contracts without following the required state bid process?"

"You know, Craig, I am glad you asked that question, because people need to understand that I rely on my presidents to do the right thing, and I decentralize my authority in order to give them as much flexibility as possible. But let me be clear, I never gave anyone the authority to ignore the state bid process. My gosh, Craig, you know my track record in the senate, and after making state laws for almost twenty years, I am certainly not the kind of guy who is going to start breaking those laws, some of which I actually voted into existence ten or fifteen years ago when I was serving in the senate."

"I am not sure you answered my question, but in the interest of time, we must move on to the point you briefly touched upon a few minutes ago. You said something about the board getting rid of O'Bryan. Tell us, what is the next step? Now that we have the findings from the hearing, what will the board do next?"

"You know, Craig, I already asked the board once before to terminate O'Bryan. I am his direct supervisor; I am telling you the man is totally insubordinate! He repeatedly ignored my calls, and he failed to report to work back in August when I was trying to reach him. You know, I am sure if he was not so damn arrogant, we could have found a much more agreeable solution. But here we are, and I will tell you that I plan to request a special board meeting and ask the board to fire this man!"

"You know Chancellor, there have been so many details to this case, but I seem to remember that you dispatched a highway patrolman on a Sunday to deliver a letter to O'Bryan and the contents of that letter prevented him from going to work and entering his office or any other building on campus. Is that correct, or did I misunderstand your early actions?"

"Craig, I am a reasonable man, and I expect my presidents to be reasonable and act respectfully."

"Chancellor, we are fast running out of time for this portion of the interview. Let me quickly ask this question. You had a team of several staff members reviewing thousands of emails after you froze O'Bryan's email account. You searched his computer hard drive and all the papers in his office that you confiscated. Tell me this, did you find anything that proved O'Bryan's culpability? To my knowledge, nothing surfaced during the hearing, so I have to ask if you are holding back some great, top secret, ultraconfidential piece of evidence?"

"You know, Craig, we did not find any direct evidence, but there were many parts and pieces that seemed to point to a presidential conspiracy. All you have to do is use a little imagination, and you can connect the dots. Plus, I must say we were dealing with a really sneaky man who clearly knows how to cover his tracks."

"Okay, before we open the phone lines and start taking call-ins, I want to ask you this last question. When this news all broke, I remember a flurry of activity at Floyd University within the faculty ranks to organize a no-confidence vote against O'Bryan, but that never developed. Why so?"

For a few brief seconds, Buzz recalls the sting from the time his department betrayed him with a no-confidence vote.

"You know, Craig, I was vaguely aware of that movement, but as the chancellor, I try to stay impartial, and I never interfere with the shared governance process on any campus. Whatever the faculty senate wants to do is fine with me."

Very irritated, the chancellor nervously chuckles aloud. Craig wants to force one more question,

"Chancellor, before we say good-bye, I want to ask, I have a few sources who tell me you plan to retire in the near future. Is that true? Are you thinking of hanging it up and taking it easy? Maybe spending a little more time out on the golf course?"

"Oh my, no, Craig, there is still a lot of fire in my belly, and I have many things to do before I ponder retirement. We are in the middle of the board's strategic planning process, and we are working hard to prepare next year's budget proposals. No, sir, as that old saying suggests, I have miles to go before I kick back and relax. I am very dedicated to this great state and the educational mission of our university system!"

Craig's phone lines are flashing like a Christmas tree, but he is required to take another commercial break.

"Thank you, Chancellor Granger! We will be right back to take your calls and hear your viewpoints after this commercial break."

———❦———

As the radio plays another River Side Ford Truck commercial, the governor's chief of staff receives a call on his private cell phone.

"Hello, Governor, how are you today?"

"Shitty, Chip, just pretty damn shitty! Did you listen to the chancellor on Craig Jacobson's talk show?"

"No, sir. I just finished a meeting with our campaign team."

"Tell me, Chip, what part of my Nebraska English do you not understand? Do you sometimes find it hard to understand my accent?"

Bracing himself for a royal ass-chewing, the chief politely responds, "Governor, I always understand your directives and guidance. How can I help?"

"Damn it, Chip, I distinctly remember telling you that I want the chancellor to retire. I want him gone! I want him out of my sight and out of the news! What part of that do you not understand?"

"Sir, I completely understand. I have been waiting—"

The governor assertively interrupted. "Waiting for what? Christmas? Damn it, Chip, the old fart just told God and everybody who was listening that he does not plan to retire because he has miles to go and years to serve! Shit!"

"Sir, I will get right on it. I thought you wanted me to wait until the O'Bryan thing was a done deal. Don't worry, I know what to do, and I will make it happen! I promise you will have his retirement letter before the Christmas break."

Larry Gene Allen is seated in the bank's conference room. He is totally engrossed with a presentation suggesting a new investment strategy that will capture and transfer the bank's entire cash account for sixty hours during the weekend. By placing this consolidated cash balance into the global money market, the bank could receive a 4.75 percent weekend interest rate, but the sixty-hour freeze on cash requires changing the level of services available to customers on Saturday mornings.

Larry's cell is muted, but it vibrates indicating an incoming call. The chancellor's name appears on the caller ID. He stops the presentation and suggests everyone take a five-minute break. Seeking private space down the hallway, Larry says, "Hello, Buzz, what can I do for you today?"

Buzz is riding high with the euphoria from his latest victory. In his mind, he just bagged a trophy kill. To him, this conquest is bigger than the 1985 trophy elk that Big Dee shot back in Montana.

"Good afternoon, Mr. Chairman. I hope you have a few minutes to talk?"

"Yes, Buzz, I can give you about five minutes. What is on your mind?"

"Well, as you know, the AG's office released the decision against O'Bryan earlier this morning. I would like to propose we call an emergency meeting of the full board. I believe we should fire O'Bryan as quickly as possible and run him out of the state!"

"Not so fast, Buzz. We walked this path once before, and it did not go well for us. The whole damn thing backfired. Why do you want an emergency meeting? Why can't we just place this on the agenda for our next regularly scheduled meeting in December?"

Buzz's temper flares.

"Well, hell, Larry! I thought we wanted to dump his ass as soon as possible. Besides, we have promises pending with half a dozen agri-business leaders across the state who want their man, Cyrus, to be named permanent president of Floyd University. Many of them have grown weary of this interim president situation that we gave Cyrus. You know how important these donors are to the governor's reelection campaign!"

"Look, Buzz, I am not going to rush into this decision. You prepare a dismissal recommendation against O'Bryan, and I will make a few calls to touch base with the board's executive committee. Right now, I plan to defuse the publicity on this hot topic and try to make it look like routine business at the next board meeting. Got to go now, but one more thing, no more news interviews or press statements on the O'Bryan decision until you hear from me! Do you understand?"

After the long Thanksgiving weekend, Larry Allen drives into Lincoln for an appointment with the governor. This meeting takes place in the governor's private office. After shaking hands and exchanging pleasantries, Larry becomes very serious.

"Governor, I have been walking the fence line and checking the pulse of every board member. Many of them are outraged with the chancellor's bizarre actions against O'Bryan. Most of them consider old Buzz a disgrace to this administration, but they are not willing to speak against him publicly. I believe that they are trying their best to remain loyal to you, Governor."

"Look, Larry, I appreciate your legwork, and I certainly understand how the board might feel about Buzz. At this point in time, I just have one question. Are you going to be able to deliver a unanimous vote during the next board meeting?"

"Yes, sir. Right now, I have all the votes. But I will tell you that the O'Bryan dismissal is going to cost us!"

"What the hell do you mean, Larry?"

"Governor, time will tell, but I predict the O'Bryan vote will be the last vote of support we get from at least three of the board members. I anticipate they will patiently wait until after the New Year begins, and then they will individually submit their resignation from the board to you. You should expect them to cite an incompatibility or inability to work with the chancellor as their reason for leaving the board."

"Larry, you know I am in the process of forcing the chancellor to retire. Do you think they will consider staying on the board if we go public with the chancellor's retirement announcement?"

"I honestly doubt it, Governor. I can try, and you most certainly have a personal connection with each member of the board so some words from you may influence them. But these philosophical differences run deep, and I don't think we can keep all of them. You need to know that many on the board believe Buzz has severely damaged the reputation of Floyd University while he has been on the rampage against O'Bryan. And since I live there at ground zero, I must concur with their observation. It will take us a decade to overcome the bad publicity that has been directed toward the university's image."

On December 15, 2016, the state board assembles in the Elkhorn Conference Room on the second floor of the state capitol building for their quarterly meeting. Casually positioned on the board's agenda, item number four is expressed with three brief words: President O'Bryan's Dismissal.

In less than twenty minutes, the board arrives at the topic everyone is anticipating. The chair asks the chancellor to introduce the O'Bryan resolution. The chancellor moves to the microphone and proudly stands before the entire room. His demeanor bubbles with arrogance as his voice screeches through the speaker system. While he is reading, the chancellor's secretary moves around the room and distributes copies of the resolution to everyone, including representatives from the news media.

> Be it resolved that the board moves to dismiss Dr. O'Bryan from his position as president of Floyd University. This removal from office becomes effective immediately on December 15, 2016. Furthermore, be it resolved that Dr. O'Bryan must vacate the presidential home at Floyd University not later than December 31, 2016.

The vice chair quickly gives his second to the motion. "Mr. Chairman, in order to expedite this resolution, and give us the chance to discuss its merits, I will second this motion so we can begin an open and frank conversation." Mr. Allen is immediately surprised and puzzled. The vice chair's tone of voice signals some discontent and unrest.

Buzz feels a giant knot forming in his stomach. He senses the political winds are changing rapidly and the sand beneath his feet is shifting. He quickly steals a glance across the room and establishes eye contact with a pair of familiar, haunting, diamond-blue eyes. Seated in the front row of guest chairs, the slender lady behind these eyes, Diana Dawson, is wearing a stunning red dress. With her hair in a ponytail, Buzz marvels that from this modest distance, she looks like a young college student.

"All right, we have a motion on the floor and a second. Is there any discussion?" Visibly stunned by the silent, rapid response, Larry looks at the four board members with their hands in the air. "Mr. Gleason, I think you were the first to raise your hand.

The chair recognizes you and asks that you direct your comments into the microphone."

"Thanks, Mr. Chair. You know, I am an old country boy with a high school diploma and a PhD from the school of hard knocks. Sometimes, this university lingo goes over my head, but my mama made sure I grew up with a heavy dose of common sense. So from my perspective, it seems to me that we are about to embark upon a hasty judgment. Maybe, a rush to injustice! As a board, we hire and fire presidents. That's one of our main jobs. Now I may sound a little old-fashioned, but from where I stand, I want to look President O'Bryan in the eye and hear what he has to say. I have been around the barn a time or two, and I am old enough to realize two great truths in life. First, some T-bone steaks are better than others, and second, there is always more than one side to any story, and right now, I want us to invite O'Bryan into the room and let him make a statement regarding these alleged charges."

Buzz squirms in his chair. His entire face flashes bright red. He feels sharp pains of stress across his chest.

"Thank you, Mr. Gleason. Your concerns are noted. The chair now recognizes Liz Nemitz."

"And I thank you, Mr. Allen. Frankly I could not agree more with this old country boy. I want JP O'Bryan to come forward and tell us his side of the story. I am tired of hearing all this secondhand gossip in the news. We are living in a high-tech world where the Internet gives everyone free license to slander anyone. Honestly, I think these say-anything blogs are an outrageous disgrace. Unfortunately, we have evolved to the point where the mouse is more lethal than a razor sharp sword. I believe we need to hear from the man we hired before we take any action to fire him!"

Larry Allen realizes he has lost control of this discussion. Baffled for words, and grasping for a lifeboat, he hastily asks his fellow board members, "In the interest of time, we may want to just move forward with a vote because I don't think it is possible to reach Dr. O'Bryan and get him to this meeting. I think we have more than enough information to make a decision. Are you ready for me to call the vote?"

Without waiting to be recognized by the chair, Liz Nemitz erupts with frustration, "Absolutely not! I happen to know Dr. O'Bryan is just down the hallway in the lobby. Furthermore, our good colleague and former chairman, Mr. Blackmore, tells me we also have a university professor in the room right now by the name of Samuel Boswell. Professor Boswell wants to testify, and I am told by Mr. Blackmore that this man has important information that we need to hear. I am convinced the professor also should be given a chance to speak after O'Bryan. I strongly suggest a five-minute break so we can invite President O'Bryan into this meeting.

Four members of the board nod their heads in agreement and mutter words of support for Ms. Nemitz's proposal.

Larry Allen is blindsided by this unexpected blitz. With great reluctance, he declares a brief recess.

As the chair quietly asks the board secretary to go down the hall and get President O'Bryan, Buzz silently implodes with anger. Unconsciously reverting to old habits, he takes his number 2 lead pencil and snaps it into two pieces. After several minutes of confusion and a flurry of cell phone activity by the reporters seated in the back of the room, the board chair hits the gavel and reconvenes the meeting,

"Let the minutes of this meeting record that we have reconvened to continue our discussion regarding the motion that is on the table, and as part of our discussion of this said motion, the board has invited President O'Bryan to address the resolution which proposes his dismissal. President O'Bryan, I ask you to begin with a brief opening statement, try to limit your remarks to five minutes. After that, I expect some of the board members will ask you questions. Please proceed and speak directly into the microphone!"

JP is ready for this moment. For many weeks, he has prayed to have this opportunity. His mind is clear. His thoughts are organized. He is speaking from the heart, extemporaneously, without any written notes. As he begins, his voice is both calm and firm.

"Thank you, Mr. Chairman. I greatly appreciate your willingness to grant me this opportunity to address our board. Please know that the charges against me are truly false accusations. I was completely surprised by—"

JP stops talking midsentence because there is an unexpected shuffle in the front of the room. A chair thuds as it hits the floor. Everyone is momentarily stunned as they realize the chancellor has collapsed and fallen out of his chair. He is moaning in pain and crumpled under the table. Two women in the back of the room scream.

As the commotion quickly escalates, Larry Allen hollers, "Someone call 911! We have an emergency and need immediate help!"

35

Haunted by the Dark Night

Mankind's moral sense is not a strong beacon of light, radiating outward to illuminate in sharp outline all that it touches. It is, rather, a small candle flame, casting vague and multiple shadows, flickering and sputtering in the strong winds of power and passion, greed and ideology.

—James W. Wilson, *On Character*

December 24, 2016
Springview, Nebraska

During the last nine days, JP O'Bryan has lived amidst chaos, confusion, and turmoil. The daily drama is intense. The news media is thriving with a frenzy of interviews, speculation, and released statements. Every senior member of state government, including the governor, is riding this crest of opportunity to be part of the daily headlines. This is an unexpected chance for the governor to take center stage and enhance his momentum for reelection.

Mr. Larry Allen is dodging more questions than he answers. When he does respond to a reporter, he is carefully following the governor's prepared script. The radio, television, and newspapers replay countless times Mr. Allen's hasty decision to suspend the board's discussion and adjourn the meeting. After the ambulance crew performs CPR on the chancellor and restores his heartbeat, they transport him to Saint Anthony's Hospital. Larry immediately asks the board to table the O'Bryan resolution and quickly adjourn so that he can rush to the hospital to be with the chancellor's wife.

JP has been swamped with requests for interviews. Every major newspaper in the Midwest is asking for a statement. Two days ago, a reporter from the *New York Times* calls, wanting to talk. JP's phone messages are packed with radio and television talk show invitations that want to feature JP as a special guest. Out of respect for the board, and in consideration of the university's reputation, JP refuses to sling mud or participate in any interviews.

It is Christmas Eve. JP and his wife, Jenn, find themselves spending most of the time alone in their basement family room. This small rectangular room has become their private safe haven. It is the only space where they can escape the relentless hounding from the paparazzi. About two o'clock in the afternoon, the doorbell rings. Jenn says, "Oh no, probably another reporter. I will go upstairs and tell them you are not available for comment."

Lost deep in thought, JP responds, "Thanks, sweetheart." About five minutes later, Jenn returns to the basement.

"JP, the chaplain from the Lincoln Hospital is waiting upstairs and really needs to talk with you. I think you should hear what he has to say!"

"You've got to be kidding, why is the chaplain at our house?"

"JP, he is here with a very serious request. You'd better go talk with him yourself."

Briskly climbing up the steps, JP walks down the hallway toward the living room. He turns left and enters the front foyer. "Hello, Chaplain, my wife tells me you want to talk. How can I help you?"

"Mr. O'Bryan, may we sit for a few minutes while I share a very private request from a dying man?" JP is stunned. He briefly pauses.

"Well, of course, please step into the living room, and let me take your coat."

"Thank you, sir."

Within minutes, both men are seated. Jenn enters the room and politely asks, "Chaplain, would you like a coffee or hot tea? I have some freshly made Christmas cookies. Can I bring you some?"

"Yes, Mrs. O'Bryan, hot tea and cookies would be great. This cold weather really takes a toll on my old bones."

"Chaplain, I must ask why you drove all the way from Lincoln to see me on Christmas Eve?"

"Dr. O'Bryan, it is a very long story, and we don't have much time to talk. I will be happy to give you all the details while we are traveling in the car. The chancellor is dying and not expected to make it through the night. He is urgently requesting a private audience with you, and I am the messenger. I am here to ask if you will jump in the car with me and go back to Lincoln right now!"

Lost for words, JP hesitates and does not respond.

"Please, Mr. President, the governor ordered the highway patrol to drive me here in the most expeditious manner. We just made the trip in about four hours. If you will consider my request and grab your coat, the patrolman is waiting outside with the car running. We can be back in Lincoln by 7:00 tonight."

JP looks at the floor as he thinks about his unusual request. Never in a hundred years did he expect this turn of events. He is reluctant to leave his wife on Christmas Eve. And the very thought of the chancellor makes his blood boil with anger. He wants to do the right thing, but there is no time to ponder these complex circumstances.

"Do you know why the hell the chancellor wants to talk with me?"

"Sir, he knows he is dying. The doctors disconnected all the life support equipment earlier today. They have given him twenty-four hours to say his farewells. He never stops talking about you. He is desperate to see you. He begged me to bring you back. He is truly haunted by this dark night!"

The tone in the chaplain's voice becomes emotionally charged. "Please come with me. We must go right now!"

"All right, let me get my coat and tell my wife that I am leaving. Please enjoy your tea while I get ready. I will be with you in about five minutes."

36

Yellow Rose

Darkness cannot drive out darkness; only light can do
that. Hate cannot drive out hate; only love can do that.

—Martin Luther King, Jr. (1929-1968)

December 24, 2016
Lincoln, Nebraska

As the highway patrol car enters the backside of St. Anthony's
hospital, JP looks at his watch. It is 7:05 p.m. It is exceptionally
dark tonight. Even the streetlights are dimmed by a cold hazy
glow around the top of each pole. Gray clouds hover overhead
blocking any possible evidence of starlight, or any view of the full
moon. He turns to the chaplain,

"This is amazing. I have never traveled by car so far, so fast.
Back in Springview, when you predicted our arrival time, I did
not believe it."

Turning to the young patrolman in the front seat, JP reaches
across and taps his shoulder,

"Young man, thanks for a safe trip. You need to get some rest after this whirlwind drive."

"Thank you, Mr. President. Our orders are very clear. There will be another patrol car waiting right here for you when you are ready to return home. You will have a fresh driver. I am going home to spend Christmas Eve with my family. Merry Christmas to both of you, gentlemen."

As the chaplain and JP walk across the loading dock, a blustery gust of wind hits them in the face. It is very bitter, and the wind chill has dropped below zero. The back parking lot is beginning to collect small, fingerlike drifts. The chaplain is extremely nervous and speaks with a rapid pace as he explains that the governor's chief of staff has made advance arrangements with the hospital administrator to let them enter through the freight door. This plan will ensure JP avoids the covey of reporters that are homesteading near the hospital's front entrance.

Approaching the door, the chaplain presses the doorbell and faces the camera that is looking directly at them. The chaplain waves as he says, "My good friend, Joey, is on duty tonight in the security room. He is expecting us, and I am sure he will respond quickly so we can get inside and out of this harsh wind."

The lock system on the door simultaneously buzzes and clicks. The chaplain immediately opens the door.

"Please follow me, Dr. O'Bryan, we have no time to lose."

After entering the building, the chaplain walks briskly on a familiar route. Like an old milk cow walking toward its favorite stall, the chaplain takes JP past a large storage room filled with janitorial supplies, then past a large double door labeled technology center and computer server room. Next they pass the back side of the hospital's kitchen. As they approach the elevator, the chaplain pulls a bright red card from his pocket and scans it across the electronic reader.

"This is a staff-only elevator, and it will take us directly to the seventh floor where the ICU is located."

"Chaplain, if you don't mind, can we find a men's room because I need to make a brief stop."

"Absolutely, there is one very close to the elevator when we get off."

The elevator ride is completed in total silence. Both men sense the seriousness of pending events. Both are nervous and lost in their own private thoughts. A muted ping signals the elevator's arrival at the seventh floor as the door automatically opens.

"Dr. O'Bryan, down the hall, two doors on the left, you will find the men's room. I will check in with the head nurse and let them know we are here."

The hand of destiny has carefully turned the wheel of fortune to align the elements of time and circumstances. This evening, the stage is set for an important event. The supporting cast is many, but only seven actors have been given a speaking role. During the next hour, the eternal destiny of two souls will be charted as the forces of dark and light compete for their desired outcome.

"Hello, Dr. O'Bryan, I am Mary Jane Laurer, and I am the charge nurse tonight for our ICU floor. Welcome to St. Anthony's. Please follow me, and I will escort you to Mr. Granger's room. He is waiting for you."

As they are walking past the nurses' work station, the chaplain reaches out to shake JP's hand,

"Thank you for coming with me. You are doing the right thing. Let me hold your top coat while you are visiting. I will be waiting right here for you. Take as much time as you need, and may God be with you."

An immediate emotional lump swells in JP's throat. He has not heard that blessing extended to him since his grandmother died almost five years ago. JP musters a modest smile as he nods his head in agreement.

Walking down the hallway, Mary Jane quietly whispers,

"You will have complete privacy with Mr. Granger. That was part of his last request. Once you are in his room, I will stand outside the door and ensure absolutely no one will enter."

JP has a huge knot in his stomach. His mouth feels dry. He urgently scans the hallway for a water fountain. There is none in sight.

In less than two minutes, they arrive at a closed door. The room number, 707, is painted with black script numbers at eye level in the center of the door. For some odd reason, JP's mind flashes to an old memory of his first overseas flight on a Boeing 707 when the army sent him to South Korea.

"Please wait here, Dr. O'Bryan."

Moving with quiet grace, Mary Jane slips through the door and disappears. The door is closed. JP hears the muffled voices from two ladies.

Unannounced, the door slowly opens, and JP is flabbergasted. He did not anticipate encountering Maggie Granger in this doorway. She looks directly at him with tearful eyes that emanate a blend of remorse, regret, fear, and deep sadness.

"Hello, Maggie!"

"JP, I can't thank you enough for being here tonight. Since they removed all the life support equipment, Buzz has not stopped talking about you. After his surgery, he was in a coma for three days. Finally, when he became conscious, he had to communicate to us by writing on a paper tablet. This past week, his lungs collapsed twice, so they decided to leave the resuscitator down his throat in order to help his lungs keep working. Now we are just trying to keep him comfortable, and the doctor removed everything from his throat. He is slipping away quickly. His voice is raspy, but he wants to spend part of his final hours talking with you."

Maggie begins to cry. She reaches to touch JP's hand. In between deep sobs, she says, "Thank you, JP. Oh, thank you."

Mary Jane steps out.

"He is ready for you, Dr. O'Bryan. Take as much time as you need. I will be right here waiting for you."

It would be a colossal understatement to say that it is difficult for JP to walk into this room. His mind races with a cascade of memories, and most of them have a bitter taste. Strangely, he feels like there is a force present that is physically shoving him through the door. He enters the room and, surprisingly, does not recognize the frail old man lying in the bed.

Speechless and overwhelmed by a dimly lit, small room that is crowded with high-tech machines, monitors with flashing lights, and a portable table lined with flowers, JP stops in his tracks and hesitates. He is not sure this is such a good idea. For a few brief seconds, he feels like it is time to flee; he wants to leave the room as quickly as possible.

Buzz interrupts JP's thoughts. He speaks, but his voice is so timid and soft, JP cannot understand him. Buzz raises his right hand and motions. He points to the chair next to his bed.

Instinctively, JP walks toward the chair and sits next to the man who has ruined his career. JP feels awkward. He feels insecure. He feels fear. This is the first time JP has sat in the chamber of death with someone. More importantly, he is not sitting with someone he loves, but rather a person he hates.

The silence is deafening. JP deliberately avoids eye contact as he scans the contents of Buzz's room. The only audible sound comes from the heart monitor that emits a gentle beep. The rhythm of this high-pitched noise is synchronized with Buzz's struggling heartbeat, and it is visually displayed by a rapidly moving line across the bright screen hanging above his head.

The opposite side of the room is lined with computer driven machines, hanging electrical cords, and television monitors. JP assumes this is the life support equipment that has been recently disconnected. There is an elevated tray reaching across the bed with a water pitcher and a small glass that contains a bent straw. At the foot of the bed, there is an impressive array of plants and flowers. From JP's seated position, he can read the names on two cards. The largest vase is filled with an assorted collection of cut flowers; a helium balloon with the words "Get Well Soon" floats above this bouquet. The card says, "From Governor Abe." The center vase contains a massive display of pristine perfect yellow roses. The card says, "Love you forever, M." Once again, JP is jolted by an old memory from his childhood. He remembers standing with his grandmother, Nan, and cutting yellow roses to put in a vase that always sat on top of the buffet in Nan's dining room. JP's eyes move down the bed and fix upon Buzz's arm. The IV wounds have been bleeding and fresh blood is visible under the Band-Aids that hold the IV needle in place. There is a clear plastic wrist band below the IV line. The identification strip says, Wilber Granger.

JP marvels as he thinks to himself, *Wilber! I had no idea that was his legal name!*

Buzz breaks the silence.

"Thanks for coming. I did not know if you would do it!"

JP remains silent as he looks directly at the face of the man who has maliciously destroyed his life. During the last nine days, Buzz has aged twenty years.

"Please help me with the water. My throat is so dry. I need some water."

Hesitant to respond, JP's movement is automatic. He is driven more by an internal sense of kindness than from a deliberate, conscious willingness to help. As he carefully holds the glass, Buzz leans toward the straw and sips a small quantity of water.

Buzz leans back into his pillow. After years of smoking, his lungs are weak, and his breathing is labored. "JP, I have been to hell and back. They tell me I was in a coma for a few days. To me, it was just a long, horrible dream. The worst nightmare ever. I want to tell you about it. Please move closer to my bed so I don't have to talk so loud."

JP complies and slides his chair over against the dying man's bed.

"I remember falling into a dark tunnel. It seemed like a very long drop that took forever. And then I was in a small room that had a big screen on it. There was a gentle voice talking to me. The voice asked me to concentrate on the screen. It was strange. I was watching a replay of my entire life, but the movie paused each time I came to an important decision. All the decision points looked like a road intersection where you have to turn either right or left. During my childhood years, the intersection signs said turn left for the easy path or turn right for the difficult path." Buzz pauses to clear his throat.

"Please, just a little more water to help my voice!"

Once again, JP holds the glass of water, and Buzz sips on the bent straw.

"Anyway, this replay of my life started to move faster and faster. I encountered hundreds of intersections, but the signs changed as I grew older. Some of them said either right or wrong, some of them said kind or cruel, and some of them said good or evil. Each time, I unfortunately selected the wrong path. I followed all the wrong guideposts during my life. My thoughts and decisions were driven by an evil agenda. Oh, how I wish for the chance to do it all over again. I remember crying with an overwhelming sense of remorse. I begged God for one more chance to get it right."

JP is listening carefully but staring at Buzz's hand rather than his eyes. When Buzz stops talking, JP looks up at his face. Tears are pouring down his cheeks.

Buzz is hoping that JP will say something, but he does not speak so Buzz elects to continue.

"Finally the movie stopped and the room went dark. I was alone. I felt hopeless. I felt lost. But most of all, I felt ashamed. After a painful eternity of time in the dark, the gentle voice returned and said that God heard my prayers and decided to give me one last chance to do the right thing. The next minute, I awoke in this room and realized that this was my last chance to make things right with you."

JP remains silent. As he reaches toward the water glass, Buzz grabs his hand with a surprisingly strong grip.

"JP, please forgive me. Please accept my apology. I did terrible things to you. I was motivated by all the wrong reasons. I lived on the dark side of life for so many years, I forgot how to be a good person. My wife tells me it is Christmas Eve. It is my sincere prayer that the spirit of Christmas is in your heart tonight. Please grant me the gift I desperately need. Please forgive me!"

JP is not prepared to respond. He does not know what to say. His mind becomes clouded with emotion. Intellectually, he is very critical of Buzz. The feelings of anger boil in JP's veins as his Irish temper simmers. However, emotionally he feels compassion toward this dying man. As he struggles to sort and balance his thoughts, he feels the chancellor's grip disappear and his hand go cold. JP knows, intuitively, Buzz does not have much time left. JP searches for words. He begins to speak from the heart. He remains reluctant to forgive this dying man. While he is talking, he looks directly into Buzz's eyes. There is a dark ring around both eyes. He truly looks like a man who has been to hell and back. His eyes convey a sense of mortality that is tempered with an understanding of eternity. There is a brightness within his pupils that JP has not noticed before.

"Chancellor, I believe the spiritual process of forgiveness is in God's hands. It sounds like you have already started that conversation with God, and I sure do not want to interfere or interrupt."

JP stops abruptly. Subconsciously, he is compelled to turn and look at the vase of yellow roses that are edged with beautiful crimson. Their distinct fragrance triggers another childhood memory. Without warning, JP privately hears his grandmother's gentle voice. During his formative years, every time he did something wrong and felt remorse, she would graciously say, "Love is patient, love is kind, love is forgiving, and love is forever."

JP looks back. Tears continue to flow down Buzz's face. A surge of compassion rushes through the fiber of JP's soul. It is like flipping an internal switch and mentally seeing a bright light. He instantly finds the words he wants to say.

"Chancellor, today, right now, we are locked in this temporal world. I understand your remorse, and I accept your apology. You have my forgiveness, and from this day forward, I will pray that God grants you the blessings and forgiveness that you desire."

Buzz sobs with bone deep relief.

"Oh thank you, thank you so much, JP. You have given me the greatest Christmas gift ever. More importantly, you have given me the final chance to do something right. As I crawl toward the finish line, I want to end my life with the knowledge that the fragile line in my soul that divides good and evil just moved a millimeter closer to good. Thank you, my dear friend. You have helped me prepare to face my eternal father."

JP sits next to Buzz in silence for a few minutes. The chancellor's hand and upper arm are now cold. The monitor above his head illustrates an increasingly irregular heartbeat, and Buzz's breathing is more shallow and labored. JP hears the early beginnings of the death rattle in Buzz's throat.

JP is surprised when Buzz breaks the silence with a clear voice.

"Go in peace, JP. Live long and prosper. You have many good things ahead of you. Before I depart, I will help balance the scales of justice in your favor. Please send my Maggie back in so I can talk with her. Ask her to bring some paper and a pen. Farewell, JP!"

For the first time in their relationship, JP is touched by Buzz's kindness. JP realizes this room currently has a sacred aura about it. Like a man quietly leaving a church, JP reverently departs. As he steps into the hallway, he notices Mary Jane on guard duty standing against the wall like a drill sergeant. With a mild voice that is fortified by a peaceful resolution, JP says, "Buzz is asking for his wife. He wants to talk with her, and she should take some paper and a pen into the room."

"I will get her immediately. She is just around the corner in our private lounge. We have fresh coffee there if you would like some. The chaplain is talking with Mrs. Granger, so you will find him there with your top coat."

"Thank you, Mary Jane. I appreciate all your thoughtful ways. I wish you and your family a very Merry Christmas!"

37

Crooked Timber

Out of the crooked timber of humanity,
no straight thing was ever made.

—Immanuel Kant,
German Philosopher, 1724–1804

January 30, 2017
Floyd University

After the holiday break, classes at Floyd University resume on January 9 in the midst of great public turmoil and frantic political maneuvering. The State Board of Higher Education conducts two special meetings during the month of January. The first, January 12, under the leadership of Mr. Allen, launches an independent investigation of Dr. O'Bryan's dismissal charges. After Mrs. Granger releases the chancellor's deathbed confession to the *Jacobson Talk Show*, it becomes clear to the general public that President O'Bryan has been framed with false accusations.

Following Mr. Allen's resignation from the board, the vice chair, Mr. Atkins, assumes the top leadership position and Ms. Nemitz moves into the vice chair role. The second special meeting on January 26 culminates with a unanimous vote to immediately restore Dr. O'Bryan as Floyd University's president.

Throughout the holidays and the January chaos, JP O'Bryan and Jenn seek refuge in the beauty of the Black Hills. They find a quiet Best Western motel that is pet-friendly. There they hibernate while remaining out of the reach of frenzied reporters and relentless television crews who continually roam the campus. Like hungry piranhas, these reporters are seeking a glimpse of the badgered, besieged president or his wife while she walks their small dog.

Monday morning, January 30, 2017, begins early for Dr. O'Bryan. He sets the alarm for 5:15 a.m. Last evening, under the cover of darkness, JP and Jenn drove into town and returned to their home on campus. Filled with optimism and hope, JP prepares for the long walk across campus to the administration building. There he will reenter the office that was pillaged almost six months ago by the chancellor's henchmen.

Jenn is excited for her husband. More than anyone else, she realizes the magnitude of this day. For her, it is like a dream come true. On this day, her husband's courage and moral compass will be vindicated. She has agreed to make this amazing "come back" walk with JP. They have been through a terrible ordeal together. Now the specter of dark sadness is out of sight and tucked under the bed. It is a time when bright joy and happiness will fill their day.

The former board chair, Mr. Blackmore, suggests that JP arrive at his office around 9:00 a.m. Mr. Blackmore hints that a few board members want to be there to extend their words of welcome and celebrate this exciting moment with JP.

About 8:50 a.m., JP and Jenn grab their coats and prepare to leave the house through the back door. Since a television crew is positioned in the front yard with cameras ready, JP elects to start this cross campus journey without the eyes of a camera focused on his first steps. As they walk together, JP notices how the bright sun sparkles across the snow drifts that have accumulated in their backyard. He points to the snow covered blue spruce tree he planted two years ago in memory of his deceased dad. There is a beautiful red cardinal perched on this little spruce tree, and JP could not be more pleased. They encounter several students on the sidewalk and exchange pleasantries. Neither JP nor Jenn are surprised when an aggressive reporter runs toward them with his camera rapidly snapping photos as they walk.

When they approach the administration building, it becomes evident that more than a few board members are waiting. The front steps are lined with students and faculty. Over the front door, there is a large banner that proclaims, "Welcome Home President O'Bryan!" JP is astonished. He turns to Jenn,

"Did you know about all this?"

"Well, JP, I must confess. Several people have been secretly planning this surprise for you. I may have made a few suggestions since they asked me about your favorite cake. After all, it is an important moment. Many of our friends want to share this celebration with you."

Upon entering the building, the crowd begins to clap. As JP maneuvers through the gathering, everyone expresses kind words as they shake his hand. There is a cluster of helium balloons tied to his office door. JP does not rush. He takes time to warmly say something to every person who shakes his hand.

Moving down the hallway, they soon enter the reception area adjacent to his office. Four board members are waiting for him. They are standing near a beautifully decorated table that displays a giant chocolate cake and a large dispenser of coffee.

During the next hour, JP is surrounded by friends, faculty members, community leaders, and students. Everyone enjoys the cake, conversation, and fellowship. It is a wonderful party. JP takes the time to hug and thank Samuel Boswell for his special courage and loyal support.

Eventually, people begin to leave. Before departing the room, Mr. Blackmore steals a private moment in the corner.

"JP, today is your day. It is a time for joy, a time to celebrate. It is a time for healing and a time for goodness to prevail. Thanks for your leadership and all the great things you do for this university!"

"Mr. Blackmore, it is I who thanks you. If you and Professor Boswell had not intervened, I would not be standing here right now."

"JP, every now and then the crooked timber of humanity yields a straight plank of beautiful wood."

"Well, sir, I am in your debt forever!"

Mr. Blackmore winks.

"Hey, JP, it is my pleasure. By the way, did you notice the *Springview Press* is not here today?"

Both men chuckle.

After the crowd disperses, Jenn takes JP's hand and silently leads him into his office. It is the first time JP has entered this work space since his abrupt dismissal six months ago. On his oak desk there is an enormous vase filled with an incredible array of yellow roses. JP opens the card and tears of happiness flow from his eyes. The handwritten note says,

> Love is patient. Love is kind. Love is forgiving. Love you forever, J.

38

Epilogue

Discover the private face of public universities

Approximately 2,500 years ago, a wise teacher wrote as an observer of life. He recognized the order in the universe and shared the following observations regarding the rhythm of our brief life.

For everything there is a season, and a time for every purpose under Heaven:

A time to be born, and a time to die;
A time to kill, and a time to heal;
A time to weep, and a time to laugh;
A time to mourn, and a time to dance;
A time to keep silent, and a time to speak;
A time to love, and a time to hate.

—Ecclesiastes 3

Wilber (Buzz) Granger

Buzz died at the age of sixty-seven just two hours after JP left his hospital room. However, before he died, he dictated a statement to his wife. She was directed to give his last confession to Craig Jacobson. Buzz was buried on December 30, 2016, in the Springview Cemetery. A harsh winter blizzard dropped seven inches of snow the night before his service. The funeral had to be delayed two hours in order to clear the snow drifts away from his grave. Buzz was buried in the plot next to his old friend, Dean Frank Warton. One night, many years ago, in their deer camp they were inspired by Jack Daniel's Old Number 7 to purchase adjoining cemetery plots so they could continue their friendship through eternity. Within a few months, Buzz was forgotten by most everyone, especially the general public who previously considered him a household name. His malicious deeds and track record quickly disappeared from everyone's memory like a dark shadow that is enveloped by the noonday sun.

Joseph Patrick O'Bryan

After the board restored Dr. O'Bryan to his presidential assignment, he successfully completed the academic year at Floyd University. Every day that year, he encountered the individual faces of those who had failed to stand with him while he walked the gauntlet. He avoided the temptation for revenge and navigated his conversations through a maze of obstacles in order to avoid reprisals or reprimands against those who had publically criticized him. Six months later, with sadness in his heart, he announced his resignation shortly after the spring commencement ceremony. The following year, he accepted another presidency at a large public university on the east coast where he served with distinction for an additional ten years.

Governor Abe Turner

As the last surviving member of the Remarkable Trinity, the governor encountered an extensive barrage of negative publicity after the chancellor's death. The rumors and innuendos suggested the governor was directly involved with the O'Bryan conspiracy. At first, the governor blamed his chief of staff and publicly sacrificed him with an immediate dismissal. Next, the governor blamed his trusted agent, Larry Gene Allen, and forced him to resign from the board. Unable to erase his culpability and the tangent evidence of judicial tampering before the O'Bryan hearing, the governor lost his reelection bid. Severely embittered, he returned to his home in Springview and spent his retirement years counting his money, drinking whiskey, and hunting in Montana.

Samuel Brenden Boswell

Thrust onto the public stage in the midst of great turmoil, Professor Boswell eventually testified before the board in support of JP O'Bryan. As his dear friend, Dr. Moreland suggested, Samuel discovered that one man with courage can become a majority. His late night phone call to Mr. Blackmore prompted an unexpected chain of events that truly altered the planned outcome of the December 15, 2016, board meeting. Dr. Boswell's courage and character prompted the Omaha World Herald to choose him as Nebraska's outstanding citizen of the year. Later during the spring semester, he was selected for a prestigious Fulbright Visiting Scholar appointment in New Zealand. After a year down under, he returned to Floyd University and taught for another three years. During that time, his newly published book on John Donne received a national award for the best nonfiction book of the year. After more than thirty-five years of teaching, Samuel retired and returned to his beloved Tortola. There he lives with his old cat, Maxie II, and a newly adopted rescue puppy named White Fang.

Diana Everett Dawson

Following Samuel Boswell's revealing testimony at the board meeting, the county prosecutor investigated the alleged charges of sexual assault and rape against minors. Since there is no statute of limitations for rape, the prosecutor eventually filed felony charges and found three men willing to testify that Diana sexually harassed and raped them during their freshman year in college. The legendary Dragon Lady was found guilty and sentenced to three years in the state's penitentiary for women. She traded her red dresses and extensive collection of Victoria's Secret lingerie for a neon orange prison jumpsuit. Challenged by numerous legal battles and two attempted appeals, she was forced to liquidate her entire wealth in order to pay the attorney fees which accumulated for her defense. After serving six months in prison, she was released on parole. She returned to downtown Kearney, Nebraska, where she resides in a modest, upstairs, one-bedroom efficiency on lower Third Street just across the corner from the old, abandoned tattoo parlor she frequented during her youth. Her parole officer helped her secure a job on the night shift at Wal-Mart where she stocks shelves.

Carol Nodland

Carol suffered a significant backlash from her colleagues at Floyd University when it became evident that she helped plan the O'Bryan dismissal. She was ignored and shunned by most, including her faculty senate buddies. Six months after Chancellor Granger's death, she was diagnosed with stage 3, rapidly growing breast cancer. She struggled with chemotherapy for five months while the cancer metastasized into her brain. Her final weeks of life were filled with excruciating pain. She died and never enjoyed one day of retirement.

Mrs. Maggie Granger

Sixty days after her husband's death, Mrs. Granger became a millionaire. Overcome with sympathy and remorse, the State Board of Higher Education surprised everyone, including the governor, and opted to pay out the remaining two years of salary that existed on Buzz's employment contract. With that salary settlement plus Buzz's life insurance policy, Mrs. Granger became a very wealthy widow. She trashed her black dress after the funeral, sold everything, and moved into a beautiful three-thousand-square-foot townhouse in a gated community next to a Florida golf course. Only a ten-minute walk from the beach, she enjoys telling all of her Nebraska friends that she will never shovel snow again!

Larry Gene Allen

Mr. Allen made a complete fool of himself after the chancellor's death. Once Craig Jacobson aired Buzz Granger's death bed confession, Mr. Allen vehemently denied his involvement with the O'Bryan fiasco. Three board members resigned citing incompatibility with the chairman and the governor. The governor desperately attempted to deflect blame and forced Mr. Allen to take the heat and resign from the board. Larry returned to his full-time work at the Springview West Gate Bank Center. Two or three times each week, he can be found at Mildred's Family Restaurant during the lunch hour eating homemade coconut cream pie with former Governor Abe Turner.

Craig Jacobson

Talk show host, Craig Jacobson, soared into stardom after Chancellor Granger's death. For many weeks, his listening audience significantly increased as he traced every step of the drama that unfolded after the chancellor's heart attack. His talk show eventually became a syndicated program across the Midwest. Six months after the chancellor's funeral, Craig was offered his own late-night talk show on one of Omaha's most popular television stations. Next to Mrs. Granger, Mr. Jacobson realized, as a second order implication, the most significant financial gain caused by this human ordeal that showcased the best and the worst aspects of human nature.

Ellen Marie Martinez

When Samuel discovered his trusted friend, Emmy, was one of the Sexy Six and an active member within the Ladies in Red girlfriend club, he immediately stopped talking to her. Saddened by this loss of friendship, Emmy became depressed. When she was forced to testify during Diana Dawson's trial, Emmy became super frazzled and started suffering from migraine headaches. As her anxiety and depression escalated, her bulimia was aggravated. Her health rapidly declined. Frail, but mobile, she was able to travel once and visit Diana at the penitentiary. However, she died before Diana was granted parole. Her death certificate recorded the cause as malnutrition and starvation.

Ronald Harvey Kronberg

As the owner and editor of the *Springview Press*, Mr. Kronberg experienced a windfall of fame and good fortune. His newspaper realized a surge in subscriptions and paid advertisements. Many of his editorials circulated nationally across the AP news line. At the end of the year, he attended the Midwest's annual newspaper conference in Chicago where he received a prestigious reporting award for his news breaking editorials. The next spring, he was recognized at Springview's annual Chamber of Commerce Dinner as the 2016 Man of the Year. His trustworthy assistant editor, Jolee McBride, became worried during the Diana Dawson investigation. As a member of the Sexy Six, she panicked and quickly moved to Kansas. She subsequently went to work for a major metropolitan newspaper. This assignment, ironically, doubled her pay and gave her a new hunting ground for her yellow journalism techniques.

Marsha Ann Montgomery

Marsha earned her tenure at Chadron State and completed a successful teaching career. After retiring as a university professor, Marsha continued to enjoy a lucrative writing career. Her poetry appealed to an international audience and garnered several prestigious writing awards. After the chancellor died, she carefully followed the news surrounding Diana Dawson's court case. When the jury found Diana guilty and the judge sentenced her to prison, Marsha was inspired to write a new poem that quickly became a national hit. This poem is entitled, "Yes, There Is a God!"

People are like stained-glass windows. They sparkle and shine when the sun is out, but when the darkness sets in; their true beauty is revealed only if there is a light from within.

—Elisabeth Kubler-Ross, 1926–2004

CPSIA information can be obtained
at www.ICGtesting.com
Printed in the USA
BVOW11s0808270118
506471BV00017B/545/P